STUDY GUIDE

Jeannie Shearer-Gillmore
University of Western Ontario

Foundations of Macroeconomics

Second Edition

Robin Bade

Michael Parkin
University of Western Ontario

Brian Lyons
Sheridan Institute of Technology and Advanced Learning

PEARSON

Addison
Wesley

We'd like to thank the original authors of the U.S. edition of the Study Guide:
• Neil Garston, *California State University, Los Angeles*
• Tom Larson, *California State University, Los Angeles*
• Mark Rush, *University of Florida*

Study Guide multiple-choice questions authored by:
• Ali Ataiifar, *Delaware County Community College*
• Diego Mendez-Carbajo, *Illinois Wesleyan University*
• William Mosher, *Assumption College*
• Cindy Tori, *Valdosta State University*
• Nora Underwood, *University of California, Davis*

ISBN 0-321-24300-5

Senior Acquisitions Editor: Gary Bennett
Developmental Editor: Michelle Harrington
Production Editor: Jennifer Handel
Production Coordinator: Deborah Starks

 3 4 5   08 07 06 05

Printed and bound in Canada.

Tejal Govande

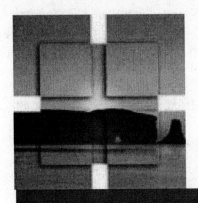

Table of Contents

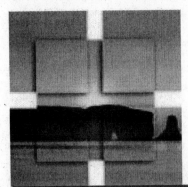

Your Complete Learning Package

■ The Complete Package

Your *Foundations of Macroeconomics* package consists of

- Textbook
- Study Guide
- Foundations Web site

The Foundations Web site is a powerful and tightly integrated online learning environment. For students, the site includes

- eText—the entire textbook in PDF format with hyperlinks to all the other components of the Web site and with Flash animations of all the textbook figures accompanied by audio explanations prepared by us

- eStudy Guide—the entire Study Guide online

- *Foundations Interactive*—tutorials, quizzes, and graphing tools that make curves shift and graphs come to life with the click of a mouse

- Diagnostic Quiz for every Checkpoint with feedback that includes hyperlinks to the eText, the tutorial and quiz in *Foundations Interactive*, and the eStudy Guide

- Economics in the News updated twice a week (or more often) during the school year

- Online "Office Hours"—ask a question via e-mail, and one of us will respond with 24 hours!

- Economic links—links to sites that keep students up to date with what's going on in the economy and that enable them to work end-of-chapter Web Exercises

■ Checklist and Checkpoints: The Glue That Holds Your Tools Together

Each chapter of your textbook opens with a Chapter Checklist that tells you what you'll be able to do when you've completed the chapter. The number of tasks varies from two to five and most often is three or four. Begin by reviewing this list thoughtfully and get a good sense of what you are about to learn.

Your Study Guide provides an Expanded Chapter Checklist that breaks down your tasks into detailed bite-size pieces.

Each part of a chapter in the textbook, Study Guide, and Foundations Web site is linked directly to a Checklist item to enable you to know exactly what you're studying and how it will enable you to accomplish your learning objective.

Each part of a chapter in the textbook ends with a Checkpoint—a page that offers you a practice problem, a worked and illustrated solution to the practice problem, and a further (parallel) exercise. The Checkpoints enable you to review what you've read when it's fresh in your mind—the most effective and productive time to do so. The Checkpoints guide you in a step-by-step approach that takes the guesswork out of learning. The Study Guide reinforces each Checkpoint by providing a more detailed solution to the textbook practice problem and an additional practice problem.

Self-test questions in the Study Guide, the Diagnostic Quiz on the Foundations Web site, and the tutorials and quizzes in *Foundations Interactive* are organized by Checkpoint. The Study Guide page numbers are listed at every textbook Checkpoint.

■ Practice Makes Perfect

As you study, distinguish between *practice* and *self-test*. Practice is part of the learning process—learning by doing. Self-test is a check. It shows you where you need to go back and reinforce your understanding, and it helps you build your confidence.

The Checkpoint Practice Problems and Exercises, the end-of-chapter Exercises, and the quizzes in *Foundations Interactive* are designed for practice. The self-test questions in the Study Guide, the Diagnostic Quiz on the Web site, and the practice exam in *Foundations Interactive* are designed to reveal your gaps in understanding and to target your final examination of the material.

■ Learn Your Learning Style

It is unlikely that you'll need to use all the tools that we've created all of the time. Try to discover how you learn best. If you learn best by reading with a marker or pencil in your hand, you'll use the textbook and Study Guide more often than the other items. If you learn best by seeing the action, you'll often use the *e*Text and Foundations Interactive Demos with their animated graphics. If you learn best by hearing, you'll use the *e*Text audio explanations of the action in key figures. If you learn best by participating and acting, you'll often use the Action and Quiz in *Foundations Interactive*.

■ Tell Us What Works for You

Please tell us the tools that you find most helpful and what you think we can improve. Email us at robin@econ100.com or michael.parkin@uwo.ca, or use the Office Hours in your Foundations Web site.

Robin Bade
Michael Parkin
Ontario, Canada
February, 2004

Your Learning Tools at a Glance

Activity	Print		eFoundations	
	Textbook	**Study Guide**	**eText and eStudy Guide**	**Foundations Interactive**
Getting into a chapter	Chapter opener— previews and places chapter in context	Chapter in perspective—a short summary of the core material		
	Chapter checklist tells you what you'll be able to do when you've completed the chapter	Expanded chapter checklist breaks down your tasks into detailed bite-size pieces		
Learning the material	Explanations; matched tables and figures; figures with numbered captions		eText has exactly the same content as the print textbook plus: dynamic figures and audio explanations	Fast track summarizes each topic. Textbook figures are interactive in Action and animated in Demo
	Key terms defined in text and in margin	Key terms list for review	Key terms with hyperlinks to definitions, examples, and related terms in both tools	
	Chapter checkpoint • Key points • Key terms list			
Practice makes perfect	Checkpoints • Practice problem • Exercise • Solution to practice problem	Checkpoints • Practice problem • Additional practice problem • Expanded solution to practice problem	eText practice problems, exercises and solutions; eStudy Guide additional practice problems and expanded solutions	Five question types in Interactive Quiz: • Fill in the blanks • True or False • Multiple Choice • Numeric • Complete the graph
	Chapter checkpoint exercises		Chapter checkpoint exercises link to external sites	
Self Test		Self Test: • Fill in the blanks • True or False • Multiple Choice • Complete the graph • Short Answer	eStudy Guide has the same content as the print Study Guide. Online quizzes with hyperlinks to eText for further review: • True or False • Multiple Choice	Self Test version of Interactive Quiz: • Fill in the blanks • True or False • Multiple Choice • Numeric • Complete the graph
Enrichment, Critical Thinking, and Applications	Eye On ... • The Canadian economy • The global economy • The past			
	Economics in the News		Economics in the News hyperlinks to news article and related sites	

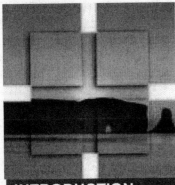

Your Course
and
Your Study
Guide

INTRODUCTION

The goal of this Study Guide is to help you to understand the course material presented by your teacher and by your textbook. The Study Guide is just one of the tools that you will use to reach your peak performance on examinations. Using this Study Guide alone is not enough to guarantee that you will earn an A. To help you overcome the problems and difficulties that many students encounter, I have some general advice on how to study economics and some specific advice on how to use this Study Guide.

Economics is difficult for many students because it studies familiar things in an unfamiliar way. Economics doesn't *describe* the economic world: it *explains* it. And to do so, economists make extensive use of *models* that are simpler than the world in which we live. In an economic model, everything remains the same except for the tiny part of the world that we are trying to explain. We make assumptions about what people and businesses are trying to achieve. Then we figure out the decisions that people will make. This approach can be demanding. It feels unfamiliar to most students and requires practice.

It is not as easy to do well in economics on the basis of your raw intelligence and high-school knowledge as it is in many other courses. Many students are frustrated and puzzled that they are receiving As and Bs in their other courses but only a C or worse in economics. They have not recognized that economics is different and requires practice.

To avoid a frustrating visit to your instructor after your first exam, I suggest you do the following.

HOW TO STUDY ECONOMICS

■ Don't rely solely on your high-school economics

If you took high-school economics, you've already studied demand and supply, which your instructor will lecture on in the first few weeks. Don't be lulled into feeling that the course will be easy. Your high-school knowledge of economic concepts will be useful, but it will not be enough to guarantee high scores on exams. Your college instructor will demand more detailed knowledge of concepts and ask you to apply them in new circumstances.

■ Keep up with the course material on a weekly basis

Read the appropriate textbook chapter before your instructor lectures on it. You'll be amazed at how your instructor's teaching ability improves when you come to class prepared. After class, work the practice problems and exercise and Foundations Interactive quiz for practice. Then use the Study Guide quiz to test your understanding. Economics requires lots of practice and self testing.

■ Make a good set of notes

Good notes are vital to focus your studying. Writing the notes is more important than reading them! The note-writing process begins when you read the textbook *before* the lecture. Make an outline set of notes at that time. List all the key terms and be sure you know their definitions. Take the outline to class and fill in the details. After class, rewrite the notes clearly so that you can easily review them later. At this time, elaborate any items that your instructor emphasizes.

■ Use your instructor and/or teaching assistants for help

When you have questions or problems with course material, ask questions. Your instructor is here to help you learn. Instructors like to be asked questions. And there are no stupid questions! So try not to be shy. The personal contact that comes from one-on-one tutoring is rewarding for instructors as well as beneficial for you.

■ Form a study group

A useful way to motivate your studying and to learn economics is to discuss the course material and problems with other students. Explaining the answer to a question out loud is a very effective way of discovering how well you understand the question. When you answer a question only in your head, you often skip steps in the chain of reasoning without realizing it. When you are forced to explain your reasoning aloud, gaps and mistakes quickly appear, and you and your fellow group members can quickly correct your reasoning. The Checkpoint practice problems and exercises are extremely good study group material.

■ Work old exams intelligently

You can usually obtain old exam papers in your school library, from your instructor, or from students who have already taken the course. Past exams give you a feel for the style of question your instructor might ask, and working them under a time constraint helps you to pace yourself and do the exam in the allotted time. But remember that you are preparing for the *next* exam

that your instructor will set, not the *last* one. You must *understand* the answer to each question. If you *memorize* answers, you are likely to fail. Every year, instructors hear students who tell them that this year's exam was much harder than last year's. In truth, it was the same paper with a few numbers and examples changed!

■ Use All Your Tools

The authors of your book, Robin Bade, Michael Parkin, and Brian Lyons, have created a rich array of learning tools that they describe in the preceding section, "Your Complete Learning Package." Make sure that you read this section and use *all* your tools! You should attempt to complete a chapter in the Study Guide only after you have read the corresponding textbook chapter and listened to your instructor lecture on the material.

HOW TO USE THE STUDY GUIDE

Each Study Guide chapter contains:

Chapter in Perspective

This first section is a short summary of the key material. It is designed to focus you quickly and precisely on the core material that you must master. You can use it to help you organize you own notes when you first read the textbook chapter. And you can use it before your exam to serve as a final check of the key concepts you have studied.

Expanded Chapter Checklist

A key point of the textbook is its use of Chapter Checklist and Checkpoints. Each Checklist item is explained in the textbook and is followed by a Checkpoint where you will work practice problems and exercises. The Study Guide repeats the Checklist learning objective and then breaks it down into a list of smaller objectives. Use this more detailed list to organize your study and for review. If you have mastered each of the detailed checklist objectives, you can be confident that you understand the material.

Key Terms

One aspect many students find difficult about economics is its vocabulary. To understand economics you must learn its vocabulary. The Study Guide lists the key terms in each chapter and gives the page in the textbook on which they are found. You can use this list to help you review for a test. Be sure that you can define each term and that you understand its definition.

After the Key Terms, the Study Guide is divided into topics that correspond to each Checkpoint in your text. At the beginning of each Checkpoint the learning objective is repeated. Always keep this objective in mind because it helps place the material in the Checkpoint into perspective.

Practice Problem

Each Checkpoint in the text contains a practice problem with answers. These practice problems are repeated in the Study Guide, but the explanations of the solutions are more detailed than in the textbook. Use these solutions to enhance your understanding of the topic.

Additional Practice Problem

After the original practice problem is explained, the Study Guide presents an additional practice problem. The additional practice problem either extends the original one or covers a related topic. Although the solution to the additional practice problem is given, try to solve it on your own first.

Following the additional practice problem is the Self Test. This section has fill in the blank, true or false, multiple choice, complete the graph, and short answer questions. The questions are designed to test your understanding of each topic.

Do the Self Test questions as if they were real exam questions, which means do them without looking at the answers. Struggling to work out the answers to a question that you find difficult is one of the most effective ways to learn. You will learn the most from right answers you had to struggle to work out and from your wrong answers and mistakes. Look at the answers, only

after you have attempted all the questions in a Checkpoint. When you finally do check the answers, be sure to understand where you went wrong and why the answer given is correct.

Fill in the Blanks

Fill in the blank questions will help you with the economics vocabulary and allow you to check that you know the definitions of the key terms and how to use them. These questions will also help you review for a test because, once completed, they serve as a *very* brief list of the main points within a Checklist item.

True or False

Some instructors use true or false questions on exams or quizzes, so these questions can prove very valuable exam practice. The answers to the questions are given along with a textbook page reference. If you do not understand the answer, turn to the textbook and study the topic. Reviewing the textbook page at this time will enable you to improve your understanding and perhaps ensure that you will not miss a similar question on your exams.

Multiple Choice

Many exams contain multiple choice questions, so pay particular attention to these questions. The answers to each of these questions also contain a textbook page reference. If you have difficulty with a question, use this page reference to review the topic in the textbook and improve your understanding. Remember that multiple choice is not multiple guess. Work out the answer. Know why an incorrect option is incorrect.

Complete the Graph

The complete the graph questions allow you to practice using one of economists' major tools, graphs. If there are essay questions on your exams, it is a safe bet that you will be expected to use some graphs in your essay. Complete the graph questions are designed to ensure that you are well prepared to draw graphs correctly.

Use the graph in the Study Guide to answer the questions. Although the answer is given, do *not* look at it before you attempt to solve the problem. It is much too easy to deceive yourself into thinking that you understand the answer when you simply look at the question and then read the answer. Involve yourself in the material by answering the question and then looking at the answer. If you cannot answer the question or if you got the answer wrong, the Study Guide gives the textbook reference. Use the text and study the material!

Short Answer

The last set of questions are short answer questions. Approach them in the same way as you approach the other question types. Answer them before you look at the answers in the Study Guide. These questions make good discussion questions for your study group. Use them to check how well your study group members understand the topic. If your group disagrees about the answer, use the textbook page references to settle the disagreements and be sure that everyone has a solid grasp of the topic.

FINAL COMMENTS

This Study Guide could not have been written without the help of many people.

Robin Bade, Michael Parkin, and Brian Lyons have written an outstanding textbook. Their intense interest in their students and their dedication to producing the best learning package possible is inspirational. It was my privilege to be one of Michael Parkin's graduate students at the University of Western Ontario. I know from experience his outstanding pedagogical principles. And Robin Bade has taught me over the last eight years that details are important and that we should always strive for excellence—a lesson we can use in all aspects of life, not just economics!

Mark Rush from the University of Florida provided the initial files upon which this Study Guide is based.

Jane McAndrew, my friend in the Economics Reference Centre at the University of Western Ontario continues to help me in my quests for data. She also managed to mitigate my stress level with her well-timed gift of the Potato-Head Family.

Richard Parkin produced all of the artwork and maintained a wonderful sense of humour when deadlines seem insurmountable.

I made two good e-mail buddies during the work on this Study Guide. My thanks to Gary Bennett and Michelle Harrington for their support during this project.

My son Andy, who is now a grade 10 student continues to inspire me with dedication to his academic responsibilities. He always manages to meet his deadlines and I try to do likewise.

Thanks go to my husband Marvin and his parents Bernice and Ross who kept the Gillmore family afloat this past holiday season while I was so busy with work. A special thank you to my mother-in-law who not only decorated my tree but also did much of my Christmas shopping!

And finally my parents, Ve and Bill Shearer, who continue to be the rocks of support behind my endeavours. My parents believe that if I set my mind to doing something, then the thing will be done. Thank you for your faith in me.

I have tried to make the Study Guide as helpful and useful as possible. Undoubtedly I have made some mistakes—mistakes that you might find. If you do find a mistake, please let me know so that I can correct any errors. If you have a question, suggestion, or comment, please contact me. My address follows, or you can e-mail me at

jeannie.gillmore@uwo.ca.

Jeannie Gillmore
Department of Economics
University of Western Ontario
London, Ontario
N6A 5C2
February, 2004.

Getting Started

Chapter

1

Chapter 1 explains what economics is, what economists do and how they think, and why even those who do not plan on becoming economists should learn the essential elements of this discipline. Future chapters will rely on the ideas and definitions presented in this chapter....

■ **Define economics, distinguish between microeconomics and macroeconomics, and explain the questions of macroeconomics.**

Economic questions exist because of scarcity, the condition that arises because the available resources are insufficient to satisfy wants. Economics is the social science that studies the choices that we make as we cope with scarcity and the incentives that influence and reconcile our choices. Microeconomics studies choices made by individuals and businesses. Macroeconomics studies the national and global economies. Macroeconomic issues are the standard of living, the cost of living, and economic fluctuations. The standard of living is the quantity of consumption of goods and services that people enjoy and is measured by average income per person. The cost of living is the number of dollars it takes to buy the goods and services that achieve a given standard of living. Economic fluctuations are reflected in the business cycle, the periodic but irregular up-and-down movement in production and jobs.

■ **Describe what economists do and some of the problems they encounter.**

Statements about what *is* are *positive* statements; statements about what *ought to be* are *normative* statements. Economists use observing and measuring, model building, and testing to develop their theories. An economic model simplifies reality by including only those features needed for the purpose at hand. *Ceteris paribus* is a Latin term that means "other things being equal" or "if all other relevant things remain the same." Correlation is the tendency for the values of two variables to move in a predictable and related way. The *post hoc* fallacy is the error of reasoning that a first event *causes* a second event because the first occurred *before* the second.

■ **Explain four core ideas that define the way economists think about macroeconomic questions.**

The four core ideas are that macroeconomic performance results from rational choices that respond to the incentives people face; the standard of living improves when production per person increases; the cost of living rises when the quantity of money increases faster than production; and economic fluctuations result from expenditure and productivity fluctuations.

■ **Explain why economics is worth studying.**

Studying economics provides understanding and expanded career opportunities. The costs of studying economics are forgone knowledge of other subjects and forgone leisure time.

EXPANDED CHAPTER CHECKLIST

When you have completed this chapter, you will be able to

1 Define economics, distinguish between microeconomics and macroeconomics, and explain the questions of macroeconomics.

- Define economics and explain the meaning of scarcity.
- Distinguish between microeconomics and macroeconomics.
- List and explain the three big macroeconomic issues.

2 Describe what economists do and some of the problems they encounter.

- Explain the difference between positive and normative statements.
- Describe the task of economic science.
- Define and discuss correlation.
- Give examples of the *post hoc* fallacy.

3 Explain four core ideas that define the way economists think about macroeconomic questions.

- Define rational choice and explain why a rational choice is made on the margin.
- Explain the role productivity plays in increasing the standard of living.
- Discuss the cause of inflation.

4 Explain why economics is worth studying.
- State two benefits of studying economics.
- State two costs of studying economics.

KEY TERMS

- Benefit (page 13)

- Business cycle (page 5)
- *Ceteris paribus* (page 10)
- Correlation (page 11)
- Cost of living (page 5)
- Deflation (page 5)
- Economic model (page 9)
- Economic theory (page 9)
- Economics (page 3)
- Goods and services (page 4)
- Great Depression (page 6)
- Incentive (page 2)
- Inflation (page 5)
- Macroeconomics (page 3)
- Margin (page 14)
- Marginal benefit (page 14)
- Marginal cost (page 14)
- Microeconomics (page 3)
- Opportunity cost (page 13)
- *Post hoc* fallacy (page 11)
- Productivity (page 15)
- Rational choice (page 13)
- Scarcity (page 2)
- Standard of living (page 4)
- Unemployment (page 4)

CHECKPOINT 1.1

■ Define economics, distinguish between microeconomics and macroeconomics, and explain the questions of macroeconomics.

Practice Problems 1.1

1. Economics studies choices that arise from one fact. What is that fact?

2. Sort the following headlines into those that deal with (i) the standard of living, (ii) the

cost of living, and (iii) economic fluctuations:

a. Production per person has grown for the tenth straight year.

b. Another price hike for consumers?

c. Firms lay off more workers as orders decline.

d. The government pays more unemployment benefits.

e. New robots boost production across a wide range of industries.

f. Money doesn't buy what it used to.

Solution to Practice Problems 1.1

These Practice Problems involve definitions, which focus on the key macroeconomic questions.

Quick Review

- *Standard of living* The quantity of consumption of goods and services that people enjoy on the average; it is measured by average income per person.

- *Cost of living* The number of dollars it takes to buy the goods and services that achieve a given standard of living.

- *Economic fluctuations* The economy fluctuates in a business cycle, a periodic but irregular up-and-down movement in production and jobs.

1. **Economics studies choices that arise from one fact. What is that fact?**

The fact is scarcity. The available resources are insufficient to satisfy wants. Scarcity influences all of economics.

2. **Sort the following headlines into those that deal with (i) the standard of living, (ii) the cost of living, and (iii) economic fluctuations:**

a. **Production per person has grown for the tenth straight year.**

Production per person affects the standard of living because with more goods and services per person being produced, income per person, which measures the standard of living, increases.

b. **Another price hike for consumers?**

A price hike raises the cost of living because it increases the number of dollars it takes to pay for goods and services.

c. **Firms lay off more workers as orders decline.**

As orders decline, production decreases and more workers become unemployed so the headline deals with economic fluctuations.

d. **The government pays more unemployment benefits.**

The government pays out more unemployment benefits when there are more unemployed workers and the economy goes into recession, so the headline deals with economic fluctuations.

e. **New robots boost production across a wide range of industries.**

By boosting production, the robots increase production per worker. So the headline deals with the standard of living.

f. **Money doesn't buy what it used to.**

More dollars are needed to purchase the same quantity of goods and services as in the past. The headline deals with the cost of living.

Additional Practice Problem 1.1a

Which of the following headlines are microeconomic in nature and which are macroeconomic?

a. Several manufacturers introduce gigabyte memory chips for personal computers.

b. Government helps farmers recover losses from poor wheat crop.

c. The unemployment rate rises.

d. The federal government decides to regulate the production and price of electricity.

Solution to Additional Practice Problem 1.1a

a.   Several manufacturers introduce gigabyte memory chips for personal computers.

This headline is about the choice made by firms to introduce new memory chips. It is a microeconomic headline.

b.   Government helps farmers recover loses from poor wheat crop.

This headline shows us the government in the market for wheat. It is a microeconomic headline.

c.   The unemployment rate rises.

An increase in the unemployment rate is a macroeconomic issue. Although it affects individuals and their choices, it involves the overall health of the national economy.

d.   The federal government decides to regulate the production and price of electricity.

Even though the federal government is involved, this issue is a matter of how a particular product is produced and sold. So it is microeconomic in nature.

■ Self Test 1.1

Fill in the blanks

Economic questions arise because ____ (wants; resources) exceed the ____ (wants; resources) available to satisfy them. Faced with ____ (scarcity; the *post hoc* fallacy), people must make choices. ____ (Macroeconomics; Microeconomics) is the study of the choices that individuals and businesses make. The big issues macroeconomics studies are ____, ____, and ____.

True or false

1.   An incentive can encourage or discourage an action.

2.   The standard of living is measured by the inflation rate.

3.   The cost of living is the number of dollars it takes to buy the goods and services to achieve a given standard of living.

4.   The worst recession ever experienced is called the Great Depression.

Multiple choice

1.   The characteristic from which all economic problems arise is

a.   political decisions.

b.   providing a minimal standard of living for every person.

c.   how to make a profit.

d.   scarcity.

2.   Scarcity results from the fact that

a.   human wants exceed the resources available to satisfy them.

b.   an incentive can be either a carrot or a stick

c.   our standard of living keeps increasing.

d.   the population keeps growing.

3.   ____ studies issues such as the standard of living, recessions, and interest rates.

a.   Macroeconomics

b.   Microeconomics

c.   International economics

d.   The history of economics

4.   Last year, a country's average income per person increased and the cost of living did not change. You can conclude that

a.   the country's standard of living decreased during the last year.

b.   scarcity is not a concern because labour resources increased.

c.   the country's standard of living increased during the last year.

d.   the country's cost of living decreased during the last year.

5. When inflation leads to a decrease in the value of the dollar, an economy experiences

a. an increasing cost of living.

b. an increasing standard of living.

c. a decreasing cost of living.

d. an expansionary period.

6. Business cycles are

a. business law irregularities.

b. the smooth, upward path of production and jobs.

c. fluctuations in prices only.

d. irregular up-and-down movement in production and jobs.

Complete the graph

■ FIGURE 1.1
Total production

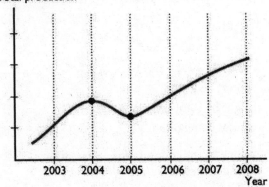

1. Figure 1.1 shows how total production changes over the years. In the figure, label the parts of the business cycle.

Short answer

1. Will there ever come a time without scarcity?

2. Explain the difference between microeconomics and macroeconomics.

3. What are the three big issues that macroeconomics studies?

CHECKPOINT 1.2

■ **Describe what economists do and some of the problems they encounter.**

Practice Problems 1.2

1. Classify the following statements as positive or normative:

a. Unemployed workers have to wait too long before being rehired.

b. Doctors earn, on the average, more than the Prime Minister.

2. Provide two examples of the *post hoc* fallacy.

Solution to Practice Problems 1.2

The key to whether a statement is positive or normative is whether the statement can be tested. If we can test the statement, it is positive; if we cannot test the statement, it is normative.

Quick Review

- *Positive statement* A positive statement tells what is currently understood about the way the world operates.

- *Normative statement* A normative statement tells what ought to be. It depends on opinions and cannot be tested.

- *Post hoc* fallacy The error of reasoning that a first event *causes* a second event because the first occurred *before* the second.

a. **Unemployed workers have to wait too long before being rehired.**

This statement cannot be tested. What one person thinks is too long, another thinks is too short. The statement is normative.

b. **Doctors earn, on the average, more than the Prime Minister.**

This statement can be tested to determine if it is correct, so it is a positive statement.

2. **Provide two examples of the *post hoc* fallacy.**

Your examples will differ. The key is that the first event does not cause the second.

i) A sale on swimsuits in April causes warm weather in June.

ii) Buying 100 shares of Bell Canada stock today causes its price to fall tomorrow.

Additional Practice Problem 1.2a

Why is it harder to test theories in macroeconomics than in laboratory sciences, such as chemistry?

Solution to Additional Practice Problem 1.2a

In laboratory sciences it is possible to do controlled experiments. You can add all the same ingredients in the same proportions, but just change the temperature of the mixture and observe the effect, or keep the temperature and everything else the same but change the amount of one ingredient. If you have a theory that predicts what the effect of each change should be, you can test the theory by matching the prediction with the results of the experiment.

In the area of macroeconomics, controlled experiments seem impossible. Even if a whole nation would consent to have an economist perform an experiment on the country to test a theory, there still would be no controlled experiment. That would require that the country (starting at the same date, with all the same conditions) go through the same period of time twice—for example once with a low inflation rate and again with a higher inflation rate. Clearly this isn't possible. Economists must use other methods to try to disentangle the effects of many things happening all at the same time.

■ Self Test 1.2

Fill in the blanks

A statement that tells what *is* is a ____ (positive; normative) statement. A statement that tells what *ought to be* is a ____ (positive; normative)

statement. An economic ____ (model; theory) simplifies the reality it describes. The process of building and testing models creates ____ (theories; natural experiments). The Latin term meaning "other things being equal" is ____ (*ceteris paribus; post hoc*).

True or false

1. The statement, "If income per person grows more rapidly, crime rates decrease" is a positive statement.

2. An economic model must include all the details about the real world.

3. Studying a situation that arises naturally in the ordinary course of economic life is called a natural experiment.

4. Assuming that one event causes another because the first occurs before the second is good economic reasoning.

Multiple choice

1. A positive statement
a. must always be right.
b. cannot be tested.
c. might be right or wrong.
d. cannot be negative.

2. Which of the following is an example of a normative statement?
a. If cars become more expensive, fewer people will buy them.
b. Car prices should be affordable.
c. If wages increase, firms will fire some workers.
d. Cars emit pollution.

3. If an economic model's predictions conflict with actual data,
a. there is zero correlation between variables.
b. the model needs adjustment.
c. it becomes an economic law.
d. the subject matter must be normative.

4. The Latin term *ceteris paribus* means
a. after this, therefore because of this.
b. other things being equal.
c. what is correct for the part is not correct for the whole.
d. when one variable increases, the other variable decreases.

5. To cope with the problem of sorting out the effects of each individual factor and to compare the effects with what a model predicts, economists use
a. natural experiments
b. econometric investigations
c. economic experiments
d. all of the above

6. "The rooster crows every morning and then the sun comes out. Sunrise, therefore, is caused by the rooster's crowing." This statement is a
a. true statement.
b. *post hoc* fallacy.
c. normative statement.
d. negative statement.

Short answer

1. Becky is writing an essay about the law that requires all passengers in a car to use a seat belt and the effectiveness of wearing a seat belt. Give an example of a positive statement and a normative statement that she might include in her essay.

2. The task of economic science is broken into three steps. List these three steps.

3. What is correlation? Give an example other than the examples in your textbook.

CHECKPOINT 1.3

■ **Explain four core ideas that define the way economists think about macroeconomic questions.**

Practice Problems 1.3

1. Kate usually plays tennis for two hours a week and her grade on math tests is usually 70 percent. Last week, after playing two hours of tennis, Kate thought long and hard about playing for another hour. She decided to play another hour of tennis and cut her study time by one additional hour. But the grade on last week's math test was 60 percent.
a. What was Kate's opportunity cost of the third hour of tennis?
b. Was Kate's decision to play the third hour of tennis rational?
c. Did Kate make her decision on the margin?

2. Classify each of the following events as (i) an influence on the standard of living or the cost of living and (ii) an expenditure or productivity source of economic fluctuations:
a. A new computer chip doubles the speed of a PC.
b. A new process lowers the cost of producing fibre-optic cable.
c. Telephone companies increase their spending on cellular networks.
d. Expenditure is increasing, prices are rising but production is stagnant.

Solution to Practice Problem 1.3

The first Practice Problem uses several ideas, including rational choice. To understand rational choice, you also need to understand marginal benefit and marginal cost because a rational choice compares the marginal benefit to the marginal cost. The second problem returns to the macroeconomic themes of this chapter, the standard of living, the cost of living, and economic fluctuations.

Quick Review

- *Marginal cost* The opportunity cost that arises from a one-unit increase in an activity. The marginal cost of something is what you *must give up* to get *one more* unit of it.

- *Marginal benefit* The benefit that arises from a one-unit increase in an activity. The marginal benefit of something is *measured by* what you are *willing to* give up to get *one more* unit of it.

- *Rational choice* A choice that uses the available resources to most effectively satisfy the wants of the person making the choice.

a. What was Kate's opportunity cost of the third hour of tennis?

The opportunity cost of the third hour of tennis was the ten-percentage point drop in her grade.

b. Was Kate's decision to play the third hour of tennis rational?

Kate's decision was rational if her marginal benefit exceeded her marginal cost.

c. Did Kate make her decision on the margin?

Kate's decision to play was made on the margin because she compared the cost and benefit of *one additional hour* of tennis.

2. Classify each of the following events as (i) an influence on the standard of living or the cost of living and (ii) an expenditure or productivity source of economic fluctuations:

a. A new computer chip doubles the speed of a PC.

The chip increases productivity and raises the standard of living. It is a productivity source of economic fluctuations.

b. A new process lowers the cost of producing fibre-optic cable.

The new process increases productivity, raises the standard of living, and lowers the cost of liv-

ing. It is a productivity source of economic fluctuations.

c. Telephone companies increase their spending on cellular networks.

The new cellular networks will increase the standard of living. The spending is an expenditure source of economic fluctuations.

d. Expenditure is increasing, prices are rising but production is stagnant.

When prices rise, the cost of living increases. The increase in expenditure is an expenditure source of economic fluctuations.

Additional Practice Problem 1.3a

Macroeconomics studies the standard of living, the cost of living, and economic fluctuations. Which of these three topics is the most important?

Solution to Additional Practice Problem 1.3a

It is impossible to state with certainty which topic is the most important because importance is a normative concept. From the vantage point of public opinion, the topic considered most important varies over time, depending on what is currently the weakest area of the nation's performance. During a recession, the topic of economic fluctuations is considered most important, while during a period of inflation, the cost of living is considered most important. In times during which there is neither a recession nor severe inflation, the standard of living is deemed key.

■ Self Test 1.3

Fill in the blanks

A choice made on the margin compares the marginal benefit of an action to its ____ (marginal cost; total benefit). The standard of living increases only when ____ (prices rise; the number of people employed increases; productivity increases). A rising cost of living is called ____ (inflation; recession) and occurs when there is an increase in the quantity of ____ (money; wages) not matched by an increase in the quantity of

____ (money; goods and services). The sources of economic fluctuations are placed in two broad groups: fluctuations in ____ (expenditure; wages; inflation) and fluctuations in ____ (marginal benefits; productivity). Most people think economic fluctuations are ____ (desirable; undesirable).

True or false

1. Instead of attending her macroeconomics class for two hours, Kim could have played tennis or watched a movie. The opportunity cost of attending class is the tennis *and* the movie she had to give up.

2. When Martha decides whether or not to watch another hour of television by comparing the marginal cost to the marginal benefit, she is making a rational choice.

3. Inflation is caused by increases in productivity.

4. Macroeconomists know how to eliminate the business cycle.

Multiple choice

1. Which of the following is NOT one of the four core macroeconomic ideas?

a. The nation's macroeconomic performance has led people to make rational choices.

b. The standard of living improves when production per person increases.

c. The cost of living rises when the quantity of money increases faster than production.

d. The economy fluctuates when expenditure and productivity fluctuates.

2. An increase in a country's standard of living *definitely* occurs if

a. prices rise.

b. the population grows.

c. the dollar value of a nation's production increases.

d. total production per person employed increases.

3. Which of the following increases the nation's standard of living?

a. an increase in the quantity of money

b. a decrease in the quantity of money

c. an increase in productivity

d. a decrease in productivity

4. When there is too much money chasing too few goods, the result is

a. inflation.

b. deflation.

c. productivity.

d. splurging.

5. The sources of economic fluctuations are fluctuations in

a. expenditures only.

b. productivity only.

c. expenditures and in productivity.

d. expenditures, in productivity, and in the seasons.

6. "Smoothing the business cycle" occurs when economists

a. predict when a recession will occur.

b. limit the damage from a recession.

c. eliminate expansions.

d. decrease productivity gains.

Short answer

1. Define opportunity cost. If you have a choice of buying dinner for $5 at Taco Bell or at KFC and you decide to eat at KFC, what is the opportunity cost of the decision?

2. What is marginal cost? What is marginal benefit?

3. What are the sources of economic fluctuations?

CHECKPOINT 1.4

■ **Explain why economics is worth studying.**

Practice Problem 1.4

A student is choosing between an economics course and a popular music course. List two opportunity costs and two benefits from taking a course in economics.

Solution to Practice Problem 1.4

This Practice Problem uses the idea of making a rational choice, which is a choice that uses the available resources to most effectively satisfy the wants of the person making the choice.

Quick Review

- *Opportunity cost* The opportunity cost of something is what you *must* give up to get it.

A student is choosing between an economics course and a popular music course. List two opportunity costs and two benefits from taking a course in economics.

The opportunity cost of taking the economics course is the forgone knowledge from the popular music course. If the popular music course does not involve as much time studying, forgone leisure is another opportunity cost. Benefits from taking the economics course are the knowledge gained from the class, a better understanding of the world, better problem-solving skills, and expanded career opportunities.

Additional Practice Problem 1.4a

What are the opportunity cost and benefits of using this *Study Guide*?

Solution to Additional Practice Problem 1.4a

The opportunity cost of using this *Study Guide* is the highest-valued forgone activity. Your highest-valued forgone activity may be one of studying for another class, watching television, playing sports, or sleeping.

The benefits from using this *Study Guide* are an enhanced understanding of the important topics in the book, which likely will lead to a higher grade in the class. Over a longer time horizon, an increased understanding might influence the future courses you take and lead to career benefits.

■ **Self Test 1.4**

Fill in the blanks

A better understanding of important issues is a ____ (benefit; cost) of studying economics. The cost of buying textbooks ____ (is; is not) an opportunity cost of studying economics rather than another subject.

True or false

1. Economics requires thinking abstractly about concrete issues.

2. Economics graduates are among the highest-paid professionals.

3. Most students find that memorization is the best way to get a good grade in an economics course.

4. The benefits to all students from majoring in economics exceed the costs.

Multiple choice

1. A benefit from studying economics is
   a. that the only jobs available to students studying economics are as economists.
   b. an understanding of many of today's events.
   c. the increased leisure time from the choice of economics as a major.
   d. that you will become as rich as Mick Jagger.

2. Economics is a good course for a ____ student.
   a. pre-med
   b. pre-law
   c. pre-MBA
   d. All of the above answers are correct.

3. On average, economics graduates earn less than ____ graduates and more than ____ graduates.

a. engineering and computer science; commerce

b. commerce; fine arts and humanities

c. commerce; engineering and computer science

d. fine arts and humanities; engineering and computer science

4. An opportunity cost of studying economics as your major rather than another subject is the

a. expense of the textbooks you buy and the tuition you pay.

b. tuition you pay but not the expense of the textbooks you buy.

c. the forgone knowledge of the other subject.

d. increased salary you might earn after you graduate.

5. Economics says that you should major in economics if

a. your instructor tells you that the benefits from the major exceed the costs.

b. you think the benefits from the major exceed the costs.

c. you think you will make lots of money regardless of the costs.

d. you are very good at memorization.

Short answer

1. What are the career benefits from taking economics courses?

2. Why do some students decide not to major in economics?

SELF TEST ANSWERS

■ CHECKPOINT 1.1

Fill in the blanks

Economic questions arise because <u>wants</u> exceed the <u>resources</u> available to satisfy them. Faced with <u>scarcity</u>, people must make choices. <u>Microeconomics</u> is the study of the choices that individuals and businesses make. The big issues macroeconomics studies are <u>the standard of living</u>, <u>the cost of living</u>, and <u>economic fluctuations</u>.

True or false

1. True; pages 2-3
2. False; page 4
3. True; page 5
4. True; page 6

Multiple choice

1. d; page 2
2. a; page 2
3. a; page 3
4. c; page 4
5. a; page 5
6. d; page 5

Complete the graph

■ FIGURE I.2

Total production

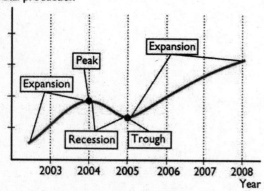

2003 2004 2005 2006 2007 2008
Year

1. Figure 1.2 labels the parts of the business cycle; page 6.

Short answer

1. There will never be a time without scarcity because human wants are unlimited; page 2.
2. Microeconomics is the study of the choices that individuals and businesses make and the way these choices respond to incentives, interact, and are influenced by governments. Macroeconomics is the study of the aggregate (or total) effects on the national economy and the global economy of the choices that individuals, businesses, and governments make; page 3.
3. The three big issues macroeconomics studies are the standard of living; the cost of living; and economic fluctuations; page 4.

■ CHECKPOINT 1.2

Fill in the blanks

A statement that tells what *is* is a <u>positive</u> statement. A statement that tells what *ought to be* is a <u>normative</u> statement. An economic <u>model</u> simplifies the reality it describes. The process of building and testing models creates <u>theories</u>. The Latin term meaning "other things being equal" is <u>ceteris paribus</u>.

True or false

1. True; page 8
2. False; page 9
3. True; page 11
4. False; page 11

Multiple choice

1. c; page 8
2. b; page 8
3. b; page 9
4. b; page 10

5. d; pages 11-12

6. b; page 11

Short answer

1. A positive statement is "People who obey the law and wear seat belts are involved in fewer road deaths." This statement can be tested. A normative statement is "People should be free to choose whether to wear a seat belt or not." This statement cannot be tested; page 8.

2. The three steps are observing and measuring; model building; and testing; page 8.

3. Correlation is the tendency for the values of two variables to move in a predictable and related way. An example is the correlation between the income a person makes and the highest level of education they have attained; page 11.

■ **CHECKPOINT 1.3**

Fill in the blanks

A choice made on the margin compares the marginal benefit of an action to its marginal cost. The standard of living increases only when productivity increases. A rising cost of living is called inflation and occurs when there is an increase in the quantity of money not matched by an increase in the quantity of goods and services. The sources of economic fluctuations are placed in two broad groups: fluctuations in expenditure and fluctuations in productivity. Most people think economic fluctuations are undesirable.

True or false

1. False; page 13

2. True; page 13

3. False; page 15

4. False; page 16

Multiple choice

1. a; page 13

2. d; page 15

3. c; page 15

4. a; page 15

5. c; page 16

6. b; page 16

Short answer

1. The opportunity cost of a decision is the highest-valued alternative forgone. The opportunity cost of eating at KFC is *not* $5. It is eating a meal at Taco Bell because that is the best alternative forgone; page 13.

2. Marginal benefit is the benefit that arises from a one-unit increase in an activity. The marginal benefit of something is measured by what you are willing to give up to get one more unit of it. Marginal cost is the opportunity cost that arises from a one-unit increase in an activity. The marginal cost of something is what you must give up to get one more unit of it; page 14.

3. The sources of economic fluctuations are expenditure fluctuations and productivity fluctuations; page 16.

■ **CHECKPOINT 1.4**

Fill in the blanks

A better understanding of important issues is a benefit of studying economics. The cost of buying textbooks is not an opportunity cost of studying economics rather than another subject.

True or false

1. True; page 19

2. True; page 19

3. False; page 20

4. False; page 20

Multiple choice

1. b; page 18

2. d; page 19

3. a; page 19

4. c; page 20

5. b; page 20

Short answer

1. Economics courses stress thinking abstractly and logically about important subjects, which are valuable skills to possess. In addition, economics courses discuss many important economic concepts. A student's career benefits from the style of thought gained in economics classes and from the economic concepts covered in the classes; page 19.

2. There are students for whom the benefit of economics as a major is less than the cost. The costs might be high because the student does not enjoy economics or because the student finds the subject difficult. These students should not major in economics; page 20.

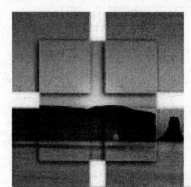

Appendix: Making and Using Graphs

1

APPENDIX IN PERSPECTIVE

This appendix reviews the graphs used in your economics course.

■ **Making and using graphs.**

A graph represents a quantity as a distance. The vertical axis is the y-axis and the horizontal axis is the x-axis. A scatter diagram is a graph of the value of one variable against the value of another variable. A time-series graph measures time on the x-axis and the variable or variables of interest on the y-axis. A cross-section graph shows the values of an economic variable for different groups in a population at a point in time. A relationship between two variables that move in the same direction is a positive or direct relationship. A relationship between two variables that move in opposite directions is a negative or inverse relationship. Some relationships have minimum or maximum points. The slope of a relationship is the change in the value of the variable measured on the y-axis divided by the change in the value of the variable measured on the x-axis. To graph a relationship among more than two variables, we use the *ceteris paribus* assumption and graph the relationship between two of the variables holding the other variables constant.

EXPANDED APPENDIX CHECKLIST

When you have completed this chapter, you will be able to

1 Interpret a scatter diagram, a time-series graph, and a cross-section graph.

- Identify the x-axis, the y-axis, and the origin in a graph.

- Explain what is plotted and identify a scatter diagram, a time-series graph, and a cross-section graph.

2 Interpret the graphs used in economic models.

- Identify a positive or direct relationship between two variables.

- Identify a negative or inverse relationship between two variables.

- Identify a relationship that has a maximum or a minimum.

- Identify when variables are unrelated.

3 Define and calculate slope.

- Present the formula used to calculate the slope of a relationship and use it to calculate slope.

4 Graph relationships among more than two variables.

- Describe how the *ceteris paribus* assumption is used to allow us to illustrate the relationship among more than two variables.

KEY TERMS

- Cross-section graph (page 26)
- Direct relationship (page 28)
- Inverse relationship (page 29)
- Linear relationship (page 28)
- Negative relationship (page 29)
- Positive relationship (page 28)
- Scatter diagram (page 26)
- Slope (page 31)
- Time-series graph (page 26)
- Trend (page 26)

CHECKPOINT A1.1

■ **Making and using graphs.**

Additional Practice Problems A1.1

1. You have data on the average monthly rainfall and the monthly expenditure on umbrellas in Halifax. What type of graph would be the best to reveal if any relationship exists between these variables?

2. The table in the next column shows the annual Canadian unemployment rate in the 1990s. In Figure A1.1, label the axes and then plot these data. What type of graph are you creating? What is the trend in the unemployment rate?

3. In Figure A1.2, draw a straight line that shows a positive relationship and another straight line that shows a negative relationship.

4. Figure A1.3 shows the relationship between the price of a paperback book and the quantity of paperback books a publisher is willing to sell. What is the slope of the line in Figure A1.3?

Year	Unemployment rate (percentage of labour force)
1990	8.2
1991	10.3
1992	11.2
1993	11.4
1994	10.3
1995	9.4
1996	9.6
1997	9.1
1998	8.3
1999	7.6

■ **FIGURE A1.1**

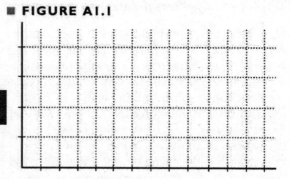

■ **FIGURE A1.2**

■ **FIGURE A1.3**

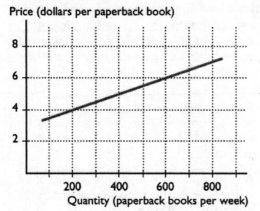

Solution to Additional Practice Problems A1.1

1. **You have data on the average monthly rainfall and the monthly expenditure on umbrellas in Halifax. What type of graph would be the best to reveal if any relationship exists between these variables?**

A scatter diagram would be the best graph to use. A scatter diagram plots average monthly rainfall on the vertical axis (the y-axis) and the monthly expenditure on umbrellas on the horizontal axis (the x-axis).

2. **The table shows the annual Canadian unemployment rate in the 1990s. In Figure A1.1, label the axes and then plot these data. What type of graph are you creating? What is the trend in the unemployment rate?**

Figure A1.4 labels the axes and plots the data in the table. The graph is a time-series graph. The trend is negative because the unemployment rate has generally been decreasing during 1990s.

■ **FIGURE A1.4**

3. **In Figure A1.2, draw a straight line that shows a positive relationship and another straight line that shows a negative relationship.**

Figure A1.5 has two lines, one that shows a positive relationship and another that shows a negative relationship. Your figure might not show exactly these lines. The key point is that the line for the positive relationship slopes up as x increases along it and the line for the negative relationship slopes down as x increases along it.

■ **FIGURE A1.5**

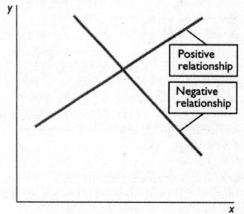

4.   What is the slope of the line in Figure A1.3?

The slope of a line is the change in the variable measured on the y-axis divided by the change in the variable measured on the x-axis. To calculate the slope of the line in the figure, use points A and B in Figure A1.6. Between A and B, y rises by 2, from 4 to 6. And x increases by 400, from 200 to 600. The slope equals 2 ÷ 400, which is 0.005.

■ **FIGURE A1.6**

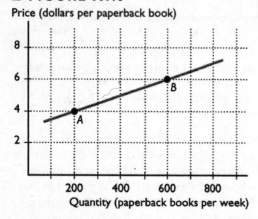

Price (dollars per paperback book)

Quantity (paperback books per week)

■ **Self Test A1.1**

Fill in the blanks

In a graph, the vertical line is called the _____ (x-axis; y-axis) and the horizontal line is called the _____ (x-axis; y-axis). A _____ (scatter diagram; time-series graph; cross-section graph) is a graph of the value of one variable against the value of another variable. A _____ (scatter diagram; time-series graph; cross-section graph) measures time on the x-axis and the variable on the y-axis. A _____ (scatter diagram; time-series graph; cross-section graph) shows the values of an economic variable for different groups in a population at a point in time. If the graph of a relationship between two variables slopes up to the right, the two variables have a _____ (positive; negative) relationship. If the graph between two variables is a vertical line, the two variables _____ (are; are not) related. The slope of a relationship is the change in the value of the variable measured on the _____ (x-axis; y-axis)

divided by the change in the value of the variable measured on the _____ (x-axis; y-axis). By using the *ceteris paribus* assumption, it _____ (is; is not) possible to graph a relationship that involves more than two variables.

True or false

1.   A point that is above and to the right of another point will have a larger value of the x-axis variable and a larger value of the y-axis variable.

2.   A scatter diagram shows the values of an economic variable for different groups in a population at a point in time.

3.   A time-series graph compares values of a variable for different groups at a single point in time.

4.   A trend is a measure of the closeness of the points on a graph.

5.   A positive relationship is always a linear relationship.

6.   A relationship that starts out sloping upward and then slopes downward has a maximum.

7.   A graph that shows a horizontal line indicates variables that are unrelated.

8.   The slope of a relationship is calculated as the change in the value of the variable measured on the x-axis divided by the change in the value of the variable measured on the y-axis.

9.   The slope at a point on a curve equals the slope of the straight line that touches the point and no other point on the curve.

Multiple choice

1.   The best way to demonstrate how a variable changes from one year to the next is to use a

a.   scatter diagram.

b.   time-series graph.

c.   linear graph.

d.   cross-section graph.

2. To show the values of a variable for different groups in a population at a point in time, it is best to use a

a. scatter diagram.
b. time-series graph.
c. linear graph.
d. cross-section graph.

3. If whenever one variable increases, another variable also increases, then these two variables have a ____ relationship.

a. positive
b. negative
c. inverse
d. cross-sectional

4. A graph of the relationship between two variables is a line that slopes down to the right. These two variables have ____ relationship.

a. a positive
b. a direct
c. a negative
d. no

5. Two variables are unrelated if the relationship is illustrated by

a. a vertical line.
b. a 45° line.
c. a horizontal line.
d. Both (a) and (c) are correct.

6. Figure A1.7 shows the relationship between the price of rutabagas and the quantity purchased. Between points A and B, what is the slope of the line?

a. 4
b. 1
c. 3
d. –3

■ FIGURE A1.7

Price (dollars per kilogram)

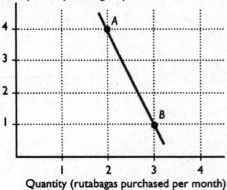

Quantity (rutabagas purchased per month)

7. In Figure A1.8 an increase in z leads to a

a. movement up along one of the lines that shows the relationship between x and y.
b. movement down along one of the lines that shows the relationship between x and y.
c. rightward shift of the line that shows the relationship between x and y.
d. leftward shift of the line that shows the relationship between x and y.

■ FIGURE A1.8

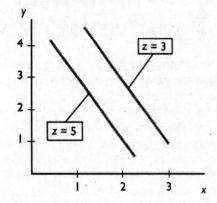

8. In Figure A1.8, *ceteris paribus*, an increase in *x* is associated with

a. an increase in *y*.

b. a decrease in *y*.

c. an increase in *z*.

d. a decrease in *z*.

Complete the graph

1. The table below has the annual average Canadian inflation rate for the decade of the 1990s. In Figure A1.9, measure time on the horizontal axis and the inflation rate on the vertical axis, and then plot these data.

Year	Inflation rate (percent per year)
1990	3.0
1991	2.7
1992	1.3
1993	1.5
1994	1.1
1995	2.2
1996	1.7
1997	0.9
1998	−0.6
1999	1.6

a. What type of graph are you creating?

b. In what year was the inflation rate the highest? The lowest?

c. Using your figure, what was the trend in the inflation rate during the 1990s?

■ **FIGURE A1.9**

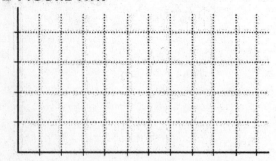

2. The table below has the annual average Canadian inflation rate and an annual interest rate for the decade of the 1990s. In Figure A1.10, measure the interest rate along the *y*-axis and the inflation rate along the *x*-axis. Then plot these data.

Year	Interest rate (percent per year)	Inflation rate (percent per year)
1990	12.8	3.0
1991	8.8	2.7
1992	6.6	1.3
1993	4.8	1.5
1994	5.5	1.1
1995	7.1	2.2
1996	4.2	1.7
1997	3.2	0.9
1998	4.7	−0.6
1999	4.7	1.6

a. What type of graph are you creating?

b. What is the relationship between the interest rate and the inflation rate that you see in your figure?

■ **FIGURE A1.10**

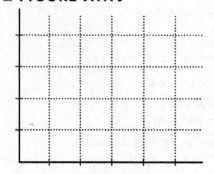

3. The number of sacks of premium cat food that cat lovers buy depends on the price of a sack of cat food. The relationship is given in the table. In Figure A1.11, plot this relationship, putting the price on the vertical axis and the quantity on the horizontal axis.

Price (dollars per sack of cat food)	Quantity (sacks of cat food per month)
1	10,000
2	8,000
3	7,000
4	4,000

a. If the price of a sack of cat food is $2, how many sacks are purchased in a month?

b. If the price of a sack of cat food is $3, how many sacks are purchased in a month?

c. Is the relationship between the price and the quantity positive or negative?

■ **FIGURE A1.11**

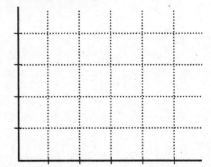

4. In Figure A1.12, label the maximum and minimum points.

■ **FIGURE A1.12**

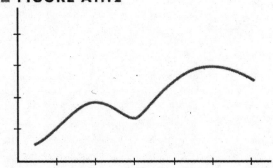

5. In Figure A1.13, draw a line through point A with a slope of 2. Label the line "1." Draw another line through point A with a slope of –2. Label this line "2."

■ **FIGURE A1.13**

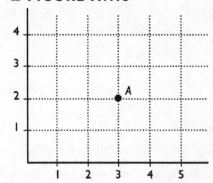

6. Bobby says that he buys fewer compact discs when the price of a compact disc is higher. Bobby also says that he will buy more compact discs after he graduates and his income is higher. The table below shows the number of compact discs Bobby buys in a month at different prices when his income is low and when his income is high.

Price (dollars per compact disc)	Quantity of compact discs purchased, low income	Quantity of compact discs purchased, high income
11	4	5
12	3	4
13	1	3
14	0	2

a. In Figure A1.14, put the price on the vertical axis and the quantity purchased on the horizontal axis. Show the relationship between the number of discs purchased and the price when Bobby's income is low.

b. On the same figure, draw the relationship between the number of discs purchased and the price when his income is high.

c. When Bobby's income increases, does the curve that graphs the relationship between the price of a compact disc and the number purchased shift rightward or leftward?

■ FIGURE A1.14

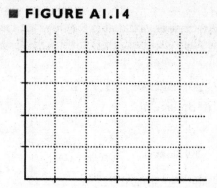

Short answer

1. What are the three types of graphs?

2. If two variables are positively related, will the slope of a graph of the two variables be positive or negative?

3. If a line slopes downward to the right, is its slope positive or negative?

4. In Figure A1.15, what is the slope of the curved line at point *A*? At point *B*?

■ FIGURE A1.15

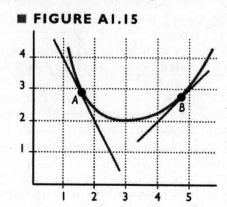

SELF TEST ANSWERS

■ CHECKPOINT A1.1

Fill in the blanks

In a graph, the vertical line is called the y-axis and the horizontal line is called the x-axis. A scatter diagram is a graph of the value of one variable against the value of another variable. A time-series graph measures time on the x-axis and the variable on the y-axis. A cross-section graph shows the values of an economic variable for different groups in a population at a point in time. If the graph of a relationship between two variables slopes up to the right, the two variables have a positive relationship. If the graph between two variables is a vertical line, the two variables are not related. The slope of a relationship is the change in the value of the variable measured on the y-axis divided by the change in the value of the variable measured on the x-axis. By using the *ceteris paribus* assumption, it is possible to graph a relationship that involves more than two variables.

True or false

1. True; page 25
2. False; page 26
3. False; page 26
4. False; page 26
5. False; page 28
6. True; page 30
7. True; page 30
8. False; page 31
9. True; page 31

Multiple choice

1. b; page 26
2. d; page 26
3. a; page 28
4. c; page 29
5. d; page 30
6. d; page 31
7. d; page 32
8. b; page 32

Complete the graph

■ **FIGURE A1.16**

Inflation rate (percent per year)
3
2
1
0
–1
1990
1992
1994
1996
1998
2000
Year

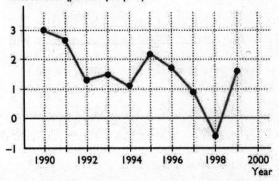

1. Figure A1.16 plots the data.
a. This is a time-series graph; page 26.
b. The inflation rate was highest in 1990 and lowest in 1998.
c. The inflation rate generally fell during the decade so the trend is negative; page 26.

■ **FIGURE A1.17**

Interest rate (percent per year)
15
12
9
6
3
–1
0
1
2
3
Inflation rate (percent per year)

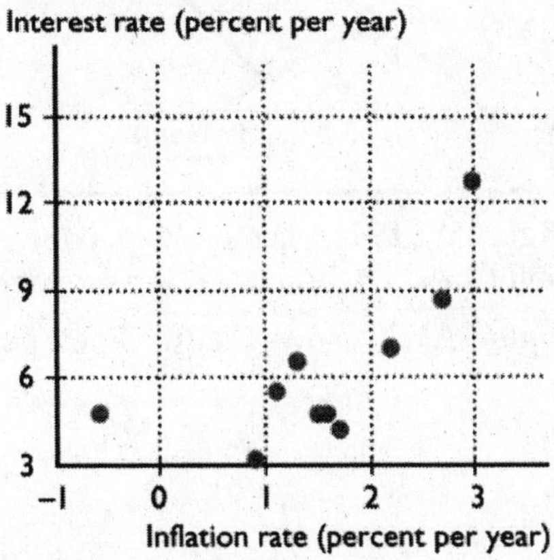

2. Figure A1.17 plots the data.

a. The figure is a scatter diagram; page 26.

b. The relationship between the interest rate and the inflation rate is positive; page 28.

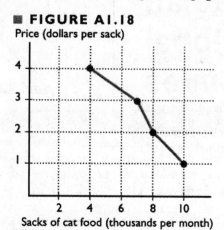

■ FIGURE A1.18

Price (dollars per sack)

Sacks of cat food (thousands per month)

3. Figure A1.18 plots the relationship.

a. If the price is $2 a sack, 8,000 sacks are purchased in a month.

b. If the price is $3 a sack, 7,000 sacks are purchased in a month.

c. The relationship between the price and quantity of sacks is negative; page 29

■ FIGURE A1.19

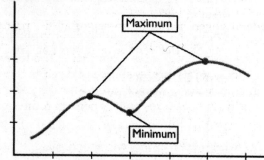

4. Figure A1.19 labels the two maximum points and one minimum point; page 30.

5. Figure A1.20 shows the two lines; page 31.

6a. Figure A1.21 plots the relationship.

b. Figure A1.21 plots the relationship.

c. An increase in Bobby's income shifts the relationship rightward; page 32.

■ FIGURE A1.20

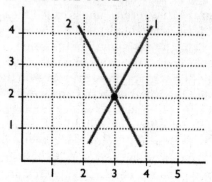

■ FIGURE A1.21

Price (dollars per compact disc)

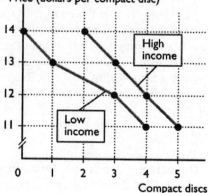

Compact discs

Short answer

1. The three types of graphs are scatter diagram, time-series graph, and cross-section graph; page 26.

2. If two variables are positively related, a graph of the relationship will have a positive slope; pages 28, 31.

3. If a line slopes downward to the right, its slope is negative; page 31.

4. The slope of the curved line at point A is −2 and the slope of the curved line at point B is 1; page 31.

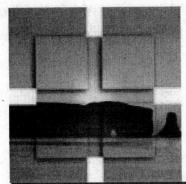

The Canadian and Global Economies

Chapter 2

Chapter 2 introduces concepts about how households, firms, markets, and government are linked together. A circular flow model is presented that shows the flow of expenditure and income from and to households, firms, and government. The three dimensions of macroeconomic performance, which are standard of living, cost of living, and economic fluctuations, are discussed.

■ **Describe what, how, and for whom goods and services are produced in Canada.**

The production of goods and services, the "what" question, is divided into four large groups: consumption goods and services, investment goods, government goods and services, and export goods and services. The "how" of production involves the factors of production: land, labour, capital, and entrepreneurship. The functional distribution of income is the distribution of income among the factors of production. The largest share of income in Canada is earned by labour. The personal distribution of income is the distribution of income among households.

■ **Use the circular flow model to provide a picture of how households, firms, and governments interact.**

The circular flow model shows that households provide factors of production and firms hire factors of production in factor markets. The circular flow also shows that households purchase goods and services and firms sell goods and services in goods markets. The decisions made by households, firms and government in these markets determine the answers to the "what," "how," and "for whom" questions. The national debt is the total amount that the federal government has borrowed in the past to finance its budget deficits. In the circular flow, the government purchases goods and services in goods markets. It makes transfers to firms and households and also receives taxes from them. The federal government's largest payment is on health and social services and its largest source of receipts is personal income taxes. 43 percent of provincial and local governments' payments are for health care. 10 percent of provincial and local governments' receipts come from sales taxes and 19 percent come from personal income taxes.

■ **Describe the macroeconomic performance—standard of living, cost of living, and economic fluctuations—of the Canadian and other economies.**

The world's economies are divided into advanced, developing, and transition economies. In Canada in 2003, the average income was about $124 a day, which is about four times the world average. Canada's unemployment rate during the past 10 years ranks in the middle of the developed economies. Along with most advanced countries, Canada has a low inflation rate. Developing and transition economies have higher inflation rates than Canada. Canada's last recession occurred in 1990–1991; Asia suffered a severe recession in 1998.

EXPANDED CHAPTER CHECKLIST

When you have completed this chapter, you will be able to

1 **Describe what, how, and for whom goods and services are produced in Canada.**

- Define consumption goods and services, investment goods, government goods and services, and export goods and services.

- Discuss the four factors of production.

- Define functional distribution of income and personal distribution of income.

2 **Use the circular flow model to provide a picture of how households, firms, and governments interact.**

- Define households and firms.

- Tell what is bought and sold in goods markets and in factor markets.

- Draw the circular flow between households and firms that shows factor markets and goods markets.

- Draw the circular flow model with the government added.

- State the major payments of the federal government and the main taxes paid to the federal government.

- State the main payments of the provincial and local governments and the main taxes paid to the provincial and local governments.

3 **Describe the macroeconomic performance—standard of living, cost of living, and economic fluctuations—of the Canadian and other economies.**

- Distinguish between advanced, developing, and transition economies and give examples of each.

- Discuss how Canada compares to other countries in terms of its standard of living, unemployment rate, inflation rate, and economic fluctuations.

KEY TERMS

- Capital (page 38)
- Circular flow model (page 42)
- Consumption goods and services (page 36)
- Entrepreneurship (page 39)
- Export goods and services (page 36)
- Factor markets (page 42)
- Factors of production (page 37)
- Firms (page 42)
- Functional distribution of income (page 39)
- Goods markets (page 42)
- Government goods and services (page 36)
- Households (page 42)
- Human capital (page 38)
- Interest (page 39)
- Investment goods (page 36)
- Labour (page 37)
- Land (page 37)
- Market (page 42)
- National debt (page 46)
- Personal distribution of income (page 40)
- Profit (or loss) (page 39)
- Rent (page 39)
- Wages (page 39)

CHECKPOINT 2.1

- Describe what, how, and for whom goods and services are produced in Canada.

Practice Problems 2.1

1. Name the four broad categories of goods and services that we use in macroeconomics, provide an example of each (different from those in the chapter), and rank them from largest to smallest in 2002.

2. Name the four factors of production and the incomes they earn.

3. Distinguish between the functional distribution of income and the personal distribution of income.

4. In Canada, which factor of production earns the largest share of income and what percentage of total income did it earn in 2002?

Solution to Practice Problems 2.1

These Practice Problems involve definitions, which we will encounter throughout our study of macroeconomics.

Quick Review

*   *Consumption goods and services* Goods and services that are bought by individuals and used to provide personal enjoyment and contribute to a person's standard of living.
*   *Investment goods* Goods that are bought by businesses to increase their productive resources.
*   *Government goods and services* Goods and services that are bought by governments.
*   *Export goods and services* Goods and services produced in one country and sold in other countries.

1. **Name the four broad categories of goods and services that we use in macroeconomics, provide an example of each (different from those in the chapter), and rank them from largest to smallest in 2002.**

The four categories are consumption goods and services, investment goods, government goods and services, and export goods and services.

Examples of consumption goods and services are manicures and cheeseburgers. Examples of in-vestment goods are assembly lines and computer software. Examples of government goods and services are highways and health care. Examples of export goods and services are the services provided by Canadians who teach English in Japan and lumber sold to the United States.

In 2002, consumption goods and services were the largest category, export goods and services the second largest, government goods and services the third largest, and investment goods the smallest.

2. **Name the four factors of production and the incomes they earn.**

Land, labour, capital, and entrepreneurship are the four factors of production. Land earns rent; labour earns wages; capital earns interest; and entrepreneurs earn a profit or incur a loss.

3. **Distinguish between the functional distribution of income and the personal distribution of income.**

The functional distribution of income shows how total income is divided among the factors of production. The personal distribution of income shows how total income is divided among households, which are grouped according to the level of their incomes.

4. **In Canada, which factor of production earns the largest share of income and what percentage of total income did it earn in 2002?**

The factor of production that earns the largest share of income in Canada is labour. In 2002, labour earned 68 percent of total income.

Additional Practice Problem 2.1a

When does the quantity of labour increase?

Solution to Additional Practice Problem 2.1a

The quantity of labour increases as the adult population increases and if a larger percentage of the population takes jobs. During the past 50 years, a larger proportion of women have taken paid work and this trend has increased the quantity of labour available.

■ Self Test 2.1

Fill in the blanks

Goods and services that are bought by individuals and used to provide personal enjoyment and to contribute to a person's standard of living are _____ (consumption; investment; factor) goods and services. Goods that are bought by businesses to increase their productive resources are _____ (consumption; investment; productive) goods. Goods and services that are produced in one country and sold in other countries are _____ (export goods and services; factors of production; investments). Of the four large groups of goods and services in Canada, _____ (consumption goods and services; investment goods; government goods and services; export goods and services) have the largest share of total production. Productive resources are called _____ and are grouped into four categories: _____, _____, _____, and _____. In 2002, _____ (labour; capital) received 68 percent of total income. The percentage distribution of income among households is called the _____ (functional; personal) distribution of income.

True or false

1. Consumption goods and services include a slice of pizza purchased to eat at home.

2. A gold mine is included in the "land" category of productive resources.

3. The income earned by people selling the services of their capital is profit or loss.

4. In Canada, the factor of production that earns the most income is labour.

5. In Canada, the richest 20 percent of families earn approximately 30 percent of total income.

Multiple choice

1. When the total Canadian production of goods and services is divided into consumption goods and services, investment goods, government goods and services, and export goods and services, the largest component is

a. consumption goods and services.

b. investment goods.

c. government goods and services.

d. export goods and services.

2. An example of an investment good is

a. a fibre-optic cable TV system.

b. an insurance policy.

c. a hair cut.

d. a slice of pizza.

3. Goods and services produced in one country and sold in other countries are called

a. consumption goods and services.

b. investment goods.

c. government goods and services.

d. export goods and services.

4. Which of the following correctly lists the categories of productive resources?

a. machines, buildings, land, and money

b. hardware, software, land, and money

c. capital, money, and labour

d. land, labour, capital, and entrepreneurship

5. Human capital is

a. solely the innate ability we are born with.

b. the money humans have saved.

c. the knowledge and skill that people obtain from education, on-the-job training, and work experience.

d. machinery.

6. Wages are paid to ____ and interest is paid to ____.

a. entrepreneurs; capital
b. labour; capital
c. labour; land
d. entrepreneurs and labour; entrepreneurs and capital

7. The factor of production that earns the greatest income in Canada is

a. labour.
b. land.
c. capital.
d. entrepreneurship.

8. The personal distribution of income in Canada shows

a. that labour receives the largest percentage of total income.
b. how profit accounts for the largest fraction of total income
c. that the richest 20 percent of families earn 24 percent of total income,
d. that the poorest 20 percent of families earn 5 percent of total income.

Short answer

1. Is an automobile a consumption good or an investment good?

2. Compare the incomes earned by the poorest and richest 20 percent of families.

CHECKPOINT 2.2

■ Use the circular flow model to provide a picture of how households, firms, and governments interact.

Practice Problem 2.2

What are the real flows and money flows that run between households, firms, and government in the circular flow model?

Solution to Practice Problem 2.2

The circular flow model shows the interactions between firms, households, and government. It is also used in later chapters to help explain some of key macroeconomic relationships between income and expenditure.

Quick Review

• *Circular flow model* A model of the economy that shows the circular flow of expenditures and incomes that result from decision makers' choices, and the way those choices interact to determine what, how, and for whom goods and services are produced.

What are the real flows and money flows that run between households, firms, and government in the circular flow model?

Start with the circular flow diagram, illustrated in Figure 2.1. The circular flow diagram illustrates the flows between households, firms, and the government. The real flows are in orange. They are the flows of the services of the factors of production through factor markets and the flows of goods and services through goods markets. In the goods markets, households and the government buy goods and services from firms. In the factor markets, households provide land, labour, capital, and entrepreneurship to firms. The money flows are in red, blue, and green. The money flows are incomes earned by factors of production (rent, wages, interest, and profit or loss), expenditures made by households and the government on goods and services, and transfers from the government to households and firms and taxes from households and firms to the government.

■ FIGURE 2.1

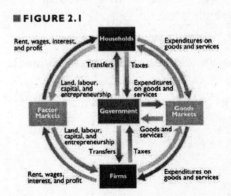

Additional Practice Problem 2.2a

In the circular flow model, describe the flow of money between households and firms and the government.

Solution to Additional Practice Problem 2.2a

Households and firms pay taxes to the government. The government makes cash payments to households and firms, which are called transfers. Taxes and transfers are direct transactions with government and do not go through the goods markets and factor markets.

■ Self Test 2.2

Fill in the blanks

The _____ (circular; economic) flow model shows the flow of expenditures and incomes. An arrangement that brings buyers and sellers together is a _____ (firm; household; market). A market in which goods and services are bought and sold is a _____ (goods; factor) market and a market in which factors of production are bought and sold is a _____ (goods; factor) market. In 2003, the federal government's receipts were equal to nearly _____ (20; 38; 75) percent of the total value of all the goods and services produced in Canada that year. In 2003, local and provincial governments spent _____ (20; 50; 75) percent more than was spent by the federal government. _____ is the largest source of federal receipts. In 2003, transfers from the federal government provided _____ (13; 38; 75) percent of provincial and local government receipts.

True or false

1. Firms own the factors of production.

2. A market is any arrangement where buyers and sellers meet face-to-face.

3. Factors of production flow from households to firms through goods markets.

4. The largest source of provincial and local government receipts is the GST.

5. The largest part of the payments of provincial and local government is education.

Multiple choice

1. Within the circular flow model, economists define households as
   a. families with at least 2 children.
   b. families living in their own houses.
   c. individuals or groups of people living together as decision-making units.
   d. individuals or groups within the same legally defined family.

2. A market is defined as
   a. the physical place where goods are sold.
   b. the physical place where goods and services are sold.
   c. any arrangement that brings buyers and sellers together.
   d. another name for a store such as a grocery store.

3. In the circular flow model,
   a. only firms sell in markets.
   b. only households buy from markets.
   c. firms sell and firms buy.
   d. the government does not transact in either the goods market or the factor market.

4. _____ choose the quantities of goods and services to produce, while _____ choose the quantities of goods and services to buy.
   a. Households; firms
   b. Firms; households and the government
   c. The government; firms
   d. Households; the government

5. A circular flow model shows the interrelationship between the ____ markets and the ____ markets.

a. household; goods

b. household; factor

c. business; household

d. goods; factor

6. In the circular flow model, the expenditures on goods and services flow in the

a. same direction as goods and services.

b. opposite direction to goods and services.

c. same direction as factor markets.

d. None of the above answers are correct.

7. The largest payment that the federal government makes is

a. education and training.

b. health and social services.

c. payments to provinces.

d. interest on the national debt.

8. The largest source of receipts for the federal government is

a. personal income taxes.

b. GST.

c. corporate income taxes.

d. lotteries.

Complete the graph

1. Figure 2.2 ignores the government and shows the flows into and out of households. Label the flows and identify who they come from and who they go to.

■ FIGURE 2.2

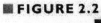
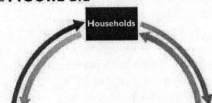

2. Figure 2.3 ignores the government and shows the flows into and out of firms. Label the flows and identify who they come from and who they go to.

■ FIGURE 2.3

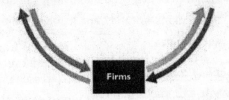

3. Figure 2.4 now includes the government and shows the money flows into and out of firms. Label the money flows.

■ FIGURE 2.4

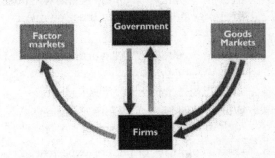

Short answer

1. Ignoring taxes and transfer payments, what funds flow into and out of firms?

2. Is it possible for something to affect households and not firms? To affect firms and not households? Explain your answer.

3. Compare the magnitude of the payments of local and provincial governments with the payments of the federal government in 2003.

4. In the circular flow, what are the sources of expenditures on goods and services?

5. Compare the amount of the federal government's spending on interest on the national debt to its spending on defence, law, and order.

CHECKPOINT 2.3

■ Describe the macroeconomic performance—standard of living, cost of living, and economic fluctuations—of the Canadian and other economies.

Practice Problems 2.3

1. What percentage of the world's population lives in developing economies and what was the range of incomes that these people earned in 2003?

2. What percentage of the world's population lives in advanced economies and what was the range of incomes that these people earned in 2003?

3. What percentage of the world's population lives in Canada and what was the average income that Canadians earned in 2003?

4. Which countries or regions experienced high inflation during the last ten years?

5. Which countries or regions experienced recession during the last ten years?

Solution to Practice Problems 2.3

These Practice Problems focus on the vast differences in economic performances throughout the world.

Quick Review

• *Advanced economies* The 28 countries (or areas) that have the highest standard of living.

• *Developing economies* The 128 countries in Africa, Asia, the Middle East, Europe, and Central and South America that have not yet achieved a high standard of living for their people.

• *Transition economies* The 28 countries in Europe and Asia that were, until the early 1990s, part of the Soviet Union or its satellites.

1. **What percentage of the world's population lives in developing economies and what was the range of incomes that these people earned in 2003?**

Almost 5 billion of the world's 6 billion people live in developing economies. So, approximately 80 percent of the world's population lives in developing economies. In 2003, their average daily incomes ranged from $8 in Africa to $29 in Central and South America.

2. **What percentage of the world's population lives in advanced economies and what was the range of incomes that these people earned in 2003?**

Almost 1 billion people, or approximately 16 percent of the world's population live in advanced economies. In 2003, their average daily incomes ranged from $81 in the new industrial economies of Asia to $140 in the United States.

3. **What percentage of the world's population lives in Canada and what was the average income that Canadians earned in 2003?**

The Canadian population in 2003 was almost 32 million, which is about one-half of one percent of the world's total population of 6 billion. The average income in Canada was $124 a day.

4. **Which countries or regions experienced high inflation during the last ten years?**

The countries and regions that experienced high inflation during the last ten years were the transition economies and parts of Central and South America.

5. **Which countries or regions experienced recession during the last ten years?**

The transition economies, Japan, and the new industrial economies of Asia experienced recession during the 1990s. The last recession in Canada occurred in 1990-1991.

Additional Practice Problem 2.3a

"For any economy, high unemployment rates mean a lower standard of living." To what extent is this statement true?

Solution to Additional Practice Problem 2.3a

If unemployment is high, society has factors of production that it is not using. These unused factors of production could be used to produce more goods and services, which means that a higher standard of living would exist. High unemployment lowers a nation's standard of living below what it could be otherwise.

■ Self Test 2.3

Fill in the blanks

The lowest standard of living is in the ____ (advanced; developing; transition) economies and the highest standard of living is in the ____ (advanced; developing; transition) economies. In Canada, average income is ____ ($104; $124; $144) a day and in India and the African continent it is ____ ($8; $4) a day. Inflation is ____ (high; low) in advanced economies. The deepest recession in the 1990s occurred in ____ (Japan; the transition economies).

True or false

1. The standard of living depends on the amount of money it takes to buy the goods and services that a typical family consumes.

2. Mexico is a transition economy.

3. Most of the people in the world live in countries that have incomes below the world average of $32 a day.

4. The transition economies have the highest inflation rates over the past ten years.

5. The deepest recession in the 1990s occurred in Canada.

Multiple choice

1. The world population is approximately ____ people.

   a. 6 million

   b. 2 trillion

   c. 6 billion

   d. 550 million

2. The percentage of the world's population that lives in the advanced economies is

   a. 75 percent.

   b. 50 percent.

   c. 25 percent.

   d. less than 20 percent.

3. Which of following groups of countries are *all* advanced economies?

   a. Australia, Brazil, and the United States

   b. Canada, Japan, France, and the United Kingdom

   c. Italy, the United States, China, and Russia

   d. Mexico, Canada, Germany, and Egypt

4. The transition economies are

   a. the largest grouping including the nations of China and India.

   b. in transition from state-owned production to free enterprises and unregulated markets.

   c. most of the nations of Western Europe.

   d. nations with some of the highest standards of living.

5. Among Canada, Russia, Germany, and the United Kingdom, the country with the highest average income per person and the highest standard of living is

   a. Canada.

   b. Russia.

   c. Germany.

   d. the United Kingdom.

6. Unemployment rates are lowest among ____ economies.

a. developing
b. transition
c. advanced
d. tropical

7. Inflation rates are lowest among ____ economies.

a. developing
b. transition
c. advanced
d. tropical

8. The deepest recession in the 1990s occurred in

a. Canada.
b. Asian countries except Japan, which had a mild recession.
c. Japan.
d. the transition economies.

Short answer

1. What are the three groups the International Monetary Fund uses to classify countries? Describe each group. Which group has the largest number of countries? The largest number of people?

2. How do inflation rates compare between advanced and developing economies?

3. Where were the deepest and most severe recessions in the 1990s?

SELF TEST ANSWERS

■ CHECKPOINT 2.1

Fill in the blanks

Goods and services that are bought by individuals and used to provide personal enjoyment and to contribute to a person's standard of living are consumption goods and services. Goods that are bought by businesses to increase their productive resources are investment goods. Goods and services that are produced in one country and sold in other countries are export goods and services. Of the four large groups of goods and services in Canada, consumption goods and services have the largest share of total production. Productive resources are called factors of production and are grouped into four categories: land, labour, capital, and entrepreneurship. In 2002, labour received 68 percent of total income. The percentage distribution of income among households is called the personal distribution of income.

True or false

1. True; page 36
2. True; page 37
3. False; page 39
4. True; page 39
5. False; page 40

Multiple choice

1. a; page 36
2. a; page 36
3. d; page 36
4. d; page 37
5. c; page 38
6. b; page 39
7. a; page 39
8. d; page 40

Short answer

1. An automobile can be either a consumption good or an investment good. It is a consumption good if it is purchased by a household but it is an investment good if it is purchased by a construction firm that uses it to transport building materials to different job sites; page 36.

2. The richest 20 percent of families have an average income of $101,628 in 2001 and earn 43 percent of total Canadian income. The poorest 20 percent of families have an average income of $11,675 and earn only 5 percent of total Canadian income; page 40.

■ CHECKPOINT 2.2

Fill in the blanks

The circular flow model shows the flow of expenditures and incomes. An arrangement that brings buyers and sellers together is a market. A market in which goods and services are bought and sold is a goods market and a market in which factors of production are bought and sold is a factor market. In 2003, the federal government's receipts were equal to nearly 20 percent of the total value of all the goods and services produced in Canada that year. In 2003, local and provincial governments spent 50 percent more than was spent by the federal government. Personal income taxes is the largest source of federal receipts. In 2003, transfers from the federal government provided 13 percent of provincial and local receipts.

True or false

1. False; page 42
2. False; page 42
3. False; pages 42-43
4. False; page 47
5. False; page 47

Multiple choice

1. c; page 42

2. c; page 42

3. c; page 42, 45

4. b; pages 42, 45

5. d; pages 42-43

6. b; pages 42-43

7. b; page 46

8. a; page 46

Complete the graph

1. Figure 2.5 labels the flows. Rent, wages, interest, and profit (or loss) flow from factor markets while land, labour, capital, and entrepreneurship flow to factor markets. Expenditures on goods and services flow to goods markets and goods and services flow from goods markets; page 43.

■ FIGURE 2.5

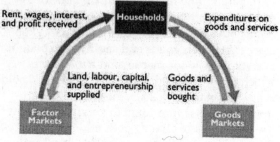

2. Figure 2.6 labels the flows. Revenue from the sale of goods and services flows into firms from goods markets and goods and services flow from firms to goods markets. Land, labour, capital, and entrepreneurship flow into firms from factor markets and rent, wages, interest, and profit (or loss) flow from firms to factor markets; page 43.

■ FIGURE 2.6

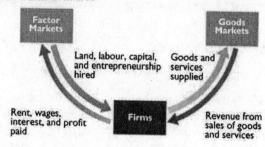

3. Figure 2.7 labels the money flows into and out of firms. Expenditures on goods and services and government expenditures on goods and services flow from goods markets to firms. Rent, wages, interest, and profit flow from firms to factor markets. Transfers flow from government to firms and taxes flow from firms to government; page 45.

■ FIGURE 2.7

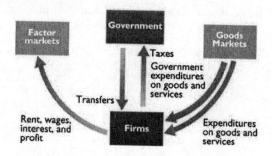

Short answer

1. Funds that flow into firms are household and government expenditures on goods and services, and transfers. Funds that flow out of firms are payments for rent, wages, interest, and profit to households in exchange for the factors of production, and taxes; pages 42, 43, 45.

2. The circular flow shows that at the macroeconomic level it is impossible for something to influence only firms or only households. An influence that changes households' buying behaviour in goods markets affects firms because firms sell to households in goods markets; pages 42-43.

3. In 2003, provincial and local governments spent about $290 billion—50 percent more than was spent by the federal government; page 44.

4. The circular flow identifies two sources of expenditures on goods and services, expenditures by households and expenditures by the government; page 45.

5. The federal government spends more on interest on the national debt than on defence, law, and order. In 2003, 13 percent of government payments was spent on interest on the national debt and 11 percent was spent on defence, law, and order; page 46.

■ CHECKPOINT 2.3

Fill in the blanks

The lowest standard of living is in the developing economies and the highest standard of living is in the advanced economies. In Canada, average income is $124 a day and in India and the African continent it is $8 a day. Inflation is low in advanced economies. The deepest recession in the 1990s occurred in the transition economies.

True or false

1. False; page 49
2. False; page 49
3. True; page 50
4. True; page 52
5. False; page 52

Multiple choice

1. c; page 49
2. d; page 49
3. b; page 49
4. b; page 50
5. a; page 50
6. c; page 51
7. c; page 52
8. d; page 52

Short answer

1. The three groups are advanced economies, developing economies, and transition economies. Advanced economies have the highest standard of living. Developing economies have yet to achieve a high standard of living. Transition economies are changing their economies from a system of state-owned production, central economic planning, and heavily regulated markets to a system of free enterprise and unregulated markets. The developing economies have the greatest number of countries, 128, and the greatest number of people, almost 5 billion; page 49.

2. Inflation rates are lowest in advanced economies and significantly higher in many developing economies; page 52.

3. The deepest and most severe recessions in the 1990s occurred in the transition economies, in particular, in Russia and Russia's neighbours; page 52.

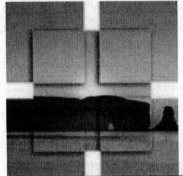

Chapter

3

The Economic Problem

Chapter 3 studies the production possibilities frontier, *PPF*. The *PPF* shows how the opportunity cost of a good or service increases as more of the good or service is produced. The *PPF* also shows how societies and individuals gain by specializing according to comparative advantage. Finally, we use the production possibilities frontier to study economic growth and its opportunity cost.

■ **Use the production possibilities frontier to illustrate the economic problem.**
The production possibilities frontier is the boundary between the combinations of goods and services that can be produced and combinations that cannot be produced, given the available factors of production and the state of technology. A production point outside the *PPF* is unattainable. Points on and inside the *PPF* are attainable. When resources are fully employed, production occurs at a point on the *PPF*. With unemployed resources, production occurs at a point inside the *PPF*. As we move along the *PPF* producing more of one good, less of another good is produced. When we move from inside the *PPF* to a point on the *PPF* more of some goods and services can be produced without producing less of others—a free lunch.

■ **Calculate opportunity cost.**
Along the *PPF* all choices involve a tradeoff. The *PPF* enables us to calculate opportunity cost—how much of one good we have to give up to get an additional unit of another good. Along the *PPF*, the opportunity cost of the good on the *x*-axis is equal to the decrease in the good on the *y*-axis divided by the increase in the good on the *x*-axis. As more of a good is produced, its opportunity cost increases.

■ **Explain how specialization and trade expand production possibilities.**
A person has a comparative advantage in an activity if that person can perform the activity at a lower opportunity cost than someone else. People gain from specializing in the production of the good in which they have comparative advantage and then trading with others. Absolute advantage occurs when one person is more productive than another person in several or even all activities. A person can have an absolute advantage in all activities but cannot have a comparative advantage in all activities.

■ **Explain how technological change and increases in capital and human capital expand production possibilities.**
A sustained expansion of production possibilities is called economic growth. Technological change, the expansion of human capital, and capital accumulation increase production possibilities and the *PPF* shifts outward. The resources used to advance technology, accumulate capital, or expand human capital cannot be used to produce current consumption goods and services. The decrease in the current production of consumption goods and services is the opportunity cost of economic growth.

EXPANDED CHAPTER CHECKLIST

When you have completed this chapter, you will be able to

1 Use the production possibilities frontier to illustrate the economic problem.

- Define the production possibilities frontier, *PPF*, and explain the relationship between the *PPF* and the available factors of production and the state of technology.
- State which production points are attainable and which are unattainable.
- Discuss production when resources are fully employed and when resources are unemployed.
- Discuss the difference between tradeoff and free lunch.

2 Calculate opportunity cost.

- Measure opportunity cost along the *PPF*.
- Describe how increasing opportunity cost is reflected in the shape of the *PPF*.

3 Explain how specialization and trade expand production possibilities.

- Define comparative advantage and explain its relationship to the gains from trade.
- Determine which of two people will specialize in the production of a good.
- Define absolute advantage and explain why it is different from comparative advantage.

4 Explain how technological change and increases in capital and human capital expand production possibilities.

- State the three key factors that influence economic growth and illustrate economic growth using a *PPF*.
- Explain the opportunity cost of economic growth.

KEY TERMS

- Absolute advantage (page 72)
- Comparative advantage (page 70)
- Economic growth (page 74)
- Production possibilities frontier (page 60)
- Tradeoff (page 63)

CHECKPOINT 3.1

■ Use the production possibilities frontier to illustrate the economic problem.

Practice Problems 3.1

1. Robinson Crusoe, the pioneer of the television program *Survivor*, lived alone on a deserted island. He spent his day fishing and picking fruit. He varied the time spent on these two activities and kept a record of his production. The table shows the numbers that Crusoe wrote in the sand. Use these numbers to make Crusoe's *PPF* if he can work only 8 hours a day.

Hours	Fish (kilograms)		Fruit (kilograms)
0	0		0
1	4.0	or	8
2	7.5	or	15
3	10.5	or	21
4	13.0	or	26
5	15.0	or	30
6	16.5	or	33
7	17.5	or	35
8	18.0	or	36

2. Which combinations (in kilograms) are attainable and which are unattainable: (i) 10 fish and 30 fruit, (ii) 13 fish and 26 fruit, (iii) 20 fish and 21 fruit?

3. Which combinations (in kilograms) use all of Crusoe's available 8 hours a day: (i) 15 fish and 21 fruit, (ii) 7 fish and 30 fruit, (iii) 18 fish and 0 fruit?

4. Which combinations (in kilograms) provide Crusoe with a free lunch and which confront him with a tradeoff when he increases fruit by 1 kilogram: (i) 18 fish and 0 fruit, (ii) 15 fish and 15 fruit, (iii) 13 fish and 26 fruit?

Solution to Practice Problems 3.1

These Practice Problems involve the construction and interpretation of a production possibilities frontier.

Quick Review

- *Production possibilities frontier* The boundary between combinations of goods and services that can be produced and combinations that cannot be produced, given the available factors of production and the state of technology.

- *Unattainable points* Production points outside the *PPF* are unattainable.

- *Full employment* At full employment, the economy produces at a point on the *PPF*.

- *Unemployment* At production points inside the *PPF* some resources are unemployed.

1. **Make Crusoe's *PPF* if he can work only 8 hours a day.**

Possibility	Fish (kilograms)		Fruit (kilograms)
A	0.0	and	36
B	4.0	and	35
C	7.5	and	33
D	10.5	and	30
E	13.0	and	26
F	15.0	and	21
G	16.5	and	15
H	17.5	and	8
I	18.0	and	0

The above table shows Crusoe's *PPF*. To calculate the *PPF*, suppose that Crusoe puts all 8 hours into gathering fruit, so that he gathers 36 kilograms—row *A*. But there is no time left for fishing, so he gets 0 kilograms of fish. If he takes an hour off from gathering fruit, he gathers 35 kilograms of fruit and has an hour in which to

fish, so he gets 4 kilograms of fish—row *B*. The rest of the *PPF* is constructed similarly.

2. **Which combinations (in kilograms) are attainable and which are unattainable: (i) 10 fish and 30 fruit, (ii) 13 fish and 26 fruit, (iii) 20 fish and 21 fruit?**

i) Row *D* shows that Crusoe can produce 10.5 fish and 30 fruit, so he can produce 10 fish and 30 fruit. So (i) is attainable.

ii) 13 fish and 26 fruit is on the production possibilities frontier—row *E*. So (ii) is attainable.

iii) 20 fish and 21 fruit is unattainable because when Crusoe spends the entire 8 hours fishing he can catch only 18 kilograms of fish—row *I*.

3. **Which combinations (in kilograms) use all of Crusoe's available 8 hours a day: (i) 15 fish and 21 fruit, (ii) 7 fish and 30 fruit, (iii) 18 fish and 0 fruit?**

i) If Crusoe spends enough time to pick 21 fruit, he can also catch 15 fish. This combination uses all his time and is on the *PPF*—row *F*.

ii) Row *C* shows that he can get 7.5 fish and 33 fruit if he works 8 hours, so combination (ii) does not require the full 8 hours. This combination is inside the *PPF*.

iii) Catching 18 fish takes 8 hours, leaving no time for picking fruit. So this combination uses all the 8 hours and is row *I* on the *PPF*.

4. **Which combinations (in kilograms) provide Crusoe with a free lunch and which confront him with a tradeoff when he increases fruit by 1 kilogram: (i) 18 fish and 0 fruit, (ii) 15 fish and 15 fruit, (iii) 13 fish and 26 fruit?**

i) 18 fish and 0 fruit is on the *PPF*—row *I*—so there is a tradeoff but no free lunch.

ii) The combination of 15 fish and 15 fruit is inside the *PPF* and so there is a free lunch.

iii) 13 fish and 26 fruit is on the *PPF*—row *E*—so there is a tradeoff but no free lunch.

Additional Practice Problem 3.1a

Use the *PPF* from Practice Problem 3.1. Can Crusoe gather 21 kilograms of fruit and catch 30 kilograms of fish? Explain your answer. Suppose that Crusoe discovers another fishing pond with more fish, so that he can catch twice as many fish as before. Now can Crusoe gather 21 kilograms of fruit and catch 30 kilograms of fish? Explain your answer.

Solution to Additional Practice Problem 3.1a

Initially, Crusoe cannot gather 21 kilograms of fruit and catch 30 kilograms of fish. This production point lies outside his *PPF* and is unattainable. When Crusoe discovers the new pond, he can gather 21 kilograms of fruit and catch 30 kilograms of fish. The *PPF* depends on the factors of production available and when the factors of production increase, Crusoe's production possibilities change.

■ Self Test 3.1

Fill in the blanks

The _____ (production possibilities; consumption) frontier is the boundary between the combinations of goods and services that can and cannot be produced given the available _____ (goods; factors of production) and _____ (number of services; state of technology). Production points outside the *PPF* _____ (are unattainable; are attainable; represent a free lunch). The possibility of a free lunch exists if production occurs _____ (inside; on; outside) the *PPF*. When resources are fully employed, we face a _____ (free lunch; tradeoff).

True or false

1. Our production capacity is limited by our available resources and by technology.

2. A point outside the production possibilities frontier is unattainable.

3. If all the factors of production are fully employed, the economy will produce at a point on the production possibilities frontier.

4. Moving from one point on the *PPF* to another point on the *PPF* illustrates a free lunch.

Multiple choice

1. A reason the production possibilities frontier exists is
   a. unlimited resources and technology.
   b. scarcity of resources.
   c. scarcity of resources and unlimited technology.
   d. unemployment.

2. The production possibilities frontier is a graph that shows the
   a. combinations of goods and services that can be produced as technology advances.
   b. combinations of goods and services that can be consumed.
   c. maximum combinations of goods and services that can be produced.
   d. minimum combinations of goods and services that can be produced.

3. The production possibilities frontier is a boundary that separates
   a. the combinations of goods that can be produced from the combinations of services.
   b. attainable combinations of goods and services that can be produced from unattainable combinations.
   c. equitable combinations of goods that can be produced from inequitable combinations.
   d. reasonable combinations of goods that can be consumed from unreasonable combinations.

4. Points inside the *PPF* are all
   a. unattainable and use fully employed resources.
   b. attainable and use fully employed resources.
   c. unattainable and have some unemployed resources.
   d. attainable and have some unemployed resources.

5. During a period of time with high unemployment, a country can increase the production of one good or service

a. without decreasing the production of something else.

b. but must decrease the production of something else.

c. and must increase the production of something else.

d. by using resources in the production process twice.

6. Moving along the production possibilities frontier illustrates

a. the existence of tradeoffs.

b. the existence of unemployment of factors of production.

c. the benefits of free lunches.

d. how free lunches can be exploited through trade.

Complete the graph

1. In Figure 3.1, draw a production possibilities frontier. Label the points that are attainable and unattainable. Label the points that have full employment and the points that have unemployment.

■ **FIGURE 3.1**
Computers (millions per year)

Food (tonnes per year)

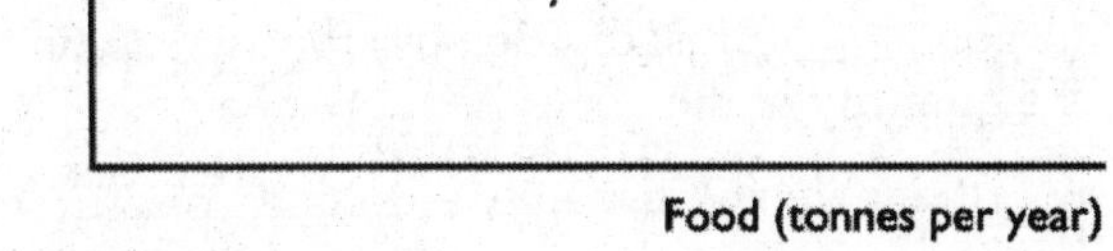

Short answer

1. What factors limit the amount of our production?

2. What is the relationship between unemployment and a free lunch? Between full employment and a tradeoff?

CHECKPOINT 3.2

■ **Calculate opportunity cost.**

Practice Problems 3.2

1. Use Robinson Crusoe's production possibilities shown in the table to calculate his opportunity cost of a kilogram of fish. Make a table that shows Crusoe's opportunity cost of a kilogram of fish as he increases the time he spends fishing and decreases the time he spends picking fruit.

Possibility	Fish (kilograms)		Fruit (kilograms)
A	0.0	and	36
B	4.0	and	35
C	7.5	and	33
D	10.5	and	30
E	13.0	and	26
F	15.0	and	21
G	16.5	and	15
H	17.5	and	8
I	18.0	and	0

2. If Crusoe increases his production of fruit from 21 kilograms to 26 kilograms and decreases his production of fish from 15 kilograms to 13 kilograms, what is his opportunity cost of a kilogram of fruit? Explain your answer.

3. If Crusoe is producing 10 kilograms of fish and 20 kilograms of fruit, what are his opportunity costs of a kilogram of fruit and a kilogram of fish? Explain your answer.

Solution to Practice Problems 3.2

Remember that opportunity cost is the highest-valued alternative forgone.

Quick Review

- *Opportunity cost is a ratio* Along a *PPF*, the opportunity cost of one good equals the quantity of the other good forgone divided by the increase in the quantity of the good.

1. **Make a table that shows Crusoe's opportunity cost of a kilogram of fish as he increases the time he spends fishing and decreases the time he spends picking fruit.**

Move from	Increase in fish (kilograms)	Decrease in fruit (kilograms)	Opportunity cost of fish (kilograms of fruit)
A to B	4.0	1	0.25
B to C	3.5	2	0.57
C to D	3.0	3	1.00
D to E	2.5	4	1.60
E to F	2.0	5	2.50
F to G	1.5	6	4.00
G to H	1.0	7	7.00
H to I	0.5	8	16.00

The opportunity cost of a kilogram of fish is the decrease in fruit divided by the increase in fish as Crusoe moves along his *PPF*. If he increases his time fishing and moves from point *A* to point *B*, he gets 4 kilograms more fish (from 0 kilograms to 4 kilograms) and he picks 1 less kilogram of fruit (he picks 35 kilograms of fruit instead of 36 kilograms). The opportunity cost of 4 kilograms of fish is 1 kilogram of fruit. The opportunity cost of 1 kilogram of fish is (1 kilogram of fruit ÷ 4 kilograms of fish), which is 0.25 kilograms of fruit. The rest of the answers in the table are calculated similarly.

2. **If Crusoe increases his production of fruit from 21 kilograms to 26 kilograms and decreases his production of fish from 15 kilograms to 13 kilograms, what is his opportunity cost of a kilogram of fruit? Explain your answer.**

If he increases fruit production from 21 kilograms to 26 kilograms, he gains 5 kilograms of fruit. Production of fish decreases from 15 kilograms to 13 kilograms, a decrease of 2 kilograms. The 5 additional kilograms of fruit cost 2 kilograms of fish. The opportunity cost of 1 kilogram of fruit equals 2 kilograms of fish forgone divided by the gain of 5 kilograms of fruit, which is 2/5 kilograms of fish.

3. **If Crusoe is producing 10 kilograms of fish and 20 kilograms of fruit, what are his opportunity costs of a kilogram of a fruit and a kilogram of fish? Explain your answer.**

This combination of fish and fruit lies inside his *PPF* so Crusoe enjoys a free lunch. He can gather more fruit without giving up fish and catch more fish without giving up fruit. His opportunity cost of fruit and of fish are zero.

Additional Practice Problem 3.2a

How does Crusoe's opportunity cost of a kilogram of fish change as he catches more fish?

Solution to Additional Practice Problem 3.2a

Crusoe's opportunity cost of a kilogram of fish increases as he catches more fish. In the table, as Crusoe moves from point *A* to point *B* and increases his quantity of fish from zero to 4 kilograms, the opportunity cost is only 0.25 kilograms of fruit per kilogram of fish. But as he catches more fish, the opportunity cost increases. As he moves from point *H* to point *I* and increases his quantity of fish to 18 kilograms, the opportunity cost increases to 16.0 kilograms of fruit per kilogram of fish.

■ **Self Test 3.2**

Fill in the blanks

Along a production possibilities frontier, the opportunity cost of obtaining one more unit of a good is the amount of another good that is ____ (forgone; gained). The opportunity cost of a good is equal to the quantity of the other good forgone ____ (plus; divided by) the increase in the quantity of the good. As more of a good is produced, its opportunity cost ____ (decreases; increases).

True or false

1. Moving from one point on the *PPF* to another point on the *PPF* has no opportunity cost.

2. When we move along the *PPF*, the quantity of CDs increases by 2 and the quantity of DVDs decreases by 1, so the opportunity cost is 2 CDs minus 1 DVD.

3. The opportunity cost of a good increases as more of the good is produced.

4. Increasing opportunity costs are common.

Multiple choice

1. The opportunity cost of one more slice of pizza in terms of pop is the
a. number of pizza slices we have to give up to get one extra pop.
b. number of pops we have to give up to get one extra slice of pizza.
c. total number of pops that we have divided by the total number of pizza slices that we have.
d. total number of pizza slices that we have divided by the total number of pops that we have.

2. Moving between two points on a *PPF*, a country gains 6 automobiles and forgoes 3 trucks. The opportunity cost of 1 automobile is
a. 3 trucks.
b. 6 automobiles – 3 trucks.
c. 2 trucks.
d. ½ of a truck.

3. A country produces only cans of soup and pens. If the country produces on its *PPF* and increases the production of cans of soup, the opportunity cost of a
a. can of soup is increasing.
b. can of soup is decreasing.
c. can of soup remains unchanged.
d. pen is increasing.

4. The bowed-out shape of the *PPF* reflects
a. different rates of unemployment.
b. increasing availability of factors of production and improved technology.
c. decreasing opportunity cost.
d. increasing opportunity cost.

5. Moving along a country's *PPF*, a reason opportunity cost increases is that
a. unemployment decreases as a country produces more and more of one good.
b. unemployment increases as a country produces more and more of one good.
c. technology declines as a country produces more and more of one good.
d. some resources are better suited for producing one good rather than the other.

6. Increasing opportunity costs exist
a. in the real world.
b. as long as there is high unemployment.
c. only in theory but not in real life.
d. for a country but not for an individual.

Complete the graph

1. The table shows the production possibilities for a nation.

Production point	MP3 players (millions per year)		DVD players (millions per year)
A	4	and	0.0
B	3	and	3.0
C	2	and	4.0
D	1	and	4.7
E	0	and	5.0

a. Placing MP3 players on the vertical axis, label the axes in Figure 3.2 and graph the production possibilities frontier.

b. What is the opportunity cost of a DVD player when moving from point *A* to point *B*? *B* to *C*? *C* to *D*? *D* to *E*? How does the opportunity cost change as more DVD players are produced?

■ **FIGURE 3.2**

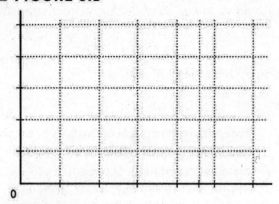

0

Short answer

1. What is the opportunity cost of increasing the production of a good while moving along a *PPF*? Why does this opportunity cost increase?

2. What does it mean for the opportunity cost to be a ratio?

CHECKPOINT 3.3

■ **Explain how specialization and trade expand production possibilities.**

Practice Problem 3.3

Tony and Patty produce scooters and snowboards. The figure shows their production possibilities per day.

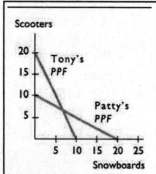

a. Calculate Tony's opportunity cost of a snowboard.

b. Calculate Patty's opportunity cost of a snowboard.

c. Who has a comparative advantage in producing snowboards?

d. Who has a comparative advantage in producing scooters?

e. If they specialize and trade, how many snowboards and scooters will they produce?

Solution to Practice Problem 3.3

This problem uses what you learned in the last checkpoint about how to measure opportunity cost along a *PPF* along with the definition of comparative advantage.

Quick Review

• *Comparative advantage* The ability of a person to perform an activity or produce a good or service at a lower opportunity cost than someone else.

Tony and Patty produce scooters and snowboards. The figure shows their production possibilities per day.

a. **Calculate Tony's opportunity cost of a snowboard.**

In the figure Tony has a constant opportunity cost because the *PPF* is a straight line. If he uses all his resources to produce scooters he can make 20, and if he uses all his resources to produce snowboards, he can make 10. Each snowboard produced decreases his scooter production by 2. The opportunity cost of a snowboard is 2 scooters.

b. **Calculate Patty's opportunity cost of a snowboard.**

If Patty uses all her resources to produce scooters she can make 10, and if she uses all her resources to produce snowboards, she can make 20. Each snowboard produced decreases her scooter production by ½. The opportunity cost of a snowboard is ½ of a scooter.

c. **Who has the comparative advantage in producing snowboards?**

The opportunity cost of a snowboard for Patty is ½ of a scooter and for Tony is 2 scooters. Patty has a lower opportunity cost. Comparative advantage is the ability of a person to perform an activity or produce a good or service at a lower opportunity cost than someone else. So Patty has the comparative advantage in producing snowboards.

d. Who has the comparative advantage in producing scooters?

The opportunity cost of a scooter for Patty is 2 snowboards and the opportunity cost of a scooter for Tony is 1/2 of a snowboard. Tony has a lower opportunity cost and so he has the comparative advantage in producing scooters.

e. If they specialize and trade, how many snowboards and scooters will they produce?

Patty specializes in snowboards and Tony specializes in scooters. Patty can produce 20 snowboards and Tony can produce 20 scooters. A total of 20 snowboards and 20 scooters will be produced.

Additional Practice Problem 3.3a

Patty buys new equipment for scooter production that lets her produce 60 scooters a day. Should Patty and Tony specialize and trade?

Solution to Additional Practice Problem 3.3a

When Patty can produce 60 scooters a day, her opportunity cost of a scooter falls to 1/3 snowboards per scooter and her opportunity cost of a snowboard rises to 3 scooters per snowboard. Patty now has the comparative advantage in scooters and Tony in snowboards. Patty and Tony should still specialize and trade, only now Patty will specialize in scooters and Tony will specialize in snowboards.

■ Self Test 3.3

Fill in the blanks

A person has ____ (a comparative; an absolute) advantage in an activity if that person can perform the activity at a lower opportunity cost than someone else. If people specialize according to ____ (comparative; absolute) advantage and then trade, they can get ____ (outside; inside) their production possibilities frontiers. A person has ____ (a comparative; an absolute) advantage if they are more productive than someone else in several or even all activities. It ____ (is; is not) possible for someone to have a comparative advantage in all activities. It ____ (is; is not) possible for someone to have an absolute advantage in all activities.

True or false

1. Martin has an absolute advantage in an activity if he can perform the activity at a lower opportunity cost than someone else.

2. If Robert can produce ice cream at a lower opportunity cost than Mary, Robert has a comparative advantage in ice cream production only if he produces more ice cream than Mary in an hour.

3. To achieve the gains from trade, a producer specializes in the product in which he or she has a comparative advantage and then trades with others.

4. Specialization and trade can make both producers better off even if one of them has an absolute advantage in producing all goods.

Multiple choice

1. Norman has a comparative advantage in the production of a good if he can produce

   a. more of all goods than another person.

   b. more of the good in which he has a comparative advantage than another person.

   c. the good in which he has a comparative advantage for a lower dollar cost than another person.

   d. that good at a lower opportunity cost than another person.

2. Bob produces baseballs and softballs. In one hour he can produce 10 baseballs or 2 softballs. Bob's opportunity cost of producing 1 softball is

   a. 2 softballs.

   b. 10 baseballs.

   c. 5 baseballs.

   d. 1 baseball.

For the next three questions, use the following information: Scott and Cindy produce only tacos and pizzas. In one hour, Scott can produce 20 pizzas or 40 tacos and Cindy can produce 30 pizzas or 40 tacos.

3. Scott's opportunity cost of producing 1 taco is

a. 1/2 of a pizza.
b. 1 pizza.
c. 2 pizzas.
d. 20 pizzas.

4. Cindy's opportunity cost of producing 1 taco is

a. 3/4 of a pizza.
b. 1 pizza.
c. 30 pizzas.
d. 40 pizzas.

5. Based on the data given,

a. Cindy has a comparative advantage in producing tacos.
b. Scott has a comparative advantage in producing tacos.
c. Cindy and Scott have the same comparative advantage when producing tacos.
d. neither Cindy nor Scott has a comparative advantage when producing tacos.

6. In one hour John can produce 20 loaves of bread or 8 cakes. In one hour Phyllis can produce 30 loaves of bread or 15 cakes. Which of the following statements is true?

a. Phyllis has a comparative advantage when producing bread.
b. John has a comparative advantage when producing cakes.
c. Phyllis has an absolute advantage in both goods.
d. John has an absolute advantage in both goods.

Complete the graph

1. Figure 3.3 shows the *PPF*s for Mark and Sue.

■ **FIGURE 3.3**

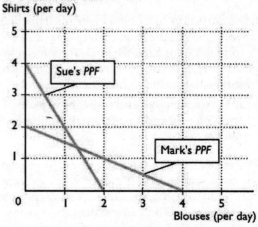

a. Who has the comparative advantage in producing shirts and who has the comparative advantage in producing blouses?

b. Who should specialize in producing blouses and who should specialize in producing shirts?

c. If Mark and Sue specialize according to their comparative advantage, indicate the total production of shirts and blouses by putting a point in Figure 3.3 that shows total production. Label the point *A*.

d. How does point *A* show the gains from trade?

Short answer

1. Why should people specialize according to their comparative advantage?

2. To achieve gains from trade, the opportunity costs of the trading partners must diverge. Why?

3. When it comes to trading one good for another, why is comparative advantage crucial and absolute advantage unimportant?

CHECKPOINT 3.4

■ **Explain how technological change and increases in capital and human capital expand production possibilities.**

Practice Problem 3.4

The table shows a nation that produces education services and consumption goods. If the nation increases the graduates from 0 to 500 a year, what is the opportunity cost of these 500 graduates?

Possibility	Education services (graduates)	Consumption goods (units)
A	1,000	0
B	750	1,000
C	500	2,000
D	0	3,000

Solution to Practice Problem 3.4

Economic growth has an opportunity cost. When we use resources to develop new technologies, educate and train people, and accumulate capital, we must decrease our current production of consumption goods and services.

Quick Review

• *Opportunity cost of growth* The opportunity cost of economic growth is the current consumption goods and services forgone.

The table shows a nation that produces education services and consumption goods. If the nation increases the graduates from 0 to 500 a year, what is the opportunity cost of these 500 graduates?

The opportunity cost of economic growth is the current production of consumption goods and services forgone. If the nation produces no graduates, it can produce 3,000 units of consumption goods. When the number of graduates increases to 500, the production of consumption goods and services falls to 2000 units. The oppor-tunity cost of the 500 graduates is the 1,000 units (3,000 – 2,000) of consumption goods forgone.

Additional Practice Problem 3.4a

Does economic growth eliminate scarcity?

Solution to Additional Practice Problem 3.4a

Economic growth increases the goods and services that can be produced but people's wants will continue to outstrip the ability to produce. While economic growth means that additional wants can be satisfied, people's wants are infinite and scarcity will continue to be present.

■ **Self Test 3.4**

Fill in the blanks

The sustained expansion of production possibilities is called ____ (economic growth; technology). The three factors that influence economic growth are ____, ____, and ____. Economic growth shifts the *PPF* ____ (inward; outward). The *PPF* shows that economic growth requires ____ (a decrease; an increase) in the current production of consumption goods and services.

True or false

1. The three key factors that influence economic growth are technological change, income, and capital accumulation.

2. Economic growth abolishes scarcity.

3. The opportunity cost of economic growth is less consumption goods in the future.

4. Production possibilities per person in Canada have remained constant during the last 30 years.

Multiple choice

1. To increase economic growth, we should

a. limit the number of college students.

b. encourage spending on goods and services.

c. encourage education because that leads to increased human capital.

d. increase current consumption.

2. Other things remaining the same, if Mexico devotes more resources to train its population than Spain,

a. Mexico will be able to eliminate opportunity cost faster than Spain.

b. Mexico will be able to eliminate scarcity faster than Spain.

c. Spain will grow faster than Mexico.

d. Mexico will grow faster than Spain.

3. If we decide to increase the current production of consumption goods, then

a. economic growth will slow down.

b. the *PPF* will shift outward.

c. the *PPF* will shift inward.

d. some factors of production will become unemployed.

4. Which of the following statements is correct?

a. As the economy grows, the opportunity cost of economic growth necessarily decreases.

b. Economic growth has no opportunity cost.

c. As the economy grows, the opportunity cost of economic growth necessarily increases.

d. The opportunity cost of economic growth is the decrease in the current production of consumption goods and services.

5. When a country's production possibilities frontier shifts outward over time, the country is experiencing

a. no opportunity cost.

b. economic growth.

c. higher unemployment of resources.

d. a decrease in the production of consumption goods and services.

6. The *PPF* shows economic growth when the *PPF*

a. shifts outward, away from the origin.

b. shifts inward, towards the origin.

c. changes from a bowed-out *PPF* to a linear *PPF*.

d. changes from a linear *PPF* to a bowed-out *PPF*.

Complete the graph

1. In Figure 3.4, illustrate what happens if there is a technological advance in the production of computers but not in the production of automobiles.

■ **FIGURE 3.4**

Automobiles (millions per year)

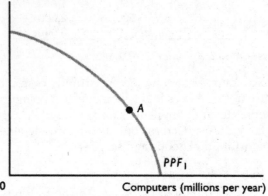

a. Suppose the economy was initially producing at point *A*. After the technological advance, is it possible for the economy to produce more computers *and* more automobiles?

Short answer

1. What are the three key factors that influence economic growth?

2. What is the opportunity cost of economic growth?

SELF TEST ANSWERS

■ CHECKPOINT 3.1

Fill in the blanks

The <u>production possibilities</u> frontier is the boundary between the combinations of goods and services that can and cannot be produced given the available <u>factors of production</u> and <u>state of technology</u>. Production points outside the *PPF* <u>are unattainable</u>. The possibility of a free lunch exists if production occurs <u>inside</u> the *PPF*. When resources are fully employed we face a <u>tradeoff</u>.

True or false

1. True; page 60
2. True; page 62
3. True; pages 62-63
4. False; pages 63-64

Multiple choice

1. b; page 60
2. c; page 60
3. b; page 62
4. d; pages 62-63
5. a; pages 63-64
6. a; pages 63-64

Complete the graph

■ FIGURE 3.5

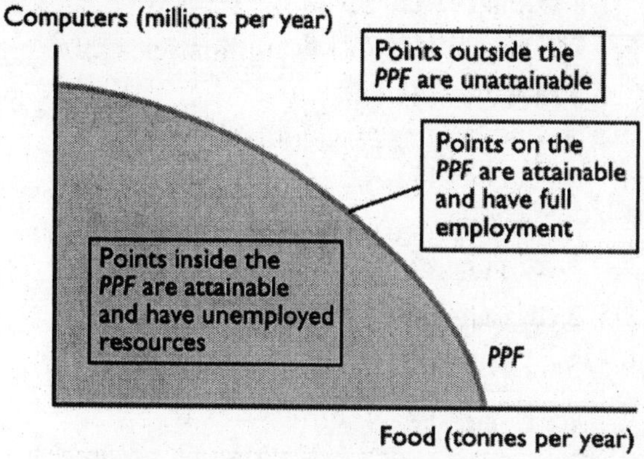

Computers (millions per year)

Points outside the *PPF* are unattainable

Points on the *PPF* are attainable and have full employment

Points inside the *PPF* are attainable and have unemployed resources

PPF

Food (tonnes per year)

1. Figure 3.5 shows a production possibilities frontier between computers and food and labels the points; pages 62-63.

Short answer

1. The factors that limit the amount of our production are the available factors of production and the state of technology; page 60.

2. When we are producing at a point with unemployment, a free lunch is possible because the production of some goods and services can be increased without decreasing the production of anything else. When we are producing at full employment, we are on the *PPF* and an increase in the production of one good or service requires a tradeoff. If the production of one good or service is increased, the production of something else must be decreased; pages 62-64.

■ CHECKPOINT 3.2

Fill in the blanks

Along a production possibilities frontier, the opportunity cost of obtaining one more unit of a good is the amount of another good that is <u>forgone</u>. The opportunity cost is equal to the quantity of the other good forgone <u>divided by</u> the increase in the quantity of the good. As more of a good is produced, its opportunity cost increases.

True or false

1. False; page 66
2. False; pages 67-68
3. True; page 68
4. True; page 68

Multiple choice

1. b; page 66
2. d; page 66
3. a; page 68
4. d; page 68
5. d; page 68
6. a; page 68

Complete the graph

1. a. Figure 3.6 illustrates the production possibilities frontier; page 66.

FIGURE 3.6

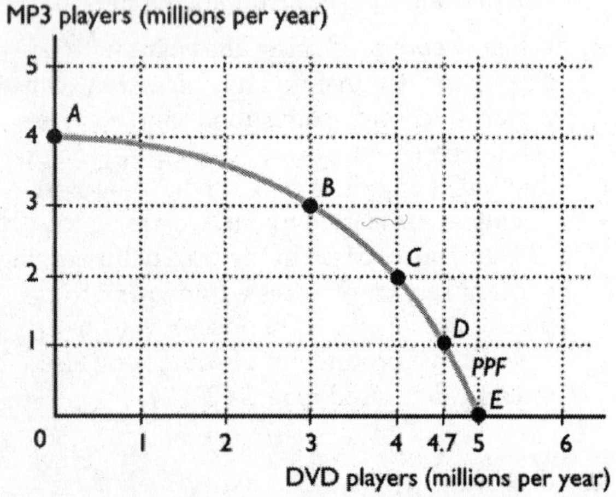
MP3 players (millions per year)
5
4
3
2
1
0
A
B
C
D
PPF
E
1
2
3
4
4.7
5
6
DVD players (millions per year)

b. The opportunity cost of moving from point *A* to point *B* is 0.33 MP3 players per DVD player; from *B* to C is 1.00 MP3 player per DVD player; from C to *D* is 1.43 MP3 players per DVD player; and, from *D* to *E* is 3.33 MP3 players per DVD player. The opportunity cost increases; page 68.

Short answer

1. The opportunity cost of increasing production of one good is the production of some other good forgone. The opportunity cost increases because resources are not equally productive in all activities. When initially increasing the production of one good, resources that are well suited for its production are used. When still more of the good is produced, resources that are less well suited must be used. Because the resources are ill suited, more are necessary to increase the production of the first good, and the forgone amount of the other good increases; page 68.
2. The opportunity cost of a good is the amount of the other good forgone to gain an additional unit of the good. We divide the quantity of the other good forgone by the increase in the good. So opportunity cost is a ratio—the change in the quantity of one good divided by the change in the quantity of another good; pages 67-68.

CHECKPOINT 3.3

Fill in the blanks

A person has a comparative advantage in an activity if that person can perform the activity at a lower opportunity cost than someone else. If people specialize according to comparative advantage and then trade, they can get outside their production possibilities frontiers. A person has an absolute advantage if they are more productive than someone else in several or even all activities. It is not possible for someone to have a comparative advantage in all activities. It is possible for someone to have an absolute advantage in all activities.

True or false

1. False; page 70
2. False; page 70
3. True; page 72
4. True; page 72

Multiple choice

1. d; page 70

2. c; page 70

3. a; page 70

4. a; page 70

5. b; page 70

6. c; page 72

Complete the graph

1. a. Sue has the comparative advantage in producing shirts. Her opportunity cost of a shirt is 1/2 of a blouse and Mark's opportunity cost of a shirt is 2 blouses. Mark has the comparative advantage in producing blouses. His opportunity cost of a blouse is 1/2 of a shirt and Sue's opportunity cost of a blouse is 2 shirts; page 70.

   b. Mark should specialize in producing blouses and Sue should specialize in producing shirts; page 72.

   c. Mark produces 4 blouses and Sue produces 4 shirts, so a total of 4 shirts and 4 blouses are produced. Figure 3.7 shows this production as point A; page 72.

   d. If the total production at point A is divided evenly, both Mark and Sue have 2 shirts and 2 blouses. When both were producing only for themselves, they could not produce 2 shirts and 2 blouses because this point is beyond both their PPFs. By specializing and trading, Mark and Sue get outside their PPFs; page 72.

■ **FIGURE 3.7**

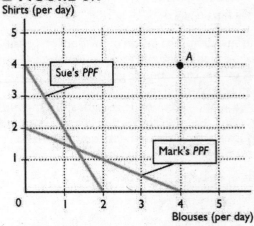

Short answer

1. When people specialize according to their comparative advantage, they produce the good at a lower opportunity cost than other people. By having this person specialize in the production of the good, it is produced at the lowest cost; pages 70, 72.

2. If the trading partners' opportunity costs are the same, there is no incentive for them to trade. For example, if two people produce gum and pop and both have the same opportunity cost of producing gum and pop, neither is willing to buy or sell to the other. Only when opportunity costs diverge will one person be willing to buy (the person with the higher opportunity cost) and the other willing to sell (the person with the lower opportunity cost); page 72.

3. People are willing to trade if they can obtain a good at a lower opportunity cost than what it costs them to produce. Even if a person has an absolute advantage in all goods, he does not have a comparative advantage in all goods. Comparative advantage determines who produces a good and who buys it; page 72.

■ **CHECKPOINT 3.4**

Fill in the blanks

The sustained expansion of production possibilities is called <u>economic growth</u>. The three factors that influence economic growth are <u>technological change</u>, <u>expansion of human capital</u>, and <u>capital accumulation</u>. Economic growth shifts the *PPF* <u>outward</u>. The *PPF* shows that economic growth requires <u>a decrease</u> in the current production of consumption goods and services.

True or false

1. False; page 74

2. False; page 74

3. False; page 74

4. False; page 74

Multiple choice

1. c; page 74

2. d; page 74

3. a; page 74

4. d; page 74

5. b; page 74

6. a; page 74

Complete the graph

1. Figure 3.8 illustrates the new production possibilities frontier. Because the technological advance did not affect automobile production, the maximum amount of automobiles that can be produced on the vertical axis does not change; pages 74-75.

■ **FIGURE 3.8**
Automobiles (millions per year)

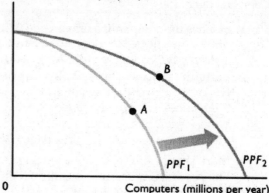

a. Figure 3.8 shows that it is possible for the production of *both* automobiles and computers to increase, as a movement from the initial point *A* to a possible new point *B* illustrates; page 75.

Short answer

1. The three key factors that influence economic growth are technological change, the expansion of human capital, and capital accumulation; page 74.

2. Economic growth requires developing new technologies, accumulating more human capital, or accumulating more capital. Each of these requirements for economic growth uses factors of production, so we must decrease our current production of consumption goods and services. This decrease in the current production of consumption goods and services is the opportunity cost of economic growth; page 74.

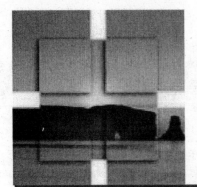

Demand and Supply

Chapter 4

Chapter 4 studies the tools of demand and supply, which determine the quantities and prices of the goods and services produced and consumed and the quantities of the factors of production employed.

■ **Distinguish between quantity demanded and demand and explain what determines demand.**

The quantity demanded is the amount of any good, service, or resource that people are willing and able to buy during a specified period at a specified price. The law of demand states that other things remaining the same, if the price of a good rises, the quantity demanded of that good decreases; and if the price of a good falls, the quantity demanded of that good increases. A demand curve is a graph of the relationship between the quantity demanded of a good and its price. A change in price leads to a *change in the quantity demanded* and a movement along the demand curve. Factors that *change demand* and shift the demand curve are prices of related goods; income; expectations; number of buyers; and preferences.

■ **Distinguish between quantity supplied and supply and explain what determines supply.**

The quantity supplied is the amount of any good, service, or resource that people are willing and able to sell during a specified period at a specified price. The law of supply states that other things remaining the same, if the price of a good rises, the quantity supplied of that good increases; and if the price of a good falls, the quantity supplied of that good decreases. A supply curve is a graph of the relationship between the quantity supplied of a good and its price. A change in price leads to a *change in the quantity supplied* and a movement along the supply curve. Factors that *change supply* and shift the supply curve are prices of related goods; prices of resources and other inputs; expectations; number of sellers; and productivity.

■ **Explain how demand and supply determine price and quantity in a market and explain the effects of changes in demand and supply.**

The equilibrium price and equilibrium quantity occur when the quantity demanded equals the quantity supplied. An increase in demand raises the price and increases the quantity. An increase in supply lowers the price and increases the quantity. An increase in both demand and supply increases the quantity and the price might rise, fall, or not change. An increase in demand and a decrease in supply raises the price and the quantity might increase, decrease, or not change. A decrease in demand and an increase in supply lowers the price and the quantity might increase, decrease, or not change. Changes in demand and supply in the opposite direction lead to reverse changes in price and quantity.

■ **Explain how price ceilings, price floors, and sticky prices cause shortages, surpluses, and unemployment.**

A price ceiling below the equilibrium price creates a shortage. A price floor above the equilibrium price creates a surplus. A sticky price creates temporary shortages or surpluses.

EXPANDED CHAPTER CHECKLIST

When you have completed this chapter, you will be able to

1 **Distinguish between quantity demanded and demand and explain what determines demand.**

- Define quantity demanded.
- State and explain the law of demand.
- List the influences on buying plans that change demand.
- Distinguish between a change in the quantity demanded and a change in demand.

2 **Distinguish between quantity supplied and supply and explain what determines supply.**

- Define quantity supplied.
- State and explain the law of supply.
- List the influences on selling plans that change supply.
- Distinguish between a change in the quantity supplied and a change in supply.

3 **Explain how demand and supply determine price and quantity in a market and explain the effects of changes in demand and supply.**

- Determine the equilibrium price and equilibrium quantity in a demand-supply graph.
- Indicate the amount of surplus or shortage if the price is not the equilibrium price.
- Illustrate the effects of a change in demand and a change in supply.

4 **Explain how price ceilings, price floors, and sticky prices cause shortages, surpluses, and unemployment.**

- Explain the effect of a price ceiling and a price floor.

- Discuss why a price might be sticky and illustrate how a sticky price can create a shortage or a surplus.

KEY TERMS

- Change in demand (page 85)
- Change in supply (page 90)
- Change in the quantity demanded (page 85)
- Change in the quantity supplied (page 90)
- Complement (page 85)
- Complement in production (page 90)
- Demand (page 83)
- Demand curve (page 84)
- Demand schedule (page 84)
- Equilibrium price (page 93)
- Equilibrium quantity (page 93)
- Inferior good (page 85)
- Law of demand (page 83)
- Law of market forces (page 94)
- Law of supply (page 88)
- Market equilibrium (page 93)
- Minimum wage law (page 103)
- Normal good (page 85)
- Price ceiling (page 101)
- Price floor (page 103)
- Quantity demanded (page 83)
- Quantity supplied (page 88)
- Rent ceiling (page 101)
- Shortage or excess demand (page 94)
- Substitute (page 85)
- Substitute in production (page 90)
- Supply (page 88)
- Supply curve (page 89)
- Supply schedule (page 89)
- Surplus or excess supply (page 94)

CHECKPOINT 4.1

■ **Distinguish between quantity demanded and demand and explain what determines demand.**

Practice Problem 4.1

In the market for scooters, several events occur, one at a time. Explain the influence of each event on the quantity demanded of scooters and on the demand for scooters. Illustrate the effects of each event by either a movement along the demand curve or a shift in the demand curve for scooters and say which event (or events) illustrates the law of demand in action. These events are

a.   The price of a scooter falls.

b.   The price of a bicycle falls.

c.   Citing rising injury rates, cities and towns ban scooters from sidewalks.

d.   Income increases.

e.   Rumour has it that the price of a scooter will rise next month.

f.   Scooters become unfashionable and the number of buyers decreases.

Solution to Practice Problem 4.1

This problem studies the difference between a change in the quantity demanded and a change in demand.

Quick Review

• *Change in the quantity demanded* A change in the quantity of a good that people plan to buy that results from a change in the price of the good.

• *Change in demand* A change in the quantity that people plan to buy when any influence on buying plans, other than the price of the good changes.

a.   **The price of a scooter falls.**

A fall in the price of a scooter increases the quantity of scooters demanded, which is shown in the figure as a movement down along the demand curve. This event illustrates the law of demand in action.

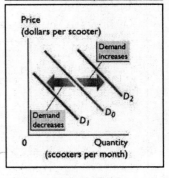

b.   **The price of a bicycle falls.**

A fall in the price of a bicycle, which is substitute for a scooter, decreases the demand for scooters. The demand curve for scooters shifts leftward in the figure from D_0 to D_1.

c.   **Citing rising injury rates, cities and towns ban scooters from sidewalks.**

The ban on scooters changes preferences. The demand for scooters decreases and the demand curve for the scooters shifts leftward in the figure from D_0 to D_1.

d.   **Income increases.**

The demand for scooters increases when income increases because a scooter is (likely) a normal good. The demand curve shifts rightward in the figure from D_0 to D_2.

e.   **Rumour has it that the price of a scooter will rise next month.**

A rise in the expected future price of a scooter increases the demand for scooters now. The demand curve shifts rightward in the figure from D_0 to D_2.

f.   **Scooters become unfashionable and the number of buyers decreases.**

When the number of buyers decrease, the demand for scooters decreases. The demand curve shifts leftward in the figure from D_0 to D_1.

Additional Practice Problem 4.1a

The table gives the demand schedule for scooters. Label the axes in Figure 4.1 and graph the demand curve.

Price (dollars per scooter)	Quantity (scooters per week)
100	0
75	10
50	40
25	60

■ **FIGURE 4.1**

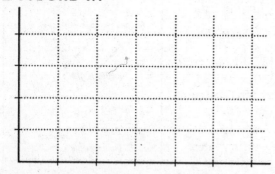

Solution to Additional Practice Problem 4.1a

The answer is given in Figure 4.2.

■ **FIGURE 4.2**

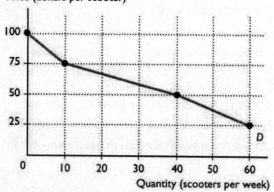

Price (dollars per scooter)

Quantity (scooters per week)

■ Self Test 4.1

Fill in the blanks

The _____ (demand schedule; law of demand) states that other things remaining the same, if the price of a good rises, the _____ (quantity demanded of; demand for) that good decreases. A _____ (demand; quantity) curve is a graph of the relationship between the quantity demanded of a good and the price when all other influences on buying plans remain the same. An increase in demand shifts the demand curve _____ (leftward; rightward). A rise in the price of a good _____ (does; does not) shift its demand curve.

True or false

1. The law of demand states that other things remaining the same, if the price of a good rises, the quantity demanded of that good increases.

2. If the quantity of ice cream demanded at each price increases and other influences on buying plans do not change, there is a movement along the demand curve for ice cream.

3. When Elizabeth's income increases, her demand for movies increases. For Elizabeth, movies are a normal good.

4. If income falls and all other influences on buying plans remain the same, the demand for computers will decrease and there will be a movement along the demand curve.

Multiple choice

1. Other things remaining the same, the quantity of a good or service demanded will increase if the price of that good or service

a. rises.

b. falls.

c. does not change.

d. rises or falls.

2. Hot dogs and hot dog buns are complements. If the price of a hot dog falls, then

a. the demand for hot dogs will increase.

b. the demand for hot dog buns will decrease.

c. the quantity demanded of hotdogs will decrease.

d. the demand for hot dog buns will increase.

3. The number of buyers in the market for sport utility vehicles decreases sharply. As a result,

a. the demand curve for sport utility vehicles shifts leftward.

b. the demand curve for sport utility vehicles shifts rightward.

c. there is neither a shift nor a movement along the demand curve for sport utility vehicles.

d. there is a movement down along the demand curve for sport utility vehicles.

4. When moving along a demand curve, which of the following changes?

a. the consumers' incomes

b. the prices of other goods

c. the number of buyers

d. the price of the good

5. If the price of a CD falls,

a. the demand for CDs will increase and the demand curve for CDs will shift rightward.

b. the demand for CDs will be unaffected, so the demand curve for CDs will not shift.

c. the quantity of CDs demanded will increase and there will be a movement along the demand curve for CDs.

d. Both answers (b) and (c) are correct.

6. Pizza and tacos are substitutes. The price of a pizza rises. Which of the following correctly indicates what happens?

a. The demand for pizzas decreases and the demand for tacos increases.

b. The demand for both goods decreases.

c. The quantity of tacos demanded increases and the quantity of pizza demanded decreases.

d. The quantity of pizza demanded decreases and the demand for tacos increases.

Complete the graph

1. The demand schedule for cotton candy is given in the following table. In Figure 4.3, draw the demand curve. Label the axes.

Price (dollars per bag of cotton candy)	Quantity (bags of cotton candy per month)
1	10,000
2	8,000
3	7,000
4	4,000

a. If the price of cotton candy is $2 a bag, what is the quantity of cotton candy demanded?

b. If the price of cotton candy is $3 a bag, what is the quantity of cotton candy demanded?

c. Does the demand curve slope upward or downward?

■ **FIGURE 4.3**

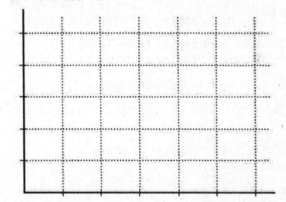

Short answer

1. Explain the difference between a change in the quantity demanded and a change in demand.

2. Explain the difference between a movement along and a shift of a demand curve.

CHECKPOINT 4.2

■ **Distinguish between quantity supplied and supply and explain what determines supply.**

Practice Problem 4.2

In the market for timber beams, several events occur one at a time. Explain the influence of each event on the quantity supplied of timber beams and the supply of timber beams. Illustrate the effects of each event by either a movement along the supply curve or a shift in the supply curve of timber beams and say which event (or events) illustrates the law of supply in action. The events are

a.   The wage rate of sawmill workers rises.

b.   The price of sawdust rises.

c.   The price of a timber beam rises.

d.   The price of a timber beam is expected to rise next year.

e.   Environmentalists convince Parliament to pass a new law that reduces the amount of forest that can be cut for timber products.

f.   A new technology lowers the cost of producing timber beams.

Solution to Practice Problem 4.2

This problem studies the difference between a change in the quantity supplied and a change in supply.

Quick Review

*   *Change in the quantity supplied* A change in the quantity of a good that suppliers plan to sell that results from a change in the price of the good.

*   *Change in supply* A change in the quantity that suppliers plan to sell when any influence on selling plans other than the price of the good changes.

a.   The wage rate of sawmill workers rises.

Sawmill workers are resources used to produce timber beams. A rise in their wage rate decreases the supply of timber beams. The supply curve in the figure shifts leftward

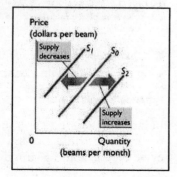

from S_0 to S_1.

b.   The price of sawdust rises.

Sawdust is produced when timber beams are produced, so sawdust and timber beams are complements in production. A rise in the price of a complement in production increases the supply of timber beams and the supply curve of timber beams in the figure shifts rightward from S_0 to S_2.

c.   The price of a timber beam rises.

A rise in the price of a timber beam increases the quantity of timber beams supplied. There is a movement up along the supply curve in the figure. This event illustrates the law of supply in action.

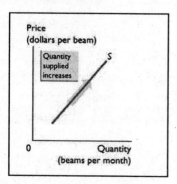

d.   The price of a timber beam is expected to rise next year.

The higher expected price decreases the current supply of timber beams because producers plan to sell their timber beams next year when the price is higher. The supply curve in the figure shifts leftward from S_0 to S_1.

e.   Environmentalists convince Parliament to pass a new law that reduces the amount of forest that can be cut for timber products.

The new law decreases the supply of trees and the price of a tree, a resource for timber beams, rises. The supply of timber beams decreases and the supply curve of timber beams in the figure shifts leftward from S_0 to S_1.

f.   A new technology lowers the cost of producing timber beams.

With the lower cost of production from the new technology, the supply of timber beams increases. The supply curve of timber beams in the figure shifts rightward from S_0 to S_2.

Additional Practice Problem 4.2a

The information in the table gives the supply schedule for scooters in a town. Label the axes in Figure 4.4 and graph the supply curve.

Price (dollars per scooter)	Quantity (scooters per week)
100	60
75	50
50	30
25	10

■ FIGURE 4.4

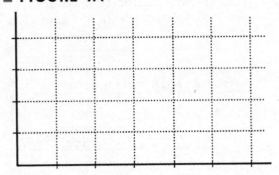

Solution to Additional Practice Problem 4.2a

The axes are labelled and the supply curve is graphed in Figure 4.5.

■ FIGURE 4.5
Price (dollars per scooter)

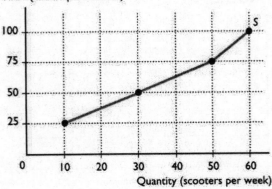

■ Self Test 4.2

Fill in the blanks

The ____ (quantity supplied; supply) of a good is the amount people are willing and able to sell during a specified period at a specified price. The law of supply states that other things remaining the same, if the price of a good rises, the quantity supplied ____ (decreases; increases). A change in the price of a good changes ____ (supply; the quantity supplied) and is illustrated by a ____ (movement along; shift of) the supply curve.

True or false

1. The law of supply states that other things remaining the same, if the price of a good rises, the quantity supplied increases.

2. If the wage rate paid to chefs rises and all other influences on selling plans remain the same, the supply of restaurant meals will increase.

3. If the price of coffee is expected to rise next month, the supply of coffee this month will decrease.

4. When new technology for producing computers is used by manufacturers, the supply of computers increases.

Multiple choice

1. The quantity supplied is the amount that people are ____ during a specified period at a specified price.
   a. able to sell
   b. willing to sell
   c. able and willing to sell
   d. willing and able to buy

2. An increase in supply is shown by a

a. rightward shift of the supply curve.

b. leftward shift of the supply curve.

c. movement up along the supply curve but no shift in the supply curve.

d. movement down along the supply curve but no shift in the supply curve.

3. If the price of pepperoni and cheese, ingredients used in the production of pizza, rise what will happen in the market for pizza?

a. The supply of pizza will decrease.

b. The quantity of pizza supplied will increase as sellers try to cover their costs.

c. Pizza will cease to be produced and sold.

d. The demand curve for pizza will shift leftward when the price of a pizza increases.

4. A rise in the price of a substitute in production for a good will lead to

a. an increase in the supply of that good.

b. a decrease in the supply of that good.

c. no change in the supply of that good.

d. a decrease in the quantity of that good supplied.

5. A technological advance in the production of jeans will bring about which of the following?

a. The quantity of jeans supplied will increase.

b. The supply of jeans will increase.

c. The demand for jeans increases because they are now more efficiently produced.

d. The impact on the supply of jeans is impossible to predict.

6. Suppose the price of leather used to produce shoes increases. As a result, there is ____ in the supply of shoes and the supply curve of shoes shifts ____.

a. an increase; rightward

b. an increase; leftward

c. a decrease; rightward

d. a decrease; leftward

Complete the graph

1. The supply schedule for cotton candy is given in the following table. In Figure 4.6, label the axes and draw the supply curve.

Price (dollars per bag of cotton candy)	Quantity (bags of cotton candy per month)
1	4,000
2	8,000
3	10,000
4	12,000

a. If the price of cotton candy is $2 a bag, what is the quantity supplied?

b. If the price of cotton candy is $3 a bag, what is the quantity supplied?

c. Does the supply curve slope upward or downward?

■ FIGURE 4.6

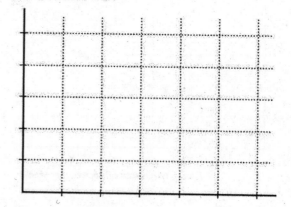

2. Figure 4.7 shows a supply curve for rubber bands. In Figure 4.7, illustrate the effect of a technological advance in the production of rubber bands.

■ FIGURE 4.7
Price (dollars per box of rubber bands)

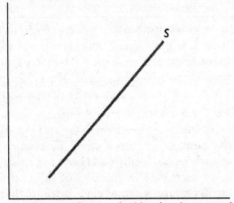

Quantity (boxes of rubber bands per year)

3. Figure 4.8 shows a supply curve for copper. The cost of the natural gas used to refine copper ore into copper rises. In Figure 4.8, show the effect of this event.

■ FIGURE 4.8
Price (dollars per tonne of copper)

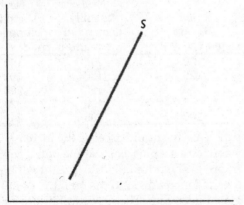

Quantity (tonnes of copper per year)

Short answer

1. What influence or influences cause a change in the quantity supplied?

2. What influence or influences cause a change in supply?

CHECKPOINT 4.3

■   Explain how demand and supply determine price and quantity in a market and explain the effects of changes in demand and supply.

Practice Problem 4.3

The table shows the demand and supply schedules for milk.

Price (dollars per carton)	Quantity demanded	Quantity supplied
	(cartons per day)	
1.00	200	110
1.25	175	130
1.50	150	150
1.75	125	170
2.00	100	190

a. What is the market equilibrium in the milk market?

b. Describe the situation in the milk market if the price is $1.75 a carton.

c. If the price is $1.75 a carton, explain how the market reaches equilibrium.

d. A drought decreases the quantity supplied by 45 cartons a day at each price. What is the new equilibrium and how does the market adjust to it?

e. Milk becomes more popular, and the quantity demanded increases by 5 cartons a day at each price. Improved feeds for dairy cows increase the quantity of milk supplied by 50 cartons a day at each price. If there is no drought, what is the new equilibrium and how does the market adjust to it?

Solution to Practice Problem 4.3

This Practice Problem studies market equilibrium and shows how changes in demand and supply change the equilibrium price and equilibrium quantity.

Quick Review

- *Market equilibrium* When the quantity demanded equals the quantity supplied — when buyers' and sellers' plans are consistent.

a.   What is the market equilibrium in the milk market?

Find the row in which the quantity supplied and the quantity demanded are equal. The quantity is 150 cartons a day, which is the equilibrium quantity, and the equilibrium price is $1.50 a carton.

b.   Describe the situation in the milk market if the price is $1.75 a carton.

When the price is higher than the equilibrium price, the quantity supplied exceeds the quantity demanded, so there is a surplus. At a price of $1.75 a carton, the surplus is 170 cartons minus 125 cartons, which is 45 cartons a day.

c.   If the price is $1.75 a carton, explain how the market reaches equilibrium.

At $1.75 a carton, there is a surplus of milk. As the price falls, the quantity demanded increases, the quantity supplied decreases, and the surplus decreases. The price falls until the surplus disappears at a price of $1.50 a carton.

d.   A drought decreases the quantity supplied by 45 cartons a day at each price. What is the new equilibrium and how does the market adjust to it?

Supply decreases by 45 cartons a day at each price. The table shows the new supply schedule and the original demand schedule.

Price (dollars	Quantity demanded	New Quantity supplied
		(cartons per day)
1.00	200	65
1.25	175	85
1.50	150	105
1.75	125	125
2.00	100	145

At the original equilibrium price of $1.50 a carton, there is a shortage of milk. The price rises, the quantity of milk demanded decreases, and the quantity supplied increases. The new equilibrium price is $1.75 a carton and the new equilibrium quantity is 125 cartons a day.

e.   Milk becomes more popular and the quantity demanded increases by 5 cartons a day at each price. Improved feeds for dairy cows increase the quantity of milk supplied by 50 cartons a day at each price. If there is no drought, what is the new equilibrium and how does the market adjust to it?

The change in preferences increases demand by 5 cartons a day at each price and the advance in technology increases supply by 50 cartons a day at each price. The table shows the new quantity demanded and the new quantity supplied.

Price (dollars per carton)	New Quantity demanded	New Quantity supplied
		(cartons per day)
1.00	205	160
1.25	180	180
1.50	155	200
1.75	130	220
2.00	105	240

The increase in supply exceeds the increase in demand, so a surplus exists at the initial equilibrium price. The price falls, the quantity of milk demanded increases, and the quantity of milk supplied decreases. The new equilibrium price is $1.25 a carton and the new equilibrium quantity is 180 cartons a day.

Additional Practice Problem 4.3a

The price of a hot dog bun falls and the number of hot dog producers increases. The effect of the fall in the price of a hot dog bun is less than the effect of the increase in the number of producers. Describe the new market equilibrium.

Solution to Additional Practice Problem 4.3a

The fall in the price of a hot dog bun, a complement of hot dogs, increases the demand for hot dogs. The demand curve for hot dogs shifts rightward in the figure from D_0 to D_1. The increase in the number of producers increases the supply of hot dogs and the supply curve shifts rightward from S_0 to S_1. The increase in supply exceeds the increase in demand so the price of a hot dog falls and the quantity increases.

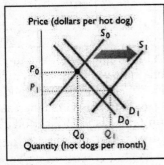

■ Self Test 4.3

Fill in the blanks

The price at which the quantity demanded equals the quantity supplied is the _____ (demand; equilibrium) price. If price exceeds the equilibrium price, the price _____ (rises; falls). An increase in demand _____ (raises; lowers) the equilibrium price and _____ (increases; decreases) the equilibrium quantity. An increase in supply _____ (raises; lowers) the equilibrium price and _____ (increases; decreases) the equilibrium quantity. If both the demand and supply increase, the equilibrium _____ (price; quantity) increases but the equilibrium _____ (price; quantity) rises, falls, or remains the same.

True or false

1. If the price of asparagus is below the equilibrium price, there is a shortage of asparagus and the price of asparagus will rise until the shortage disappears.

2. When the demand for skateboards decreases and the supply of skateboards remains un-changed, the quantity supplied of skateboards decreases as the price rises.

3. As winter sets in, the demand for and supply of hamburger buns decrease. The price of a hamburger bun will definitely remain the same.

4. The number of buyers of grapefruit juice increases and at the same time severe frost decreases the supply of grapefruit. The price of grapefruit juice will rise.

Multiple choice

1. At the equilibrium price, the

a. quantity of the good demanded equals the quantity of the good supplied.

b. quantity of the good demanded is greater than the quantity of the good supplied.

c. quantity of the good demanded is less than the quantity of the good supplied.

d. demand for the good is equal to the supply of the good.

2. Which of the following is correct?

a. A surplus puts downward pressure on the price of a good.

b. A shortage puts upward pressure on the price of a good.

c. There is no surplus or shortage at equilibrium.

d. All of the above answers are correct.

3. Which of the following is the best explanation for why the price of gasoline rises during the summer months?

a. Oil producers have lower costs of production in the summer.

b. More people walk or ride their bicycles to work in the summer.

c. Car travel increases in the summer as families go on their annual vacations.

d. Oil refineries increase production in the summer.

4. The price of lettuce used to produce tacos increases. The equilibrium price of a taco ____ and the equilibrium quantity ____.
   a. rises; increases
   b. rises; decreases
   c. falls; increases
   d. falls; decreases

5. Advances in technology associated with manufacturing computers have led to a _____ in the equilibrium price of a computer and ____ in the equilibrium quantity.
   a. rise; an increase
   b. rise; a decrease
   c. fall; an increase
   d. fall; a decrease

6. If the supply of gasoline decreases by a greater amount than the demand for gasoline increases, then the equilibrium price of gasoline _____ and the equilibrium quantity _____.
   a. rises; decreases
   b. rises; increases
   c. rises; does not change
   d. falls; does not change

Complete the graph

1. Figure 4.9 shows the demand and supply curves for cotton candy.
   a. Describe the market for cotton candy when the price of cotton candy is $1 a bag.
   b. Describe the market for cotton candy when the price of cotton candy is $3 a bag.
   c. What is the equilibrium price and equilibrium quantity of cotton candy?

■ **FIGURE 4.9**

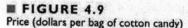
Price (dollars per bag of cotton candy)

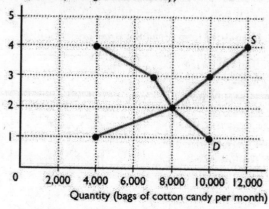

Quantity (bags of cotton candy per month)

Short answer

1. Define shortage and surplus.

2. The table gives the demand and supply schedules for sweatshirts.

Price (dollars per sweatshirt)	Quantity demanded (sweatshirts per season)	Quantity supplied (sweatshirts per season)
35	13	32
30	15	25
25	19	19
20	27	12
15	37	8

   What is the equilibrium quantity and the equilibrium price of sweatshirts?

3. People read that drinking orange juice helps prevent heart disease. What is the effect on the equilibrium price and the equilibrium quantity of orange juice?

4. The cost of memory chips used in computers falls. What is the effect on the equilibrium price and equilibrium quantity of computers?

5. The demand for veterinarian services increases and at the same time the supply of veterinarian services decreases. What is the effect on the equilibrium price of veterinarian services?

CHECKPOINT 4.4

■   **Explain how price ceilings, price floors, and sticky prices cause shortages, surpluses, and unemployment.**

Practice Problems 4.4

1. The figure shows the rental market for apartments in a Winnipeg suburb.

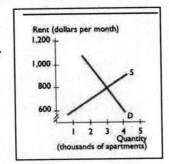

a.   What is the rent and how many apartments are rented?

b.   If the city of Winnipeg imposes a rent ceiling of $900 a month, what is the rent and how many apartments are rented?

c.   If the city of Winnipeg imposes a rent ceiling of $600 a month, what is the rent and how many apartments are rented?

2.   The figure shows the market for tomato pickers in southern Ontario:

a.   What is the equilibrium wage rate of tomato pickers and what is the equilibrium quantity of tomato pickers employed?

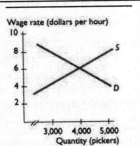

b.   If Ontario introduces a minimum wage for tomato pickers of $4 an hour, how many tomato pickers are employed and how many are unemployed?

c.   If Ontario introduces a minimum wage for tomato pickers of $8 an hour, how many tomato pickers are employed and how many are unemployed?

Solution to Practice Problems 4.4

These problems show the effects of a price ceiling and a price floor in a market.

Quick Review

• *Price ceiling* The highest price at which it is legal to trade a particular good, service, or factor of production. A rent ceiling is an example of a price ceiling.

• *Price floor* The lowest price at which it is legal to trade a particular good, service, or factor of production. A minimum wage law is an example of a price floor.

1a.   What is the rent and how many apartments are rented?

At equilibrium, the quantity supplied equals the quantity demanded. The equilibrium rent is $800 a month and 3,000 apartments are rented.

1b.   If the city of Winnipeg imposes a rent ceiling of $900 a month, what is the rent and how many apartments are rented?

With a rent ceiling of $900 a month, apartments cannot be rented for more than $900. Because the equilibrium rent is below $900, this rent ceiling is ineffective. The rent remains at $800 a month and 3,000 apartments are rented.

1c.   If the city of Winnipeg imposes a rent ceiling of $600 a month, what is the rent and how many apartments are rented?

The rent ceiling is below the equilibrium rent so the rent cannot rise to the equilibrium rent. The figure shows that when the rent ceiling is $600 a month, the rent is $600 a month and the quantity of

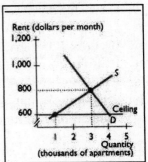

apartments rented is 1,000, determined by the supply curve.

2a. What is the equilibrium wage rate of tomato pickers and what is the equilibrium quantity of tomato pickers employed?

At equilibrium, the quantity supplied equals the quantity demanded. The equilibrium wage rate is $6 an hour and 4,000 pickers are employed.

2b. If Ontario introduces a minimum wage for tomato pickers of $4 an hour, how many tomato pickers are employed and how many are unemployed?

The minimum wage of $4 an hour is less than the equilibrium wage rate, so the minimum wage is ineffective. The wage rate remains at $6 an hour. Zero pickers are unemployed and 4,000 pickers are employed.

2c. If Ontario introduces a minimum wage for tomato pickers of $8 an hour, how many tomato pickers are employed and how many are unemployed?

The minimum wage is above the equilibrium wage rate so the wage rate cannot fall to its equilibrium level. The figure shows that when the minimum wage is $8 an hour, 3,000 tomato pickers are employed (on the demand curve), and 5,000 people would like to work as tomato pickers (on the supply curve). So 5,000 – 3,000, which is 2,000 people are unemployed.

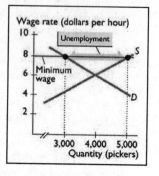

Additional Practice Problem 4.4a

What is a sticky price and how can a sticky price in the labour market create unemployment?

Solution to Additional Practice Problem 4.4a

A sticky price occurs when buyers and sellers agree on a price for a fixed period of time or a seller sets a price that changes infrequently. Many workers have contracts with employers in which the wage rate to be paid for several years

is specified. This sticky wage rate can create unemployment when the demand for labour decreases. The wage rate cannot fall to its new equilibrium value. At the relatively high sticky wage, the quantity of labour demanded is less than the quantity of labour supplied. The surplus of workers are unemployed.

■ Self Test 4.4

Fill in the blanks

A price _____ (ceiling; floor) is the highest price at which it is legal to trade a particular good, service, or factor of production. A price floor is effective when it is set _____ (above; below) the equilibrium price. A minimum wage law is an example of a price _____ (ceiling; floor). A minimum wage creates unemployment when it is set _____ (above; below) the equilibrium wage rate. Sticky prices _____ (can; cannot) create unemployment.

True or false

1. A rent ceiling always lowers the rent paid.

2. A minimum wage is an example of a price ceiling.

3. Firms hire labour, so they determine how much labour to supply in a market.

4. When firms enter into long-term contracts with labour unions that fix wage rates for several years, the wage rate is sticky.

Multiple choice

1. A price ceiling

a. prevents the market price from going above a certain value.

b. prevents the market price from going below a certain value.

c. keeps the market prices higher than would otherwise be the case.

d. matches the quantity demanded with the quantity supplied of any good or service.

2. When the government imposes a price ceiling on a product below the equilibrium price, the government creates

a. a shortage.

b. a surplus.

c. equilibrium in the market.

d. None of the above answers is correct.

3. To be effective, a price floor must be set

a. above the equilibrium price.

b. below the equilibrium price.

c. at the equilibrium price.

d. at zero.

4. A minimum wage law is an example of

a. an equilibrium price.

b. a price floor.

c. a price ceiling.

d. None of the above answers is correct.

5. A three-year labour contract is an example of a

a. price ceiling.

b. price floor.

c. sticky price.

d. shortage.

6. The result of a sticky price in a market is

a. quicker adjustment of prices.

b. no adjustment of prices.

c. slower adjustment of prices.

d. to change the price but not the quantity bought and sold.

Complete the graph

1. Figure 4.10 shows the demand and supply curves for cotton candy.

a. Describe the market for cotton candy if the government imposes a price ceiling of $1 a bag on cotton candy.

b. Describe the market for cotton candy if the government imposes a price floor of $3 a bag on cotton candy.

■ FIGURE 4.10

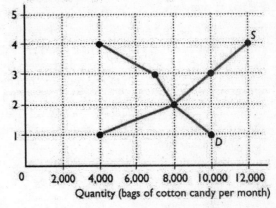

Price (dollars per bag of cotton candy)

Short answer

1. The table gives the demand and supply schedules for electricity.

Price (cents per kilowatt-hour)	Quantity demanded (kilowatt-hours)	Quantity supplied (kilowatt-hours)
7	2,700	2,700
6	2,900	2,600
5	3,100	2,500
4	3,300	2,400
3	3,500	2,300
2	3,700	2,100

At what price is the quantity demanded equal to the quantity supplied? Suppose the government tries to keep the price of electricity low by setting a price ceiling of 4¢ per kilowatt-hour. What is the impact of this price ceiling?

2. What is the effect of a minimum wage set below the equilibrium wage rate? Set above the equilibrium wage rate?

SELF TEST ANSWERS

■ **CHECKPOINT 4.1**

Fill in the blanks

The <u>law of demand</u> states that other things remaining the same, if the price of a good rises, the <u>quantity demanded of</u> that good decreases. A <u>demand</u> curve is a graph of the relationship between the quantity demanded of a good and the price when all other influences on buying plans remain the same. An increase in demand shifts the demand curve <u>rightward</u>. A rise in the price of a good <u>does not</u> shift its demand curve.

True or false

1. False; page 83

2. False; page 85

3. True; page 85

4. False; page 85

Multiple choice

1. b; page 83

2. d; page 85

3. a; page 86

4. d; page 86

5. d; page 86

6. d; pages 85-86

Complete the graph

1. Figure 4.11 shows the demand curve.

   a. 8,000 bags a month

   b. 7,000 bags a month

   c. The demand curve slopes downward; pages 83-84

Short answer

1. A change in the quantity demanded occurs when the price of the good changes. A change in demand occurs when any influence on buying plans other than the price of the good changes; page 85.

2. A movement along a demand curve shows a change in the quantity demanded. A shift of a demand curve shows a change in demand; page 86.

■ **FIGURE 4.11**
Price (dollars per bag of cotton candy)

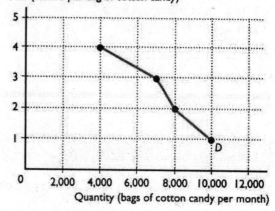

■ **CHECKPOINT 4.2**
Fill in the blanks

The <u>quantity supplied</u> of a good is the amount people are willing and able to sell during a specified period at a specified price. The law of supply states that other things remaining the same, if the price of a good rises, the quantity supplied <u>increases</u>. A change in the price of a good changes <u>the quantity supplied</u> and is illustrated by a <u>movement along</u> the supply curve.

True or false

1. True; page 88

2. False; page 90

3. True; page 90

4. True; page 91

Multiple choice

1. c; page 88

2. a; page 91

3. a; page 90

4. b; page 90

5. b; page 91

6. d; pages 90-91

Complete the graph

1. Figure 4.12 shows the supply curve.

   a. 8,000 bags a month.

   b. 10,000 bags a month.

   c. The supply curve slopes upward; page 89

■ FIGURE 4.12
Price (dollars per bag of cotton candy)

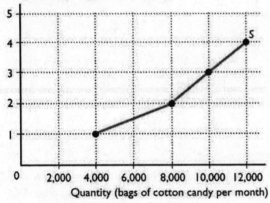

2. An advance in technology increases supply. Figure 4.13 shows the rightward shift of the supply curve from S_0 to S_1; page 91.

■ FIGURE 4.13
Price (dollars per box of rubber bands)

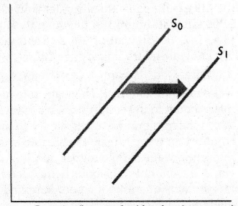

Quantity (boxes of rubber bands per year)

3. A rise in the price of a resource decreases supply. Figure 4.14 shows the leftward shift of the supply curve from S_0 to S_1; pages 90-91

■ FIGURE 4.14
Price (dollars per tonne of copper)

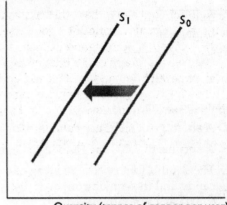

Quantity (tonnes of copper per year)

Short answer

1. Change in the price of the good; page 90.

2. Changes in: prices of related goods; prices of resources and other inputs; expectations; number of sellers; and productivity; page 90.

■ CHECKPOINT 4.3

Fill in the blanks

The price at which the quantity demanded equals the quantity supplied is the equilibrium price. If price exceeds the equilibrium price, the price falls. An increase in demand raises the equilibrium price and increases the equilibrium quantity. An increase in supply lowers the equilibrium price and increases the equilibrium quantity. If both the demand and supply increase, the equilibrium quantity increases but the equilibrium price rises, falls, or remains the same.

True or false

1. True; page 94

2. False; page 95

3. False; pages 98-99

4. True; page 99

Multiple choice

1. a; page 93

2. d; page 94

3. c; page 95

4. b; page 96

5. c; page 96

6. a; page 99

Complete the graph

1. a. A shortage of 6,000 bags a month; page 94.

   b. A surplus of 3,000 bags a month; page 94.

   c. The equilibrium price is $2 a bag of cotton candy and the equilibrium quantity is 8,000 bags a month; page 93.

Short answer

1. A shortage is a situation in which the quantity demanded exceeds the quantity supplied. A surplus is a situation in which the quantity supplied exceeds the quantity demanded; page 94.

2. The equilibrium price is $25 a sweatshirt. The equilibrium quantity is 19 sweatshirts a season; page 93.

3. The change in preferences increases the demand for orange juice. The equilibrium price of orange juice rises and the equilibrium quantity increases; page 95.

4. The fall in the cost of the memory chips increases the supply of computers. The equilibrium price of a computer falls and the equilibrium quantity increases; page 96.

5. When demand increases and supply decreases, the equilibrium price rises; page 99.

■ **CHECKPOINT 4.4**

Fill in the blanks

A price ceiling is the highest price at which it is legal to trade a particular good, service, or factor of production. A price floor is effective when it is set above the equilibrium price. A minimum wage law is an example of a price floor. A minimum wage creates unemployment when it is set above the equilibrium wage rate. Sticky prices can create unemployment.

True or false

1. False; page 102

2. False; page 103

3. False; page 103

4. True; pages 104-105

Multiple choice

1. a; page 101

2. a; page 102

3. a; pages 103-104

4. b; page 103

5. c; pages 104-105

6. c; pages 104-105

Complete the graph

1. a. With a price ceiling of $1 a bag, there is a shortage of 6,000 bags a month; page 102.

   b. With a price floor of $3 a bag, there is a surplus of 3,000 bags a month; page 104.

Short answer

1. The quantity demanded equals the quantity supplied at a price of 7¢ a kilowatt-hour. At the price ceiling, the quantity demanded is 3,300 kilowatt-hours and the quantity supplied is 2,400 kilowatt-hours, so a shortage of 900 kilowatt-hours exists; page 102.

2. A minimum wage set below the equilibrium wage rate has no effect. The wage rate remains equal to the equilibrium wage rate. When the minimum wage is set above the equilibrium wage rate, the wage rate is the minimum wage. At the higher minimum wage, the quantity of labour demanded is less than the quantity of labour supplied and unemployment results; page 104.

GDP and the Standard of Living

5

Chapter 5 describes the methods of measuring GDP. The chapter explains why the value of production equals income, which equals expenditure. It explains the difference between real and nominal GDP, and the limitations of GDP as a measure of the standard of living.

■ **Define GDP and explain why the value of production, income, and expenditure are the same for an economy.**

Gross domestic product, GDP, is the market value of all the final goods and services produced within a country in a given time period. Only final goods and services are included in GDP; intermediate goods and services are not included. Total expenditure is the sum of consumption expenditure (C), invest-ment (I), government expenditure on goods and services (G), and net exports of goods and services (NX). Firms pay out everything they receive as incomes to the factors of production. We call total in-come Y. The circular flow shows that total expenditure equals total income so that $Y = C + I + G + NX$.

■ **Describe how economic statisticians measure GDP in Canada.**

The expenditure approach to measuring GDP adds together consumption expenditure; investment; government expenditure on goods and services; and net exports of goods and services. The income approach to measuring GDP adds together wages, salaries, and supplementary labour income; interest and investment income; profits of corporations and government enterprises; and income from farms and unincorporated businesses. The sum of these four categories is net domestic product at factor cost. Net domestic product plus indirect taxes minus subsidies plus depreciation equals GDP. Value added is the value of a firm's production minus the value of the intermediate goods it buys from other firms. Gross national product is GDP minus net investment income paid to non-residents.

■ **Distinguish between nominal GDP and real GDP and define the GDP deflator.**

GDP changes when prices or production change. Real GDP is the value of the final goods and services produced in a given year when valued at constant prices; nominal GDP is the value of the final goods and services produced in a given year valued at the prices that prevailed in that year. The GDP defla-tor is an average of current prices expressed as a percentage of base-year prices and equals (Nominal GDP ÷ Real GDP) × 100.

■ **Explain and describe the limitations of real GDP as a measure of the standard of living.**

GDP measures the value of goods and services that are bought in markets. It does not measure house-hold production; underground production; the value of leisure time; the environment quality; or health and life expectancy, and political freedom and social justice.

EXPANDED CHAPTER CHECKLIST

When you have completed this chapter, you will be able to

1 Define GDP and explain why the value of production, income, and expenditure are the same for an economy.

- Define GDP.

- Explain the difference between a final good or service and an intermediate good or service and tell why only final goods and services are included in GDP.

- Discuss the four types of expenditure.

- State why the value of production equals income, which equals expenditure.

2 Describe how economic statisticians measure GDP in Canada.

- Explain the expenditure approach to measuring GDP.

- Discuss why used goods and financial assets are not included in GDP.

- Explain the income approach to measuring GDP and discuss each of the components.

- State what adjustments must be made to convert net domestic product at factor cost to GDP.

- Define and calculate value added.

- Define gross national product and explain the relationship between gross national product and gross domestic product.

3 Distinguish between nominal GDP and real GDP and define the GDP deflator.

- Define nominal GDP and real GDP, and explain the difference between them.

- Calculate nominal GDP.

- Calculate real GDP using the traditional method and the new method.

- Define the GDP deflator and calculate it.

4 Explain and describe the limitations of real GDP as a measure of the standard of living.

- List the goods and services omitted from GDP and explain why each of these goods and services are not measured in GDP.

- Discuss how these omitted factors affect the standard of living.

KEY TERMS

- Consumption expenditure (page 113)

- Depreciation (page 120)

- Exports of goods and services (page 114)

- Final good or service (page 112)

- GDP deflator (page 127)

- Government expenditure on goods and services (page 114)

- Gross domestic product (GDP) (page 112)

- Gross national product (GNP) (page 122)

- Imports of goods and services (page 114)

- Intermediate good or service (page 112)

- Investment (page 113)

- Net domestic product at factor cost (page 120)

- Net exports of goods and services (page 114)

- Net taxes (page 114)

- Nominal GDP (page 125)

- Personal disposable income (page 122)

- Real GDP (page 125)

- Value added (page 121)

CHECKPOINT 5.1

■ **Define GDP and explain why the value of production, income, and expenditure are the same for an economy.**

Practice Problems 5.1

1. Classify each of the following items as a final good or service or an intermediate good or service:

a. Banking services bought by a student.

b. New cars bought by Hertz, the car rental firm.

c. Newsprint bought by *The Globe and Mail* from Abitibi Paper.

d. Ice cream bought by a diner and used to produce sundaes.

2. During 2003 on Lotus Island, net taxes were $10 billion; consumption expenditure was $30 billion; government expenditure was $12 billion; investment was $15 billion; and net exports were $3 billion. Calculate

a. Total expenditure.

b. Total income.

c. GDP.

Solution to Practice Problems 5.1

For the first question, ask if the good is to be used as a component of a final good or service. If so, it is an intermediate good. For the second question, remember the equality between total expenditure, total income, and GDP.

Quick Review

- *Total expenditure* Total expenditure is the total amount received by producers of final goods and services and equals $C + I + G + NX$.

- *Total income* Total income is the income paid to all factors of production and equals total expenditure.

1a. Banking services bought by a student.

Because the student uses the services and does not use them to produce or sell anything else, the banking services are a final service.

b. New cars bought by Hertz, the car rental firm.

Hertz is the final buyer of the cars so the cars are a final good. The new cars are additions to capital and are part of investment when they are purchased.

c. Newsprint bought by *The Globe and Mail* from Abitibi Paper.

Because the newsprint is processed into newspapers that will be sold to others, it is an intermediate good. The newspapers are the final goods, not the newsprint.

d. Ice cream bought by a diner and used to produce sundaes.

The sundaes are the final goods. The ice cream that was bought by the diner to make the sundaes is an intermediate good.

2. During 2003 on Lotus Island, net taxes were $10 billion; consumption expenditure was $30 billion; government expenditure was $12 billion; investment was $15 billion; and net exports were $3 billion. Calculate

a. Total expenditure.

Total expenditure is the sum of consumption expenditure, investment, government expenditure on goods and services, and net exports of goods and services. Total expenditure = $C + I + G + NX$, which is $30 billion + $15 billion + $12 billion + $3 billion = $60 billion.

b. Total income.

Total income is equal to total expenditure, so total income is $60 billion.

c. GDP.

GDP can be measured either as total income or as total expenditure. So GDP is $60 billion.

Additional Practice Problem 5.1a

Last year consumption expenditure was $70 billion, investment was $16 billion, government expenditure on goods and services was $12 billion, exports were $4 billion, and imports were $3 billion. This year imports increased to $5 billion. If all the other types of expenditure stay the same, what was GDP last year, GDP this year, and how did GDP change from last year?

Solution to Additional Practice Problem 5.1a

To solve this problem use the equality between GDP and expenditure, GDP = $C + I + G + NX$. Last year's GDP was $70 billion + $16 billion + $12 billion + ($4 billion – $3 billion) = $99 billion. This year, imports increased from $3 billion to $5 billion, so replace the $3 billion in the calculation with $5 billion and GDP for this year is $97 billion. The $2 billion increase in imports results in a $2 billion decrease in GDP.

■ Self Test 5.1

Fill in the blanks

The market value of all the final goods and services produced within a country in a given time period is ____ (GDP; investment). ____ (Two; Three; Four) groups buy the final goods and services produced. Net exports of goods and services equals the value of ____ (imports; exports) of goods and services minus the value of ____ (imports; exports) of goods and services. $C + I + G + NX$ equals ____ and ____.

True or false

1. The computer chip that Dell Corp. buys from Intel Corp. is a final good.

2. Expenditure on a bulldozer is consumption expenditure.

3. The value of net exports of goods and services can be negative.

4. The value of production equals income, which equals expenditure.

Multiple choice

1. The abbreviation "GDP" stands for
   a. gross domestic product.
   b. gross domestic prices.
   c. general domestic prices.
   d. great domestic prices.

2. GDP is equal to the ____ value of all the final goods and services produced within a country in a given time period.
   a. production
   b. market
   c. wholesale
   d. retail

3. The following are all *final* goods except
   a. flour used by the baker to make cupcakes.
   b. bread eaten by a family for lunch.
   c. pencils used by a 6th grade student in class.
   d. Nike shoes used by a basketball player.

4. Investment is defined as
   a. the purchase of a stock or bond.
   b. financial capital.
   c. what consumers do with their savings.
   d. the purchase of new capital goods and additions to inventories.

5. In one year a firm increases its production by $9 million worth of goods and increases its sales by $8 million. Which of the following is true, all other things in the economy remaining the same?
   a. GDP increases by $8 million.
   b. GDP increases by $9 million.
   c. Inventory investment decreases by $1 million.
   d. GDP increases by $8 million and investment increases by $1 million.

6. Total expenditure equals

a. $C + I + G + NX$.

b. $C + I + G - NX$.

c. $C + I - G + NX$.

d. $C - I + G + NX$.

Short answer

1. Why aren't intermediate goods or services counted in GDP?

2. Classify each of the following according to the component of Canadian GDP into which they fall:

a. The purchase of a Sony DVD player made in Japan.

b. A family's purchase of a birthday cake at the local Zehrs grocery store.

c. Your college's purchase of 100 new computers.

d. The purchase of a new pizza oven by a pizzeria.

e. The government's purchase of 15 transport planes.

3. Why does total expenditure equal total income?

CHECKPOINT 5.2

■ **Describe how economic statisticians measure GDP in Canada.**

Practice Problem 5.2

1. The table gives some of the items in Canada's national accounts in 1998.

a. Calculate Canada's GDP in 1998.

b. Did you use the expenditure approach or the income approach to make this calculation?

c. How much did Canadian governments spend on goods and services in 1998?

d. By how much did capital in the Canadian economy depreciate in 1998?

Item	Amount (billions of dollars)
Wages, salaries, and supplementary labour income	475
Consumption expenditure	534
Indirect taxes *less* subsidies	120
Interest and investment income	48
Profits of corporations and government enterprises	93
Capital consumption	122
Investment	167
Net exports	17
Income from farms and unincorporated businesses	60

Solution to Practice Problem 5.2

This question focuses on calculating GDP. To solve problems such as this, you need to know how to use the expenditure approach and the income approach. The expenditure approach adds four expenditure categories. The income approach adds four income categories and then makes some additional adjustments.

Quick Review

• *Expenditure approach* GDP equals the sum of consumption expenditure; investment; government expenditure on goods and services; and net exports of goods and services.

• *Income approach* GDP equals the sum of wages, salaries, and supplementary labour income; interest and investment income; profits of corporations and government enterprises; and income from farms and unincorporated businesses plus indirect taxes minus subsidies plus depreciation. The sum of the first four income categories is net domestic product at factor cost.

a. **Calculate Canada's GDP in 1998.**

To calculate GDP using the expenditure approach we need to know the values of consumption expenditure; investment; government expenditure; and net exports of goods and services. The table does not give the value of government expenditure, so we cannot find GDP using the expenditure approach. To calculate GDP using the income approach we need to know the values of wages, salaries, and supplementary labour income; interest and investment income; profits of corporations and government enterprises; income from farms and unincorporated businesses; indirect taxes less subsidies; and depreciation, called capital consumption. All these items are listed in the table, so GDP can be calculated using the income approach. In this case,

GDP = $475 billion + $48 billion + $93 billion + $60 billion + $120 billion + $122 billion = $918 billion.

b. Did you use the expenditure approach or the income approach to make this calculation?

The only way you can calculate GDP in (a) is by the income approach, which is the approach used.

c. How much did Canadian governments spend on goods and services in 1998?

You calculated GDP in (a) using the income approach. The expenditure approach tells us that GDP = $C + I + G + NX$. Subtract C, I, and NX from both sides of the equation to show that $G = $ GDP $- C - I - NX$. Using the values of GDP, C, I, and NX gives $G = $918 billion $-$ $534 billion $-$ $167 billion $-$ $17 billion $=$ $200 billion.

d. By how much did capital in the Canadian economy depreciate in 1998?

Depreciation is the decrease in the value of capital that results from its use and obsolescence. Depreciation is also called "capital consumption," so the amount of depreciation is the amount of capital consumption, listed in the table as $122 billion.

Additional Practice Problem 5.2a

What are the ways value added can be calculated? Suppose that total expenditures of the local Harvey's are $700,000. It pays $300,000 for wages, $180,000 for ingredients, $20,000 for paper products, $150,000 for rent, and has a profit of $50,000. What is Harvey's value added?

Solution to Additional Practice Problem 5.2a

Value added equals the value of a firm's production minus the value of the intermediate goods it buys. Value added also equals the sum of the incomes (including profits) a firm pays for the factors of production it uses.

The value of Harvey's production is $700,000. The intermediate goods Harvey's uses are the ingredients and paper products. Harvey's value added equals $700,000 $-$ $180,000 $-$ $20,000, which is $500,000. Alternatively, Harvey's paid people incomes in the form of wages, rent, and profit. From this approach, value added equals the sum of the incomes, which is $300,000 + $150,000 + $50,000 = $500,000.

■ Self Test 5.2

Fill in the blanks

The _____ approach and the _____ approach are two methods used to calculate GDP. Expenditure on used goods _____ (is; is not) included in GDP. Profits of corporations and government enterprises is part of the _____ (expenditure; income) approach to calculating GDP. To calculate GDP, depreciation is _____ (added to; subtracted from) net domestic product at factor cost. The value of a firm's production minus the value of the intermediate goods it buys from other firms is called the firm's _____ (profit; valued added).

True or false

1. The expenditure approach measures GDP by using data on consumption expenditure, investment, government expenditure on goods and services, and net exports of goods and services.

2. In Canada, expenditure on used goods is becoming an increasingly large fraction of GDP.

3. The income approach uses data on consumption expenditure, investment, government expenditure on goods and services, and net exports of goods and services to calculate GDP.

4. A firm's value added equals the value of its production minus the incomes it pays to the factors of production it uses.

5. Gross national product equals GDP plus net investment income paid to non-residents.

6. Personal disposable income equals personal income minus net taxes.

Multiple choice

1. To calculate GDP, economists

a. add together total expenditure and total income.

b. can measure total expenditure, total income, or value added.

c. add together total income and value added.

d. subtract total income from total expenditure.

2. Using the expenditure approach, GDP is the sum of

a. wages, salaries, and supplementary labour income; interest and investment income; profits of corporations and government enterprises; and income from farms and unincorporated businesses.

b. the value added by each industry.

c. the total values of final goods, intermediate goods, used goods, and financial assets.

d. consumption expenditure; investment; government expenditure on goods and services; and net exports of goods and services.

3. Suppose GDP is $10 billion, consumption expenditure is $7 billion, investment is $2 billion, and government expenditure on goods and services is $2 billion. Net exports of goods and services must be

a. $1 billion.

b. −$1 billion.

c. $2 billion.

d. −$2 billion.

4. According to the expenditure approach to measuring GDP in Canada in 2003, the largest component of GDP is

a. consumption expenditure.

b. investment.

c. government expenditure on goods and services.

d. net exports of goods and services.

5. Which of the following is <u>NOT</u> one of the income categories used in the income approach to measuring GDP?

a. Interest and investment income

b. Profits of corporations and government enterprises

c. Income from farms and unincorporated businesses

d. Tax revenues paid by persons

6. To calculate GDP using the income approach, we add together the values of the four categories of income and then

a. add the amount of income saved and spent.

b. add indirect taxes and depreciation and subtract subsidies.

c. subtract indirect taxes and subsidies and add depreciation.

d. do nothing because the income sum equals GDP.

7. Personal disposable income equals

a. national income minus undistributed profits minus net taxes.

b. national income minus undistributed profits plus net taxes.

c. personal income plus undistributed profits plus depreciation.

d. GNP plus net investment income paid to non-residents.

Short answer

1. What adjustments must be made to net domestic product at factor cost to convert it to GDP? Why must these adjustments be made?

2. Suppose a driller sells a litre of oil to a refinery for $0.40. The refinery converts the litre of oil to gasoline and sells it to a consumer for $0.75. What is the increase in GDP when the consumer buys the litre of gasoline? The driller uses no intermediate goods. What is the driller's value added? The refiner's? What is the sum of the driller's value added and the refiner's value added?

3. The table below gives data for a small nation:

Item	Amount (dollars)
Wages, salaries, and supplementary labour income	3,900
Consumption expenditure	4,000
Indirect taxes minus subsidies	400
Interest and investment income	300
Profits of corporations and government enterprises	800
Government expenditure	1,000
Investment	1,100
Net exports	300
Income from farms and unincorporated businesses	300

a. What is the nation's GDP?

b. What is the net domestic product at factor cost?

c. What does depreciation equal?

CHECKPOINT 5.3

■ **Distinguish between nominal GDP and real GDP and define the GDP deflator.**

Practice Problem 5.3

An island economy produces only bananas and coconuts. The table gives the quantities produced and prices in 2003 and 2004. The base year is 2003.

Item	Data for 2003 Quantity	Data for 2003 Price	Data for 2004 Quantity	Data for 2004 Price
Bananas	100	$10 a bunch	110	$15 a bunch
Coconuts	50	$12 a bag	60	$10 a bag

Calculate

a. Nominal GDP in 2003.

b. Nominal GDP in 2004.

c. The value of 2004 production in 2003 prices.

d. Percentage increase in production when valued at 2003 prices.

e. The value of 2003 production in 2004 prices.

f. Percentage increase in production when valued at 2004 prices.

g. Real GDP in 2003 and 2004.

h. The GDP deflator in 2004.

Solution to Practice Problem 5.3

This question gives you practice calculating real GDP and the GDP deflator. Take each part step-by-step to arrive at the answer for the GDP deflator.

Quick Review

• *Nominal GDP* The value of the final goods and services produced in a given year valued at the prices that prevailed in that same year.

a. Nominal GDP in 2003.

Nominal GDP in 2003 equals the 2003 expenditure on the bananas, $(100 \times \$10)$, plus the expenditure on coconuts, $(50 \times \$12)$, which is $1,000 + $600 = $1,600.

b. Nominal GDP in 2004.

Similar to part (a), nominal GDP in 2004 = $(110 \times \$15) + (60 \times \$10)$, which is $1,650 + $600 = $2,250.

c. The value of 2004 production in 2003 prices.

The value of 2004 production in 2003 prices equals the expenditure on bananas, $(110 \times \$10)$, plus expenditure on coconuts, $(60 \times \$12)$, which is $1,100 + $720 = $1,820.

d. Percentage increase in production when valued at 2003 prices.

In 2003 prices, the value of production increases from $1,600, in part (a), to $1,820, in part (c). The increase is $220, so the percentage increase is equal to ($220 ÷ $1,600) × 100, which is 13.75 percent.

e. The value of 2003 production in 2004 prices.

The value of 2003 production in 2004 prices equals the expenditure on bananas, (100 × $15), plus the expenditure on coconuts, (50 × $10), which is $1,500 + $500 = $2,000.

f. Percentage increase in production when valued at 2004 prices.

In 2004 prices, the value of production increases from $2,000, in part (e), to $2,250, in part (b). The increase is $250, so the percentage increase is equal to ($250 ÷ $2,000) × 100, which is 12.50 percent.

g. Real GDP in 2003 and 2004.

Because 2003 is the base year, real GDP in 2003 equals nominal GDP in 2003, which is $1,600. To calculate real GDP in 2004 it is necessary to compute the growth rate of real GDP between 2003 and 2004. That growth rate is the average of the growth rates between 2003 and 2004 using prices from 2003 and using prices from 2004. Using the answers to parts (d) and (f), the average percentage increase is 13.125 percent. Real GDP in 2004 is 13.125 percent greater than real GDP in 2003. Real GDP in 2003 is $1,600, so real GDP in 2004 equals ($1,600) × (1.13125), which is $1,810.

h. The GDP deflator in 2004.

GDP deflator = (Nominal GDP ÷ Real GDP) × 100 = ($2,250 ÷ $1,810) × 100 = 124.3.

Additional Practice Problem 5.3a

Answer the following questions.

a. Nominal GDP = $10 trillion, real GDP = $9 trillion. What is the GDP deflator?

b. Real GDP = $8 trillion, GDP deflator = 120. What is nominal GDP?

c. Nominal GDP = $12 trillion, GDP deflator = 120. What is real GDP?

Solution to Additional Practice Problem 5.3a

a. Nominal GDP = $10 trillion, real GDP = $9 trillion. What is the GDP deflator?

GDP deflator = (Nominal GDP ÷ Real GDP) × 100 = ($10 trillion ÷ $9 trillion) × 100 = 111.1.

b. Real GDP = $8 trillion, GDP deflator = 120. What is nominal GDP?

Rearranging the formula used in part (a) gives (GDP deflator) × (Real GDP) ÷ 100 = Nominal GDP, so (120) × ($8 trillion) ÷ 100 = $9.6 trillion.

c. Nominal GDP = $12 trillion, GDP deflator = 120. What is real GDP?

Rearranging the formula used in part (a) gives (Nominal GDP ÷ GDP deflator) × 100 = Real GDP, so ($12 trillion ÷ 120) × 100 = $10 trillion.

■ **Self Test 5.3**

Fill in the blanks

_____ (Real; Nominal) GDP is the value of the final goods and services produced in a given year when valued at constant prices; _____ (real; nominal) GDP is the value of the final goods and services produced in a given year valued at the prices that prevailed in that same year. The GDP deflator equals 100 times _____ (real; nominal) GDP divided by _____ (real; nominal) GDP.

True or false

1. Nominal GDP increases only if the production of final goods and services increases.

2. Real GDP is just a more precise name for GDP.

3. Real GDP equals nominal GDP in the base year.

4. If real GDP is $600 billion and nominal GDP is $750 billion, then the GDP deflator is 125.

Multiple choice

1. Nominal GDP can change

a. only if prices change.

b. only if quantities of good and services produced change.

c. only if prices increase.

d. if either prices or quantities of goods and services produced change.

2. The traditional method of calculating real GDP

a. always gives a larger value for real GDP than the new method of calculating real GDP.

b. values the quantities produced in each year at the prices of the base year.

c. always gives a smaller value for real GDP than the new method of calculating real GDP.

d. puts a greater weight on net exports than the new method of calculating real GDP.

3. Real GDP measures the value of goods and services produced in a given year when valued at

a. constant prices.

b. prices that prevail in the same year.

c. prices in some previous year.

d. future prices.

4. If nominal GDP increases, then real GDP

a. must decrease.

b. must increase.

c. must not change.

d. could increase, decrease, or not change.

5. The GDP deflator is a measure of

a. taxes and subsidies.

b. changes in quantities.

c. prices.

d. depreciation.

6. The GDP deflator is calculated as

a. (nominal GDP ÷ real GDP) × 100.

b. (real GDP ÷ nominal GDP) × 100.

c. (nominal GDP + real GDP) ÷ 100.

d. (nominal GDP − real GDP) ÷ 100.

Short answer

1. An economy produces only pizza and pop. The table gives the quantities produced and prices in 2003 and 2004. The base year is 2003.

Item	Data for 2003		Data for 2004	
	Quantity	Price	Quantity	Price
Pizza	100	$10 each	150	$20 each
Pop	50	$2 each	75	$4 each

a. What is nominal GDP in 2003?

b. What is real GDP in 2003?

c. What is nominal GDP in 2004?

d. What is real GDP in 2004?

2. If you want to measure the change in production is it better to use nominal GDP or real GDP? Why?

3. How does the term "chain linking" apply to real GDP?

CHECKPOINT 5.4

■ **Explain and describe the limitations of real GDP as a measure of the standard of living.**

Practice Problem 5.4

The International Monetary Fund reports the following data for real GDP per person in 2000: China $3,976; Russia, $8,377; Canada, $27,840; United States, $34,142. Other information suggests that household production is similar in Canada and the United States and smaller in these two countries than in the other two. The underground economy is largest in Russia and

China and a similar proportion of the economy in these two cases. Canadians and Americans enjoy more leisure hours than do the Chinese and Russians. Canada and the United States spend significantly more to protect the environment, so air, water, and land pollution is less in those countries than in China and Russia. Given this information and ignoring any other influences on the standard of living

a. In which pair (or pairs) of these four countries is it easier to compare the standard of living? Why?

b. In which pair (or pairs) of these four countries is it more difficult to compare the standard of living? Why?

c. What more detailed information would we need to be able to make an accurate assessment of the relative standard of living in these four countries?

d. Do you think that the differences in real GDP per person correctly rank the standard of living in these four countries?

Solution to Practice Problem 5.4
Comparing GDP per person is perhaps the most common method of comparing the standard of living among different countries. This question reminds us that other factors also matter when it comes to determining the standard of living.

Quick Review

• *Goods and services omitted from GDP* Household production, underground production, leisure time, and environment quality are omitted from GDP.

a. **In which pair (or pairs) of these four countries is it easier to compare the standard of living? Why?**

The factors that affect the standard of living, but which are not measured by real GDP per person, are similar in Canada and the United States. Comparing the standard of living of these two countries based on real GDP per person likely would give a proper ranking. Similarly, Russia and China are stated to be similar in the areas not

measured by real GDP per person, so a comparison between these two countries based on measurement of real GDP per person is likely to rank their standard of living correctly.

b. **In which pair (or pairs) of these four countries is it more difficult to compare the standard of living? Why?**

Comparing either the United States or Canada to Russia or China would be the most difficult. Let's look at a comparison between Canada and Russia when the standard of living is measured by real GDP per person. The fact that household production in Russia is a larger proportion of the economy than in Canada and the underground economy is larger in Russia than in Canada decreases the standard of living gap between the two countries. Russia does less to protect the environment than Canada, so the difference in environment quality increases the standard of living gap between the two countries. Less leisure time in Russia also increases the standard of living gap. Similar difficulties occur when we compare the United States to China, the United States to Russia, and Canada to China.

c. **What more detailed information would we need to be able to make an accurate assessment of the relative standard of living in these four countries?**

If we knew the value of the underground economy, the value of household production, the value of leisure, and the value of environment quality differences we could adjust real GDP per person to make a more accurate assessment of the relative standard of living.

d. **Do you think that the differences in real GDP per person correctly rank the standard of living in these four countries?**

The areas where real GDP per person fails to measure the standard of living are similar in the United States and Canada, so the comparison between the United States and Canada based on real GDP per person is probably correct. Similarly, it is likely that an accurate measure of the standard of living would place Russia ahead of

China, just as real GDP per person does. Finally, the gap between real GDP per person in Canada and in Russia is so large that the ranking based on real GDP per person is probably correct.

Additional Practice Problem 5.4a

How do you think the standard of living in Canada today compares with the standard of living 150 years ago?

Solution to Additional Practice Problem 5.4a

Even though no totally accurate data on real GDP per person is available from 150 years ago, it is certain that real GDP per person is much higher today even after taking account of the fact that household production was more common 150 years ago. The underground economy is larger today, which boosts today's standard of living, and people today enjoy significantly more leisure time, which also boosts today's standard of living. Perhaps the edge on environment quality goes to the past. Considering health and life expectancy, and political freedom and social justice, people today are much better off than people 150 years ago.

■ Self Test 5.4

Fill in the blanks

The value of household production ____ (is; is not) included in GDP. The value of people's leisure time ____ (is; is not) included in GDP. GDP ____ (does; does not) subtract the value of environment degradation resulting from production. Real GDP ____ (takes; does not take) into account the extent of a country's political freedom.

True or false

1. As currently measured, real GDP does not include the value of home production.

2. Production in the underground economy is part of the "investment" component of GDP.

3. The production of anti-pollution devices installed by electric utilities is not counted in GDP because the devices are designed only to eliminate pollution.

4. The measure of a country's real GDP does not take into account the extent of political freedom in the country.

Multiple choice

1. The measurement of GDP handles household production by

   a. estimating a dollar value of the goods purchased to do housework.

   b. estimating a dollar value of the services provided.

   c. ignoring it.

   d. including it in exactly the same way that all other production is included.

2. You hire some friends to help you move. You pay them a total of $200 and buy them dinner at a local pizzeria. Which of the following is true?

   a. The $200 is counted as part of GDP but not the dinner at the pizzeria.

   b. If your friends do not report the $200 on their income tax returns, it becomes part of the underground economy.

   c. The dinner at the pizzeria is counted as part of GDP and so is the $200.

   d. Neither the $200 nor the dinner at the pizzeria is counted as part of GDP.

3. The value of leisure time is

   a. directly included in GDP.

   b. excluded from GDP.

   c. zero.

   d. None of the above answers is correct.

4. A new technology is discovered that results in new cars producing less pollution. The technology costs nothing to produce. Now the number of visits people make to doctors to complain of breathing difficulties decreases. Which of the following is true?

a. GDP will decrease because of fewer doctor services being provided.

b. GDP is not affected.

c. GDP will increase to reflect the improvement in the health of the population.

d. GDP will increase to reflect the improvement in the health of the population, and the likely increase in the cost of the car.

5. The calculation of GDP using the income approach excludes

a. wages.

b. interest and investment income.

c. environment quality.

d. profits of corporations.

6. Good health and life expectancy are included in

a. GDP but not in our standard of living.

b. GDP and our standard of living.

c. our standard of living but not in GDP.

d. neither our standard of living nor in GDP.

Short answer

1. What general categories of goods and services are omitted from GDP? Why is each omitted?

2. If you cook a hamburger at home, what happens to GDP? If you go to Burger King and purchase a hamburger, what happens to GDP?

SELF TEST ANSWERS

■ **CHECKPOINT 5.1**

Fill in the blanks

The market value of all the final goods and ser-vices produced within a country in a given time period is <u>GDP</u>. <u>Four</u> groups buy the final goods and services produced. Net exports of goods and services equals the value of <u>exports</u> of goods and services minus the value of <u>imports</u> of goods and services. $C + I + G + NX$ equals <u>total expenditure</u> and <u>total income</u>.

True or false

1. False; page 112
2. False; page 113
3. True;   page 114
4. True;   page 115

Multiple choice

1. a; page 112
2. b; page 112
3. a; page 112
4. d; page 113
5. b; page 113
6. a; page 114

Short answer

1. Intermediate goods or services are not counted in GDP because if they were, they would be double counted. A computer pro-duced by Dell Corp. is included in GDP. But if the Intel chip that is part of the computer is also included in GDP, then that production is counted twice: once when it is produced by Intel, and again when it is included in the computer produced by Dell; page 112.

2a. Imports of goods and services; page 114

b. Consumption expenditure; page 113

c. Investment; page 113

d. Investment; page 113

e. Government expenditure on goods and ser-vices; page 114

3. Total expenditure is the amount received by producers of final goods and services. Be-cause firms pay out everything they receive as incomes to the factors of production, total expenditure equals total income. From the viewpoint of firms, the value of production is the cost of production, which equals income. From the viewpoint of consumers of goods and services, the value of production is the cost of buying it, which equals expenditure; page 115.

■ **CHECKPOINT 5.2**

Fill in the blanks

The <u>expenditure</u> approach and the <u>income</u> ap-proach are two methods used to calculate GDP. Expenditure on used goods <u>is not</u> included in GDP. Profits of corporations and government enterprises is part of the <u>income</u> approach to calculating GDP. To calculate GDP, depreciation is <u>added to</u> net domestic product at factor cost. The value of a firm's production minus the value of the intermediate goods it buys from other firms is called the firm's <u>valued added</u>.

True or false

1. True;   page 117
2. False; page 118
3. False; page 119
4. False; page 121
5. False; page 122
4. True;   page 122

Multiple choice

1. b; pages 117, 119, 121
2. d; page 117
3. b; page 117
4. a; page 117
5. d; page 119
6. b; page 120
7. a; page 122

Short answer

1. To change net domestic product at factor cost to GDP, two sets of adjustments must be made. First, net domestic product at factor cost is measured at firms' costs; to convert costs to equal the market prices paid, taxes must be added and subsidies subtracted. Second, net domestic product does not include depreciation but GDP does. Depreciation must be added; page 120.

2. GDP increases by $0.75, the market value of the final product, the litre of gasoline. Because the driller uses no intermediate goods, the driller's value added is $0.40. The refiner's value added is equal to the market value of the gasoline, $0.75, minus the value of the intermediate good, the oil at $0.40. The refiner's value added is $0.35. The sum of the driller's value added and the refiner's value added is $0.75, the same as the increase in GDP; page 121.

3. a. GDP = $6,400, the sum of consumption expenditure, investment, government expenditure on goods and services, and net exports of goods and services; page 117.

   b. Net domestic product at factor cost equals $5,300, the sum of wages, salaries, and supplementary labour income; interest and investment income; profits of corporations and government enterprises; and income from farms and unincorporated businesses; page 119.

   c. The difference between GDP and net domestic product at factor cost ($1,100) is indirect taxes minus subsidies plus depreciation. Indirect taxes minus subsidies equals $400, so depreciation equals $700; page 120.

■ **CHECKPOINT 5.3**

Fill in the blanks

Real GDP is the value of the final goods and services produced in a given year when valued at constant prices; nominal GDP is the value of the final goods and services produced in a given year valued at the prices that prevailed in that same year. The GDP deflator equals 100 times nominal GDP divided by real GDP.

True or false

1. False; page 125
2. False; page 125
3. True; page 125
4. True; page 127

Multiple choice

1. d; page 125
2. b; page 126
3. a; page 125
4. d; page 125
5. c; page 127
6. a; page 127

Short answer

1. a. Nominal GDP = (100 × $10) + (50 × $2) = $1,100, the sum of expenditure on pizza and expenditure on pop; page 125.

   b. Because 2003 is the base year, real GDP = nominal GDP, so real GDP = $1,100; page 125.

   c. Nominal GDP = (150 × $20) + (75 × $4) = $3,300, the sum of expenditure on pizza and expenditure on pop; page 125.

d. Using 2003 prices, GDP grew from $1,100 in 2003 to $1,650 in 2004, an increase of 50 percent. Using 2004 prices, GDP grew from $2,200 in 2003 to $3,300 in 2004, an increase of 50 percent. The average growth is 50 percent, so real GDP in 2004 is 50 percent higher than in 2003. Real GDP in 2004 equals $1,650; page 126.

2. To measure the change in production, it is necessary to use real GDP. Nominal GDP changes whenever production *or* prices change. Real GDP uses constant prices and changes only when production changes; page 125.

3. Real GDP in one year is compared with real GDP in the preceding year. Real GDP in 2004 is linked to real GDP in 2003 by the percentage change from 2003, and real GDP in 2003 in turn is linked to real GDP in 2002 by the percentage change from 2002, and so on. These links are like the links in a chain that link real GDP back to the base year and the base year prices; page 126.

■ **CHECKPOINT 5.4**

Fill in the blanks

The value of household production <u>is not</u> included in GDP. The value of people's leisure time <u>is not</u> included in GDP. GDP <u>does not</u> subtract the value of environment degradation resulting from production. Real GDP <u>does not take</u> into account the extent of a country's political freedom.

True or false

1. True; page 129

2. False; page 129

3. False; page 130

4. True; page 131

Multiple choice

1. c; page 129

2. b; page 129

3. b; page 130

4. a; page 130

5. c; page 130

6. c; page 130

Short answer

1. Goods and services omitted from GDP are household production, underground production, leisure time, and environment quality. GDP measures the value of goods and services that are bought in markets. Because household production, leisure time, and environment quality are not purchased in markets, they are excluded from GDP. Even though underground production is bought in markets, the activity is unreported and is not included in GDP; pages 129-130.

2. If you cook a hamburger at home, the meat you purchase is included in GDP. The production of the hamburger is not included in GDP because it is household production. If you purchase a hamburger at Burger King, the production of the hamburger is included in GDP; page 129

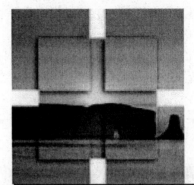

The CPI and the Cost of Living

Chapter 6

Chapter 6 discusses the Consumer Price Index, explains how it is constructed, and examines its biases. Chapter 6 demonstrates how to adjust money values for changes in the price level. This chapter also discusses the real wage rate and the real interest rate, and shows how both are calculated.

■ **Explain what the Consumer Price Index (CPI) is and how it is calculated.**

The Consumer Price Index (CPI) is a measure of the average of the prices paid by households for a fixed market basket of consumer goods and services. The CPI compares the cost of a fixed market basket of goods and services at one time with the cost of the fixed market basket in the base period. The CPI in the base period is 100. If the CPI is now 150, it costs 50 percent more to buy the same goods and services than it cost in the base period. Each month employees of Statistics Canada record the prices of the 600 goods and services in the CPI basket in retail outlets across Canada. To calculate the CPI, the cost of the CPI basket at current prices is divided by the cost of the CPI basket at base period prices and the result is multiplied by 100. The inflation rate is the percentage change in the price level from one year to the next and is equal to [(CPI in current year − CPI in previous year) ÷ (CPI in previous year)] × 100.

■ **Adjust money values for inflation and calculate real wage rates and real interest rates.**

Comparing values measured in dollars in different years is misleading if the value of money changes. To make the comparison, the nominal values must be converted to real values. A change in the real wage rate measures the change in the quantity of goods and services that an hour's work can buy. The real wage rate equals the nominal wage rate multiplied by 100 and divided by the GDP deflator. The real interest rate equals the nominal interest rate minus the inflation rate.

■ **Explain the limitations of the CPI as a measure of the cost of living.**

The main sources of bias in the CPI that lead to an inaccurate measure of the cost of living are the new goods bias (new goods replace old goods), the quality change bias (goods and services increase in quality), the commodity substitution bias (changes in relative prices lead consumers to change the items they buy), and the outlet substitution bias (consumers switch to shopping more often in discount stores). The U.S. CPI bias has been estimated to overstate inflation by 1.1 percentage points a year. Canada's CPI bias is believed to be less than 1.1 percentage points a year. The CPI bias distorts private agreements and increases government payments. The GDP deflator is constructed using, in part, the CPI and so the GDP deflator inherits the same biases as the CPI. The GDP deflator is not an alternative to the CPI as a good measure of the cost of living because GDP is the sum of expenditures on all final goods and services, not just consumption expenditures.

EXPANDED CHAPTER CHECKLIST

When you have completed this chapter, you will be able to

1 **Explain what the Consumer Price Index (CPI) is and how it is calculated.**

- Define Consumer Price Index and discuss the meaning of the CPI numbers.
- Explain the construction of the CPI, including the role played by the CPI basket and the base period.
- Explain how the CPI is calculated.
- Define and calculate the inflation rate.

2 **Adjust money values for inflation and calculate real wage rates and real interest rates.**

- Explain how changes in the price level are used when comparing the price of a good at different dates.
- Discuss the difference between the nominal wage rate and the real wage rate.
- Explain how the real wage rate is calculated.
- Define the nominal interest rate and the real interest rate.
- Discuss the difference between the nominal interest rate and the real interest rate.
- Explain how the real interest rate is calculated.
- Discuss why the distinction between nominal and real values matters

3 **Explain the limitations of the CPI as a measure of the cost of living.**

- Explain the new goods bias.
- Explain the quality change bias.
- Explain the commodity substitution bias.

- Explain the outlet substitution bias.
- Discuss the magnitude of the CPI bias.
- Explain the consequences of the CPI bias for private agreements and government payments.
- Compare the GDP deflator and the CPI as measures of the cost of living.

KEY TERMS

- Base period (page 138)
- Consumer Price Index (CPI) (page 138)
- Cost of living index (page 152)
- Expected inflation rate (page 150)
- Inflation rate (page 141)
- Money wage rate (page 145)
- Nominal interest rate (page 148)
- Nominal wage rate (page 145)
- Real interest rate (page 148)
- Real wage rate (page 145)

CHECKPOINT 6.1

■   **Explain what the Consumer Price Index (CPI) is and how it is calculated.**

Practice Problems 6.1

1. The Survey of Household Spending in Sparta shows that people consume only juice and cloth. In 2003, the year of the survey and also the base period, the average household spent $40 on juice and $25 on cloth. The price of juice in 2003 was $4 a bottle and the price of cloth was $5 a metre. In the current year, 2004, the price of juice is $4 a bottle and the price of cloth is $6 a metre. Calculate

a. The CPI basket.

b. The percentage of the average household budget spent on juice in the base period.

c. The CPI in 2004.

2. The table shows the CPI in Russia. Calculate Russia's inflation rate in 2001 and 2002. Did the price level rise or fall in 2002? Did the inflation rate increase or decrease in 2002?

Year	CPI
2000	225
2001	274
2002	310

Solution to Practice Problems 6.1

To solve the first question, you need to know the cost of the CPI basket in the period being examined and the cost of the CPI basket in the base period. The second question requires that you use the formula for the inflation rate.

Quick Review

- *CPI formula* The CPI equals

$$\frac{\text{Cost of CPI basket at current period prices}}{\text{Cost of CPI basket at base period prices}} \times 100.$$

- *Inflation rate* The inflation rate equals

$$\frac{(\text{CPI in current year} - \text{CPI in previous year})}{\text{CPI in previous year}} \times 100.$$

1a. The CPI basket.

In the base year, the price of juice was $4 a bottle and the average household spent $40 on juice. The household bought 10 ($40 ÷ $4) bottles of juice. In the base year, the price of cloth was $5 a metre and the average household spent $25 on cloth. The household bought 5 ($25 ÷ $5) metres of cloth. The CPI basket is the quantities of goods and services purchased during the survey year, so the CPI basket is 10 bottles of juice and 5 metres of cloth.

b. The percentage of the average household budget spent on juice in the base period.

The household's budget in the base period was $65 — $40 on juice plus $25 on cloth. The percentage of the budget spent on juice is the amount spent on juice divided by the budget, multiplied by 100, which is ($40 ÷ $65) × 100 = 61.5 percent.

c. The CPI in 2004.

In 2004, the 10 bottles of juice in the CPI basket cost $4 each and the 5 metres of cloth cost $6 each. So the total cost of the CPI basket in 2004 is $70. The CPI basket in the base period, 2003, cost $65. The CPI is equal to the cost of the CPI basket in 2004 divided by the cost of the CPI basket in 2003, all multiplied by 100, which is ($70 ÷ $65) × 100 = 107.7.

2. Calculate Russia's inflation rate in 2001 and 2002. Did the price level rise or fall in 2002? Did the inflation rate increase or decrease in 2002?

The inflation rate is the percentage change in the price level from one year to the next. In 2000, the CPI was 225 and in 2001, it was 274. The inflation rate in 2001 is [(274 – 225) ÷ 225] × 100, which is 21.8 percent. The inflation rate in 2002 is [(310 – 274) ÷ 274] × 100, which is 13.1 percent. The CPI is higher in 2002 than in 2001, so the price level increased in 2002. The inflation rate in 2001 was 21.8 percent and the inflation rate in 2002 was 13.1 percent, so the inflation rate decreased in 2002.

Additional Practice Problem 6.1a

In the current year, which is the year following the base period, the inflation rate is 100 percent a year. Calculate the CPI in the current year.

Solution to Additional Practice Problem 6.1a

The CPI in the base period is 100. The inflation rate in the year following the base period is [(CPI in current year − 100) ÷ 100] × 100 = 100 percent a year. By rearranging the equation, we find that the CPI in the current year is 200.

■ **Self Test 6.1**

Fill in the blanks

The ____ (Consumer Price Index; inflation rate) is a measure of the average of the prices paid by households for a fixed market basket of consumer goods and services. In the base period, the CPI equals ____ (1; 100). The CPI equals the cost of the CPI basket at current period prices ____ (plus; divided by) the cost of the CPI basket at base period prices all multiplied by 100.

True or false

1. In the base period, the CPI equals 1.0.

2. The CPI basket is changed from one month to the next.

3. If the cost of the CPI basket at current period prices equals $320, then the CPI equals 320.

4. If the cost of the CPI basket at current period prices exceeds the cost of the CPI basket at base period prices, the inflation rate between these two periods is positive.

5. If the CPI increases from 110 in one year to 121 in the next year, the inflation rate is 11 percent a year.

Multiple choice

1. The Consumer Price Index is a measure of

a. the prices of all consumer goods

b. the prices of consumer goods and services that rose in the past year.

c. the average of the prices paid by households for a fixed market basket of consumer goods and services.

d. consumer confidence in the economy.

2. The CPI is reported once every

a. year.

b. quarter.

c. month.

d. week.

3. If a country has a CPI of 105.0 in 2002 and a CPI of 102.0 in 2003, then

a. the average prices of goods and services increased between 2002 and 2003.

b. the average prices of goods and services decreased between 2002 and 2003.

c. the average quantity of goods and services decreased between 2002 and 2003.

d. there was an error when calculating the CPI in 2003.

4. The period for which the Consumer Price Index is defined to equal 100 is called the

a. base period.

b. survey period.

c. starting point.

d. zero inflation period.

5. The good or service given the most weight in the CPI basket when calculating the CPI is

a. food.

b. taxes.

c. shelter.

d. transportation.

6. Suppose a basket of consumer goods and services costs $180 using the base period prices and $300 using the current period prices. The CPI for the current period equals

a. 166.7.

b. 66.7.

c. 160.0.

d. 60.0.

7. If the CPI in 2000 is 113.4 and in 2001 is 116.4, then the inflation rate in 2001 is

a. 2.6 percent.

b. 9.8 percent.

c. 2.9 percent.

d. 1.6 percent.

8. On average, the inflation rate in Canada during the 1990s

a. was higher than in the 1980s.

b. was higher than in the 1970s.

c. was lower than in the 1980s.

d. was zero.

Short answer

1. The table gives the expenditures of households in the small nation of Studenvia. In Studenvia, 2002 is the base period.

Item	Quantity (2002)	Price (2002)	Quantity (2003)	Price (2003)
Pizza	10	$10 each	15	$10 each
Burritos	20	$1 each	25	$0.75 each
Rice	30	$0.50 a box	20	$1 a box

a. What is the cost of the CPI basket in 2002?

b. What is the cost of the CPI basket in 2003?

c. What is the CPI in 2002?

d. What is the CPI in 2003?

e. What is the inflation rate in 2003?

2. Suppose the CPI was 100.0 in 2000, 110.0 in 2001, 121.0 in 2002, and 133.1 in 2003. What is the inflation rate in 2001, 2002, and 2003?

3. If the price level rises slowly, is the inflation rate positive or negative? Why?

CHECKPOINT 6.2

■ **Adjust money values for inflation and calculate real wage rates and real interest rates.**

Practice Problems 6.2

1. The table shows some gas prices and the CPI for three years.

Year	Price of gasoline (cents per litre)	CPI (1992 = 100)
1970	10	24.2
1985	51	75.0
2001	75	115.6

a. Calculate the real price of gasoline in each year in 1992 dollars.

b. In which year was gasoline the most costly in real terms?

c. By how much did the real price of gasoline change from 1985 to 2001?

2. Canadian Industries Ltd. agreed to pay its workers $22 an hour in 2002, a 10 percent increase over the 2000 wage rate of $20 an hour. The GDP deflator for these years was 105.4 in 2000 and 107.5 in 2002.

a. Calculate the real wage rate in each year.

b. What was the change in the real wage rate between 2000 and 2002?

3. Sally worked hard all year so she could go to school full time the following year. She put her savings into a mutual fund that paid a nominal interest rate of 7 percent a year. The CPI was 123 at the beginning of the year and 132 at the end of the year. What was the real interest rate that Sally earned?

Solution to Practice Problems 6.2

To convert the nominal wage rate into the real wage rate, divide the nominal wage rate by the GDP deflator and multiply by 100. To convert the nominal interest rate into the real interest rate, subtract the inflation rate from the nominal interest rate.

Quick Review

- *Real wage rate* The average hourly wage rate measured in the dollars of a given base year.

- *Real interest rate* The percentage return on a loan expressed in purchasing power.

1a. Calculate the real price of gasoline in each year in 1992 dollars.

To convert the nominal prices in the table to real prices divide the nominal price by the CPI in that year and then multiply by 100. In 1970, the nominal price of gas is 10 cents a litre and the CPI is 24.2, so the real price of gasoline is (10 cents ÷ 24.2) × 100, which is 41.3 cents a litre. In 1985 the nominal price is 51 cents a litre, the CPI is 75.0, and the real price is (51 cents ÷ 75.0) ×

100, which is 68 cents a litre. In 2001 the nominal price is 75 cents a litre a litre, the CPI is 115.6, and the real price is 64.9 cents a litre.

b.   In which year was gasoline the most costly in real terms?

The highest real price for gasoline was in 1985 when the real price was 68 cents a litre. In 1985 you gave up more in terms of other goods and services to buy a gallon of gas than in 1970 or 2001.

c.   By how much did the real price of gasoline change from 1985 to 2001?

The real price of gasoline fell from 68 cents a litre in 1985 to 64.8 cents a litre in 2001, a decrease of 4.7 percent.

2.   Canadian Industries Ltd. agreed to pay its workers $22 an hour in 2002, a 10 percent increase over the 2000 wage rate of $20 an hour. The GDP deflator for these years was 105.4 in 2000 and 107.5 in 2002.

a.   Calculate the real wage rate in each year.

The real wage rate equals the nominal wage rate divided by the GDP deflator and multiplied by 100. The nominal wage rate in 2000 was $20 an hour, and the GDP deflator was 105.4, so the real wage rate was ($20 ÷ 105.4) × 100, which is $18.98 an hour. Similarly, the real wage in 2002 was ($22 ÷ 107.5) × 100, which is $20.47 an hour.

b.   What was the change in the real wage rate between 2000 and 2002?

The workers received a real pay raise of ($20.47 – $18.98), which is $1.49 an hour.

3.   Sally worked hard all year so she could go to school full time the following year. She put her savings into a mutual fund that paid a nominal interest rate of 7 percent a year. The CPI was 123 at the beginning of the year and 132 at the end of the year. What was the real interest rate that Sally earned?

The real interest rate equals the nominal interest rate minus the inflation rate. Sally earned a nominal interest rate of 7 percent a year. The in-

flation rate is the percentage change in the price level from one year to the next, which is [(132 – 123) ÷ 123] × 100 = 7.3 percent. The real interest rate is 7 percent a year – 7.3 percent a year, which is –0.3 percent a year.

Additional Practice Problem 6.2a

Suppose Sally (from Practice Problem 3) wants to receive a 3 percent a year real interest rate on her savings. What nominal interest rate does she need to receive if the inflation rate is 7 percent a year?

Solution to Additional Practice Problem 6.2a

The real interest rate equals the nominal interest rate minus the inflation rate. Rearranging this formula shows that the nominal interest rate equals the real interest rate plus the inflation rate. To receive a 3 percent a year real interest rate with a 7 percent a year inflation rate, Sally needs the nominal interest rate to equal 3 percent a year plus 7 percent a year, which is 10 percent a year.

■ **Self Test 6.2**

Fill in the blanks

The nominal wage rate is the average hourly wage rate measured in _____ (current; base year) dollars. The real wage rate is the average hourly wage rate measured in dollars of the _____ (current; given base) year. The real wage rate equals the nominal wage rate (plus; times; divided by) the GDP deflator and multiplied by 100. The real interest rate equals the nominal interest rate _____ (plus; minus; divided by) the _____ (CPI; inflation rate).

True or false

1.   The CPI was 113.5 in 2000 and 15.0 in 1950, so prices on the average were more than 7 times higher in 2000 than in 1950.

2.   Real GDP equals nominal GDP divided by the CPI, and multiplied by 100.

3. A change in the real wage rate measures the change in the quantity of goods and services that an hour's work can buy.

4. A nominal interest rate is the percentage return on a loan expressed in dollars and a real interest rate is the percentage return on a loan expressed in purchasing power.

5. When the inflation rate exceeds the expected inflation rate, the real interest rate and the real wage rate fall.

Multiple choice

1. Apples cost $1.49 a basket in 2002. Suppose the CPI was 120 in 2002 and 140 in 2003. If there is no change in the real value of an apple in the year 2003, how much would a basket of apples sell for in 2003?

a. $2.74

b. $1.69

c. $1.66

d. $1.74

2. The price of a local phone call is $0.10 in 1970. What is the price of this phone call in 2003 dollars if the CPI was 25 in 1970 and in 2003 it was 110?

a. $1.42

b. $0.39

c. $1.72

d. $0.44

3. The nominal wage rate is the

a. minimum hourly wage that a company can legally pay a worker.

b. average hourly wage rate measured in the dollars of a given base year.

c. minimum hourly wage rate measured in the dollars of a given base year.

d. average hourly wage rate measured in current dollars.

4. In 2002, the average starting salary for an economics major is $29,900. If the GDP deflator in 2002 is 107.5, the real salary is

a. $27.81 an hour.

b. $27,814.

c. $32,1435.

d. $35,953.

5. If we compare the nominal wage rate and the real wage rate in Canada between1983 and 2002, we see that the

a. real wage rate increased steadily.

b. nominal wage rate increased more than the real wage rate.

c. real wage rate increased more than the nominal wage rate.

d. nominal wage rate increased at an uneven pace and the increase in the real wage rate was steady and constant.

6. The real interest rate is equal to the nominal interest rate

a. plus the inflation rate.

b. minus the inflation rate.

c. times the inflation rate.

d. divided by the inflation rate.

7. You borrow at a nominal interest rate of 10 percent a year. If the inflation rate is 4 percent a year, then the real interest rate is

a. the $10 in interest you have to pay.

b. 16 percent a year.

c. 2.5 percent a year.

d. 6 percent a year.

8. In Canada between 1982 and 2002, the

a. nominal and real interest rates both generally increased.

b. gap between the nominal and real interest rates grew larger.

c. real interest rate was constant and the nominal interest rate fluctuated.

d. nominal interest rate was greater than the real interest rate.

Short answer

1. Often the cost of living varies from province to province or from large city to small city. After you graduate, suppose you have job offers in 3 locales. The nominal salary and the GDP deflator for each location are given in the table.

Job	Salary (dollars per year)	GDP deflator
Job A	20,000	105
Job B	25,000	120
Job C	34,000	170

a. Which job offers the highest real salary?

b. Which job offers the lowest real salary?

c. In determining which job to accept, what is more important: the real salary or the nominal salary? Why?

2. The table gives the real interest rate, nominal interest rate, and inflation rate for various years in a foreign country. Complete the table.

Year	Real interest rate (percent per year)	Nominal interest rate (percent per year)	Inflation rate (percent per year)
2000	____	10	5
2001	____	6	1
2002	4	6	____
2003	5	____	3

3. In one year the nominal interest rate is 12 percent a year and in another year the nominal interest rate is 8 percent a year. In which year would you rather save $1,000?

CHECKPOINT 6.3

■ **Explain the limitations of the CPI as a measure of the cost of living.**

Practice Problem 6.3

1. Economists in the Statistics Bureau decide to check the substitution bias in the CPI. To do so, they conduct an expenditure survey in both 2001 and 2002. The table shows the results of the survey. It shows the items that consumers buy and their prices.

Item	2001 Quantity	2001 Price	2002 Quantity	2002 Price
Broccoli	10	$3.00	15	$3.00
Carrots	15	$2.00	10	$4.00

The Statistics Bureau fixes the base period as 2001 and asks you to

a. Calculate the CPI in 2002 using the 2001 CPI basket.

b. Calculate the CPI in 2002 using the 2002 CPI basket.

c. Explain whether there is any substitution bias in the CPI that uses the 2001 basket.

Solution to Practice Problem 6.3

The commodity substitution bias is one of the four sources that make the CPI a biased measure of changes in the cost of living. The CPI, which uses a fixed basket, does not account for these changes in buying patterns.

Quick Review

• *Commodity substitution bias* People cut back on their purchases of items that become relatively more costly and increase their consumption of items that become relatively less costly.

a. Calculate the CPI in 2002 using the 2001 CPI basket.

The CPI basket in 2001 consists of 10 broccoli and 15 carrots. The cost of the basket in 2001 prices is $(10 \times \$3) + (15 \times \$2)$, which is $60, and its cost in

2002 prices is $(10 \times \$3) + (15 \times \$4)$, which is $90. The CPI in 2002, using the 2001 basket, equals the cost of the basket in 2002 prices divided by the cost of the basket in 2001 prices, all multiplied by 100, which is $(\$90 \div \$60) \times 100 = 150$.

b. Calculate the CPI in 2002 using the 2002 CPI basket.

The CPI basket in 2002 consists of 15 broccoli and 10 carrots. The cost of the basket in 2001 is $(15 \times \$3) + (10 \times \$2)$, which is $65 and its cost in 2002 is $(15 \times \$3) + (10 \times \$4)$, which is $85. The CPI in 2002, using the 2002 basket is $(\$85 \div \$65) \times 100$, which equals 131.

c. Explain whether there is any substitution bias in the CPI that uses the 2001 basket.

There is substitution bias. The price of broccoli is the same in both years, but the price of carrots increases between 2001 and 2002. Households substitute the now relatively cheaper broccoli for the now relatively more expensive carrots. In 2002 people bought more broccoli and fewer carrots than in 2001. Consumers spend $60 on vegetables in 2001 and $85 in 2002, an increase of 42 percent. They would have spent $90 if they had not substituted the now relatively less costly broccoli. By using a fixed CPI basket, the CPI ignores the substitution. The CPI, using the 2001 CPI basket, concludes that the cost of vegetables rises 50 percent, which overstates the actual impact of the price rise because it ignores the ability of households to partially escape the increased price of carrots by substituting broccoli. Because consumers make substitutions, the cost of vegetables increases by only 42 percent.

Additional Practice Problem 6.3a

When households buy broccoli, they discard 20 percent of it because it is bruised. Now new, genetically engineered broccoli is developed that does not bruise so that all broccoli that is purchased can be used. People switch to buying the new broccoli. If the price of the new broccoli is 10 percent higher than the old, what actually happens to the CPI and what would happen to the CPI if it accurately reflects the change in the broccoli purchases?

Solution to Additional Practice Problem 6.3a

With the introduction of the new broccoli, the CPI will rise because the new broccoli's price is 10 percent higher than the old broccoli. But, if the CPI accurately reflects the change in the broccoli purchases, then the CPI decreases because people pay only 10 percent more for 20 percent more useable broccoli. This problem illustrates how the quality change bias can bias the CPI upward.

■ Self Test 6.3

Fill in the blanks

The sources of bias in the CPI as a measure of changes in the cost of living are the ____, ____, ____, and ____. The CPI bias leads to ____ (an increase; a decrease) in government payments. The CPI and the GDP deflator follow ____ (divergent; similar) paths.

True or false

1. The CPI does not try to measure all the components of the cost of living.

2. Commodity substitution bias refers to the ongoing replacement of old goods by new goods.

3. The bias in the CPI in Canada is believed to overstate inflation by less than 1.1 percentage points a year.

4. The CPI bias can distort private agreements.

5. The GDP deflator and the CPI are alternative measures of the cost of living.

Multiple choice

1. All of the following can lead to bias in the CPI except the

a. new goods bias.

b. outlet substitution bias.

c. commodity substitution bias.

d. GDP deflator bias.

2. An example of the new goods bias in the calculation of the CPI is a price increase in

a. butter relative to margarine.

b. an MP3 player relative to a Walkman.

c. antiques.

d. textbooks bought through the campus bookstore relative to textbooks bought at a textbook warehouse.

3. Since 1990, the price of a dishwasher has remained relatively constant while the quality of dishwashers has improved.

a. The CPI is adjusted monthly to reflect this improvement in quality.

b. The CPI is increased monthly to reflect the increased quality of dishwashers.

c. The CPI has an upward bias if it is not adjusted to take account of the higher quality.

d. None of the above.

4. Joe buys chicken and beef. If the price of beef rises and the price of chicken does not change, Joe will buy _____ and help create a _____ bias for the CPI.

a. more beef; new goods

b. more chicken; commodity substitution

c. the same quantity of beef and chicken; commodity substitution

d. less chicken and beef; quality change

5. It is believed that the bias in Canada's CPI is

a. about 5 percentage points a year.

b. more than 5 percentage points a year.

c. less than 1.1 percentage points a year.

d. equal to 5 percentage points a year.

6. A consequence of the CPI bias is that it

a. decreases government payments.

b. increases international trade.

c. reduces outlet substitution bias.

d. distorts private agreements.

7. If the CPI is a biased measure of the inflation rate then government payments will

a. increase at a faster rate than the actual inflation rate.

b. increase at the same rate as the actual inflation rate.

c. increase at a slower rate than the actual inflation rate.

d. None of the above, because the bias in inflation measured using the CPI has nothing to do with government payments.

8. If we compare the recent measurements of inflation as recorded by the CPI and the GDP deflator we find that the

a. two measures fluctuate together.

b. CPI has consistently been at least 5 percentage points above the GDP deflator.

c. GDP deflator has consistently been at least 5 percentage points above the CPI.

d. two measures give very different inflation rates for most years.

Short answer

1. What are the sources of bias in the CPI? Briefly explain each.

2. When you graduate, you move to a new town and sign a long-term lease on a townhouse. You agree to pay $1,000 a month rent and to change the monthly rent annually by the percentage change in the CPI. For the next 4 years, the CPI increases 5 percent each year. What do you pay in monthly rent for the second, third, and fourth years of your lease? Suppose the CPI overstates the inflation rate by 1 percentage point a year. If the CPI bias was eliminated, what do you pay in monthly rent for the second, third, and fourth years?

SELF TEST ANSWERS

■ CHECKPOINT 6.1

Fill in the blanks

The <u>Consumer Price Index</u> is a measure of the average of the prices paid by households for a fixed market basket of consumer goods and services. In the base period, the CPI equals <u>100</u>. The CPI equals the cost of the CPI basket at current period prices <u>divided by</u> the cost of the CPI basket at base period prices all multiplied by 100.

True or false

1. False; page 138
2. False; page 138
3. False; pages 140-141
4. True;   page 141
5. False; page 141

Multiple choice

1. c; page 138
2. c; page 138
3. b; page 138
4. a; page 138
5. c; page 139
6. a; pages 140-141
7. a; page 141
8. c; pages 141-142

Short answer

1. a. The cost is $135; page 140.

   b. The cost is $145. The quantities used to calculate this cost are the base period, 2002, quantities; page 140.

   c. The CPI is 100; page 138.

   d. The CPI is 107.4; page 141.

   e. The inflation rate is 7.4 percent; page 141.

2. The inflation rate for each year is 10 percent a year; page 141.

3. Whenever the price level rises, the inflation rate is positive. If the price level rises slowly, the inflation rate is small; if the price level rises rapidly, the inflation rate is large; page 141.

■ CHECKPOINT 6.2

Fill in the blanks

The nominal wage rate is the average hourly wage rate measured in <u>current</u> dollars. The real wage rate is the average hourly wage rate measured in dollars of the <u>given base</u> year. The real wage rate equals the nominal wage rate <u>divided by</u> the GDP deflator and multiplied by 100. The real interest rate equals the nominal interest rate <u>minus</u> the <u>inflation rate</u>.

True or false

1. True; page 144
2. False; page 144
3. True; page 146
4. True; page 148
5. True; page 150

Multiple choice

1. d; page 144
2. d; page 144
3. d; page 145
4. b; page 145
5. b; page 146
6. b; page 148
7. d; page 148
8. d; page 148

Short answer

1. a. Real salary equals (nominal salary ÷ GDP deflator) × 100. The real salary is $19,048 for Job A, $20,833 for Job B, and $20,000 for Job C. The real salary is highest for Job B; page 145

   b. The real salary is lowest for Job A; page 145

   b. The real salary is more important than the nominal salary because the real salary measures the quantity of goods and services you will be able to buy; pages 145-146

2. The completed table is below; page 148.

Year	Real interest rate (percent per year)	Nominal interest rate (percent per year)	Inflation rate (percent per year)
2000	5	10	5
2001	5	6	1
2002	4	6	2
2003	5	8	3

3. You cannot determine in which year you want to save $1,000. Savers are interested in the real interest rate because the real interest rate is expressed in purchasing power. Without knowing the inflation rate there is not enough data given to compute the real interest rate; page 148.

■ CHECKPOINT 6.3

Fill in the blanks

The sources of bias in the CPI as a measure of changes in the cost of living are the new goods bias, quality change bias, commodity substitution bias, and outlet substitution bias. The CPI bias leads to an increase in government payments. The CPI and the GDP deflator follow similar paths.

True or false

1. True; page 152

2. False; page 153

3. True; page 153

4. True; page 154

5. False; pages 154-155

Multiple choice

1. d; page 152

2. b; page 152

3. d; page 152

4. b; page 153

5. c; page 153

6. d; pages 153- 154

7. a; page 154

8. a; page 155

Short answer

1. The four main sources of bias in the CPI are: the new goods bias, the quality change bias, the commodity substitution bias, and the outlet substitution bias. The new goods bias refers to the fact that new goods replace old goods. The quality change bias occurs because at times price increases in existing goods are the result of increased quality. The commodity substitution bias occurs because consumers buy fewer goods and services when their prices rise compared to other, comparable products. The outlet substitution bias refers to the fact that when prices rise, people shop more frequently at discount stores to take advantage of the lower prices in these stores; pages 152-153.

2. The monthly rent increases by 5 percent each year. For the second year the monthly rent equals $1,000 × 1.05, which is $1,050. For the third year the monthly rent equals $1,050 × 1.05, which is $1,102.50. And for the fourth year the monthly rent equals $1,102.50 × 1.05, which is $1,157.63. If the CPI bias was eliminated, the monthly rent would increase by 4 percent each year. The monthly rent would be $1,040 for the second year, $1,081.60 for the third year, and $1,124.86 for the fourth year; page 154.

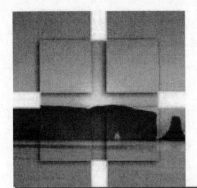

Unemployment and the Business Cycle

CHAPTER IN PERSPECTIVE

Chapter 7 defines the main labour market indicators and explains how these indicators change over time. Chapter 7 also discusses the relationship between unemployment and real GDP.

■ **Define the unemployment rate and other labour market indicators.**

The Labour Force Survey is a monthly survey of 54,000 Canadian households, which is the basis for the nation's labour market statistics. The working-age population is the total number of people aged 15 years and over. The labour force is the total number of people employed plus the number unemployed. The unemployment rate is the percentage of the people in the labour force who are unemployed. The labour force participation rate is the percentage of the working-age population who are members of the labour force. A person who does not have a job, is available and willing to work but has not made specific efforts to find a job within the previous four weeks is a discouraged worker. Part-time workers are people who usually work less than 30 hours a week. Aggregate hours are the total number of hours worked by all the people employed, both full time and part time, during a year.

■ **Describe the trends and fluctuations in the indicators of labour market performance in Canada.**

Between 1962 and 2002, the average unemployment rate in Canada was 7.7 percent. The lowest unemployment rates occurred in the 1960s. Unemployment is classified into four types: frictional, structural, seasonal, and cyclical. Full employment occurs when there is no cyclical unemployment, or, equivalently, when all the unemployment is frictional, structural, and seasonal. The unemployment rate at full employment is called the natural unemployment rate. Between 1976 and 2002, the labour force participation rate of women increased while that of men decreased. Part-time workers are an increasing proportion of the labour force, up from 13 percent in 1977 to 18.7 percent in 2002.

■ **Describe the relationships between unemployment, real GDP, and inflation over the business cycle.**

The level of real GDP that the economy would produce at full employment is potential GDP. The gap between real GDP and potential GDP is called the output gap. If real GDP exceeds potential GDP, the output gap is positive and is called an inflationary gap. If potential GDP exceeds real GDP, the output gap is negative and is called a deflationary gap. When the output gap is negative, cyclical unemployment is positive and the inflation rate slows. When the output gap is positive, cyclical unemployment is negative and the inflation rate speeds up.

EXPANDED CHAPTER CHECKLIST

When you have completed this chapter, you will be able to

1 Define the unemployment rate and other labour market indicators.

- Define working-age population and labour force.

- Classify persons as employed or unemployed.

- Define and calculate the unemployment rate and the labour force participation rate.

- Define discouraged worker.

- Classify a worker as full time or part time.

- Define involuntary part-time workers.

- Define and calculate aggregate hours.

2 Describe the trends and fluctuations in the indicators of labour market performance in Canada.

- Describe how the unemployment rate changed between 1962 and 2002.

- Tell what happens to the unemployment rate in recessions and in expansions.

- Describe the four types of unemployment.

- Define full employment and the natural unemployment rate.

- Describe the duration and demographics of unemployment in Canada

- Describe how the labour force participation rate changed between 1976 and 2002 and give reasons for the change.

- Describe the changes in the percentage of part-time workers between 1977 and 2002.

- Tell how the percentage of workers who are involuntary part-time workers changes in recessions.

3 Describe the relationships between unemployment, real GDP, and inflation over the business cycle.

- Define and calculate the output gap.

- Describe an inflationary gap and a deflationary gap.

- Describe the relationship between the output gap and cyclical unemployment.

- Describe the relationship between the output gap and the inflation rate.

KEY TERMS

- Aggregate hours (page 165)
- Cyclical unemployment (page 169)
- Deflationary gap (page 175)
- Discouraged worker (page 164)
- Frictional unemployment (page 168)
- Full employment (page 170)
- Full-time workers (page 164)
- Inflationary gap (page 175)
- Involuntary part-time workers (page 164)
- Labour force (page 162)
- Labour force participation rate (page 164)
- Natural unemployment rate (page 170)
- Output gap (page 175)
- Part-time workers (page 164)
- Potential GDP (page 175)
- Seasonal unemployment (page 169)
- Structural unemployment (page 169)
- Unemployment rate (page 163)
- Working-age population (page 162)

CHECKPOINT 7.1

■ **Define the unemployment rate and other labour market indicators.**

Practice Problem 7.1

Statistics Canada reported that in January 2001, the labour force was 15.9 million; employment was 14.7 million; and the working-age population was 24.5 million. Average weekly hours were 34.5. Calculate for that month the

a. Unemployment rate.

b. Labour force participation rate.

c. Aggregate hours worked in a week.

Solution to Practice Problem 7.1
This question focuses on the calculations required to determine three labour market indicators.

Quick Review

- Unemployment rate The percentage of the people in the labour force who are unemployed. That is,

$$\text{Unemployment rate} = \frac{\text{Number of people unemployed}}{\text{Labour force}} \times 100$$

- *Labour force participation rate* The percentage of the working-age population who are members of the labour force. That is,

$$\text{Labour force participation rate} = \frac{\text{Labour force}}{\text{Working - age population}} \times 100$$

- *Aggregate hours* The total number of hours worked by all the people employed, both full time and part time, during a year.

a. **Unemployment rate**

The labour force equals the sum of the number of people employed and the number of people un-employed. Subtracting the number employed from the labour force gives the number of unemployed. The labour force is 15.9 million and the number of employed is 14.7 million, so the number unemployed is 15.9 million – 14.7 million, which is 1.2 million. To calculate the unemployment rate, divide the number of unemployed by the labour force and multiply by 100. The unemployment rate equals (1.2 million ÷ 15.9 million) × 100, which is 7.5 percent.

b. **Labour force participation rate**

The labour force participation rate is the percentage of the working-age population who are members of the labour force. The labour force participation rate equals the labour force divided by the working-age population all multiplied by 100, which is (15.9 million ÷ 24.5 million) × 100 = 64.9 percent.

c. **Aggregate hours worked in a week**

In January 2001, 14.7 million people worked an average of 34.5 hours, so the aggregate hours worked in a week is 14.7 million × 34.5 hours, which is 507.15 million hours.

Additional Practice Problem 7.1a

Determine the labour market status of each of the following people:

a. Don is 21 and a full-time college student.

b. Shirley works for 20 hours a week as an administrative assistant and is looking for a full-time job.

c. Clarence was laid off from his job selling keyboards to computer manufacturers and is actively seeking a new job.

d. Pat quit her job as an account executive 6 months ago. She is unable to find a new position and has stopped actively searching.

Solution to Additional Practice Problem 7.1a

a. **Don is 21 and a full-time college student.**

Don is neither working nor looking for work, so he is not in the labour force.

b. **Shirley works for 20 hours a week as an administrative assistant and is looking for a full-time job.**

Shirley is part of the labour force. She is working less than 30 hours a week, so she is a part-time worker. Because she is looking for a full-time job, Shirley is an involuntary part-time worker.

c. **Clarence was laid off from his job selling keyboards to computer manufacturers and is actively seeking a new job.**

Clarence is actively seeking a new job, so he is unemployed. Clarence is part of the labour force.

d. **Pat quit her job as an account executive 6 months ago. She is unable to find a new position and has stopped actively searching.**

Pat is neither working nor actively looking for work, so she is not in the labour force. Pat is a discouraged worker.

■ Self Test 7.1

Fill in the blanks

The _____ (working-age population; labour force) is the total number of people aged 15 years and over. The unemployment rate equals the _____ (number of involuntary part-time workers plus the number unemployed; number of people unemployed) divided by the _____ (labour force; working-age population), all multiplied by 100. The labour force participation rate equals the _____ (number of people employed; labour force) divided by the _____, (labour force; working-age population) all multiplied by 100. Involuntary part-time workers _____ (are; are not) counted as employed. The total number of hours worked in a year by all the employed people are _____ (aggregate hours; GDP hours).

True or false

1. When contacted by Statistics Canada, Bob states that he has been laid off by Ford Motor Corporation, but expects to be recalled within the next three weeks. Bob is considered part of the labour force.

2. People are counted as unemployed as long as they are working less than 40 hours a week.

3. The unemployment rate decreases when unemployed workers find jobs.

4. The labour force participation rate measures the percentage of the labour force that is employed.

5. If the number of discouraged workers increases, the unemployment rate will increase.

Multiple choice

1. If the population is 30 million, the working-age population is 24 million, 15 million are employed, and 0.6 million are unemployed, what is the size of the labour force?

a. 30 million

b. 24 million

c. 15.6 million

d. 15 million

2. Which of the following statements about Canada is <u>FALSE</u>?

a. The size of the labour force is greater than the number of employed people.

b. The size of the labour force is greater than the number of unemployed people.

c. The number of unemployed people is greater than the number of employed people.

d. None of the above because they are all true statements.

3. If you are available and willing to work but have not actively looked for work in the past month then

a. you are part of the labour force because you are willing to work.

b. you are counted as unemployed because you are willing to work and do not have a job.

c. you are not part of the labour force because you are not looking for a job.

d. you are part of the labour force but are not counted as unemployed.

4. The unemployment rate equals 100 times

a. (number of people without a job) ÷ (population)

b. (number of people unemployed) ÷ (labour force)

c. (number of people without a job) ÷ (working-age population)

d. (number of people unemployed) ÷ (population)

5. A discouraged worker is

a. counted as employed by Statistics Canada but is not part of the labour force.

b. counted as employed by Statistics Canada and is part of the labour force.

c. counted as unemployed by Statistics Canada and is part of the labour force.

d. not part of the labour force.

6. While in school, Kim spends 20 hours a week working as a computer technician in the college computer lab and studies 30 hours a week.

a. Kim is classified as a full-time worker, working 50 hours a week.

b. Kim is classified as a part-time worker, working 30 hours a week.

c. Kim is classified as a part-time worker, working 20 hours a week.

d. Because Kim is a student, she is not classified as working.

7. If the number of part-time workers is 2 million, the number of involuntary part-time workers is 850,000 and the labour force is 15.6 million, then the involuntary part-time rate is

a. 5.4 percent.

b. 4.3 percent.

c. 3.0 percent.

d. 1.3 percent.

8. To determine the total amount of labour employed, we measure labour

a. in jobs.

b. by counting the number of full-time workers.

c. by multiplying the number of full-time workers by average hours per week.

d. in hours.

Short answer

1. The table gives information about the Canadian population in 1996.

Category	Millions of people
Total population	29.7
Working-age population	23.0
Not in the labour force	8.1
Employed	13.5

a. What is the size of the labour force?

b. What is the number of unemployed workers?

c. What is the unemployment rate?

d. What is the labour force participation rate?

2. The table gives information about the Canadian population in 1999.

Category	Millions of people
Working-age population	24.0
Unemployed	1.2
Employed	14.5

a. What is the size of the labour force?

b. What is the unemployment rate?

c. What is the labour force participation rate?

3. When is a person counted as unemployed?

4. What is a discouraged worker? Why is a discouraged worker not part of the labour force?

5. Is an involuntarily part-time worker counted as employed or unemployed?

CHECKPOINT 7.2

■ Describe the trends and fluctuations in the indicators of labour market performance in Canada.

Practice Problem 7.2

Use the link on your Foundations Web site and view the data for Figures 7.2, 7.5, and 7.6. Then answer the following questions:

a. In which decade—the 1960s, 1970s, 1980s, or 1990s—was the unemployment rate the lowest? What brought low unemployment in that decade?

b. In which decade was the unemployment rate the highest? What brought high unemployment in that decade?

c. Describe the trends in the participation rates of men and women and all workers. Why did these trends occur?

d. Describe the trends and fluctuations in part-time work. Why is part-time work on the increase?

Solution to Practice Problem 7.2

This question focuses on labour market trends.

Quick Review

• *Labour force participation rate* The percentage of the working-age population who are members of the labour force.

• *Unemployment rate* The percentage of the people in the labour force who are unemployed.

a. In which decade—the 1960s, 1970s, 1980s, or 1990s—was the unemployment rate the lowest? What brought low unemployment in that decade?

The average unemployment rate was lowest in the 1960s, at 5.0 percent, reaching a low of 3.3 percent in 1966. The low unemployment rate was due to a strong economic expansion generated by large increases in government spending on social programs and increasing exports to the United States.

b. In which decade was the unemployment rate the highest? What brought high unemployment in that decade?

The unemployment rate was the highest during the 1990s when it averaged 9.6 percent. A deep recession in 1990-1991 was followed by a slow recovery.

c. Describe the trends in the participation rates of men and women and all workers. Why did these trends occur?

The labour force participation rate of women has an upward trend and the labour force participation rate of men has a downward trend. Overall, the labour force participation rate of all workers has an upward trend. There are several reasons why women have entered the labour force. First, more women attend college and increase their earning power. Technological change has decreased the time necessary to work in the home and has increased the number of white-collar jobs with flexible hours. Also, more families want both spouses to work to earn more income. Men have withdrawn from the labour force because more men remain in full-time education longer and because increases in wealth allow more men to retire at earlier ages. Also, some men are forced into "early retirement" at an age at which finding a new job is difficult.

d. Describe the trends and fluctuations in part-time work. Why is part-time work on the increase?

As a percentage of all workers, the number of part-time workers increased gradually from 1976 to 2002 and fluctuated with the business cycle. Part-time jobs can be attractive to employers because they don't have to pay benefits to part-time workers and are less constrained by government regulations. Many people desire part-time work because it provides flexible hours.

Additional Practice Problem 7.2a

Describe the unemployment rate in Canada from 1996 to 2002.

Solution to Additional Practice Problem 7.2a

Between 1996 and 2000 the Canadian economy was in a strong expansion, led by rising exports to the United States. During this strong expansion, the unemployment rate fell rapidly to below its long-term average. In 2001, the U.S economy went into recession and the U.S. recovery in 2002 was very weak. The Canadian economy slowed and the unemployment rate began to rise.

■ Self Test 7.2

Fill in the blanks

The unemployment rate in 2002 was ____ (equal to; higher than; lower than) the average between 1962 and 2002. Between 1976 and 2002, the male labour force participation rate ____ (decreased; increased) and the female labour force participation rate ____ (decreased; increased). Between 1977 and 2002, the percentage of workers who had part-time jobs ____ (increased; decreased). The unemployment that arises from normal labour market turnover is called ____ (frictional; structural) unemployment and the unemployment that fluctuates over the business cycle is called ____ (cyclical; seasonal) unemployment. When ____ (frictional; structural; cyclical) unemployment equals zero, the economy is experiencing ____ (full; potential) employment.

True or false

1. The unemployment rate at full employment is the full employment rate.

2. The unemployment rate for young people (age 15-24) is three times as high as for people over 25.

3. Between 1976 and 2002, the female labour force participation rate increased but it remained less than the male labour force participation rate.

4. The percentage of all workers who are involuntary part-time workers rises during a recession.

5. The amount of frictional unemployment is influenced by unemployment compensation.

Multiple choice

1. Between 1962 and 2002, the average unemployment rate in Canada was

a. 3.3 percent.

b. 7.7 percent.

c. 11.9 percent.

d. 11.3 percent.

2. During the _____ of the late 1990s, unemployment in Canada _____ its long-term average.

a. expansion; fell to below

b. expansion; rose to above

c. recession; fell to below

d. recession; rose to above

3. Which of the following statements about the Canadian labour market is correct?

a. Between 1976 and 2002, both the male and female labour force participation rates increased.

b. Between 1976 and 2002, the male labour force participation rate decreased rapidly, the female labour force participation rate decreased slowly, and the two rates are now equal.

c. Between 1976 and 2002, the male labour force participation rate decreased and the female labour force participation rate increased.

d. Between 1976 and 2002, both the male and female labour force participation rates decreased slowly.

4. The total Canadian labour force participation rate increased between 1976 and 2002 because

a. the female labour force participation rate increased.

b. more men are retiring early.

c. fewer women are attending college.

d. many blue-collar jobs with rigid work hours have been created in the last decade.

5. The labour force participation rate of women increased between 1976 and 2002 because

a. technological change created a large number of white-collar jobs.

b. technological change in the home increased the time available for paid employment.

c. families looked increasingly to a second income to balance tight budgets.

d. All of the above.

6. _____ unemployment is the unemployment that arises because of seasonal weather patterns.

a. Winter

b. Seasonal

c. Cyclical

d. Periodic

7. In Canada, involuntary part-time workers

a. decreased as a percentage of all workers between 1977 and 2002.

b. decrease during a recession.

c. increase during an expansion.

d. decreased as a percentage of all workers during the 1990s expansion.

8. The more generous the unemployment compensation, the

a. greater the frictional unemployment.

b. smaller the frictional unemployment.

c. greater the cyclical unemployment.

d. smaller the cyclical unemployment.

9. Natural unemployment is

a. zero at full employment.

b. equal to cyclical unemployment.

c. the unemployment rate at full employment.

d. 7.7 percent a year.

Short answer

1. During a recession, what happens to:

a. the unemployment rate?

b. cyclical unemployment?

c. the number of involuntary part-time workers?

2. Discuss the Canadian unemployment rate in the

a. 1960s.

b. 1970s.

c. 1980s.

CHECKPOINT 7.3

■ **Describe the relationships among unemployment, real GDP, and inflation over the business cycle.**

Practice Problem 7.3

The table sets out real GDP and potential GDP in an economy from 1993 to 2003.

Year	Real GDP (billions of 1997 dollars)	Potential GDP (billions of 1997 dollars)
1993	1,200	1,000
1994	1,100	1,100
1995	1,000	1,200
1996	1,100	1,300
1997	1,200	1,400
1998	1,400	1,500
1999	1,600	1,600
2000	1,800	1,700
2001	2,000	1,800
2002	2,100	1,900
2003	2,000	2,000

a. In which years was the economy at full employment?

b. In which years was the output gap positive?

c. In which years was there a deflationary gap?

Solution to Practice Problem 7.3

This question focuses on the relationship between potential GDP and real GDP and the output gap.

Quick Review

*   *Output gap* Real GDP minus potential GDP expressed as a percentage of potential GDP.

*   *Deflationary gap* The output gap when potential GDP exceeds real GDP.

*   *Inflationary gap* The output gap when real GDP exceeds potential GDP.

a. In which years was the economy at full employment?

The economy is at full employment when real GDP equals potential GDP. Real GDP equals potential GDP in 1994, 1999, and 2003.

b. In which years was the output gap positive?

The output gap equals real GDP minus potential GDP expressed as a percentage of potential GDP. The output gap is positive in 1993, and 2000-2002.

c. In which years was there a deflationary gap?

A deflationary gap is the output gap when potential GDP exceeds real GDP. Potential GDP exceeds real GDP in 1995-1998.

Additional Practice Problem 7.3a

The table sets out real GDP and potential GDP in an economy from 1992 to 2002.

a. In which years was the economy at full employment?

b. In which years did the inflation rate increase?

c. In which years was there an inflationary gap?

Year	Real GDP (billions of 1997 dollars)	Potential GDP (billions of 1997 dollars)
1992	1,200	1,200
1993	1,100	1,300
1994	1,000	1,400
1995	1,100	1,500
1996	1,200	1,600
1997	1,400	1,700
1998	1,600	1,800
1999	1,800	1,900
2000	2,000	2,000
2001	2,100	2,100
2002	2,000	2,200

Solution to Additional Practice Problem 7.3a

a. The economy is at full employment when real GDP equals potential GDP. Real GDP equals potential GDP in 1992, 2000, and 2001.

b. The inflation rate increases when the output gap is positive. There are no years when the output gap is positive, so the inflation rate does not increase.

c. An inflationary gap exists when real GDP exceeds potential GDP. There are no years when real GDP exceeds potential GDP, so there is no inflationary gap.

■ Self Test 7.3

Fill in the blanks

The real GDP that the economy would produce at full employment is called _____ (output GDP; potential GDP). If potential GDP exceeds real GDP, the output gap is _____ (negative; positive) and is called _____ (a deflationary; an inflationary) gap. When the output gap is positive, the inflation rate _____ (slows; speeds up).

True or false

1. Statistics Canada measures real GDP and the unemployment rate monthly.

2. The output gap is calculated as a percentage of real GDP.

3. If real GDP exceeds potential GDP, the output gap is negative and is called a deflationary gap.

4. Canada has had more inflationary gaps than deflationary gaps during the past twenty years.

5. When the output gap is negative, the inflation rate slows.

Multiple choice

1. Real GDP

a. provides a good guide to where the economy was three to six months ago

b. measures the current state of the economy

c. is revised monthly

d. fluctuates around the natural unemployment rate

2. The output gap equals

a. (Real GDP + Potential GDP) × 100/Potential GDP.

b. (Real GDP – Potential GDP) × 100/Real GDP.

c. (Real GDP + Potential GDP) × 100/Real GDP.

d. (Real GDP – Potential GDP) × 100/Potential GDP.

3. If real GDP exceeds potential GDP, the output gap is _____ and is called _____ gap.

a. positive; an inflationary

b. negative; a deflationary

c. positive; a deflationary

d. negative; an inflationary

4. A deflationary gap occurs when

a. the output gap is positive

b. the output gap is negative

c. real GDP exceeds potential GDP

d. real GDP equals potential GDP

5. When the output gap is positive,

a. seasonal unemployment is positive.

b. frictional unemployment is positive.

c. seasonal unemployment is negative.

d. cyclical unemployment is negative.

6. During the past twenty years, Canada has had

a. more inflationary gaps than deflationary gaps.

b. more deflationary gaps than inflationary gaps.

c. more output gaps than inflationary gaps.

d. an equal number of deflationary gaps and inflationary gaps.

7. When the output gap is _____, the inflation rate _____.

a. negative; speeds up

b. negative; slows

c. zero; speeds up

d. positive; slows

8. Statistics Canada measures real GDP every _____ and the unemployment rate is measured every _____.

a. quarter; month

b. month; quarter

c. month; year

d. year; month

Short answer

1. The table sets out real GDP and potential GDP in an economy from 1990 to 2000.

a. In which years was the economy at full employment?

b. In which years was the output gap positive?

c.   In which years was there a deflationary gap?

d. In which years did the inflation rate increase?

e. In which years was there an inflationary gap?

f.   In which years did the inflation rate slow?

Year	Real GDP (billions of 1997 dollars)	Potential GDP (billions of 1997 dollars)
1990	1,200	900
1991	1,100	1,000
1992	1,000	1,100
1993	1,100	1,200
1994	1,200	1,300
1995	1,400	1,400
1996	1,600	1,500
1997	1,800	1,600
1998	2,000	1,700
1999	2,100	1,800
2000	2,000	1,900

SELF TEST ANSWERS

■ CHECKPOINT 7.1

Fill in the blanks

The <u>working-age population</u> is the total number of people aged 15 years and over. The unemployment rate equals the <u>number of people unemployed</u> divided by the <u>labour force</u>, all multiplied by 100. The labour force participation rate equals the <u>labour force</u> divided by the <u>working-age population</u>, all multiplied by 100. Involuntary part-time workers <u>are</u> counted as employed. The total number of hours worked in a year by all the employed people are <u>aggregate hours</u>.

True or false

1. True; page 162
2. False; page 162
3. True; page 163
4. False; page 164
5. False; page 164

Multiple choice

1. c; page 162
2. c; page 162
3. c; page 162
4. b; page 163
5. d; page 164
6. c; page 164
7. a; page 164
8. d; page 165

Short answer

1. a.   14.9 million; page 162
    b.   1.4 million; page 162
    c.   9.4 percent; page 163
    d.   64.8 percent; page 164

2. a.   15.7 million; page 162
    b.   7.6 percent; page 163
    c.   65.4 percent; page 164

3. The person must be without employment, available for work, and on temporary layoff with an expectation of recall or actively looking for work during the past four weeks or had a new job to start within four weeks; page 162.

4. A discouraged worker is a person who does not have a job, is available and willing to work, but has not made specific efforts to find a job within the previous four weeks. A discouraged worker is not part of the labour force. He is not unemployed because he is not actively seeking work; page 164.

5. Employed; page 164.

■ CHECKPOINT 7.2

Fill in the blanks

The unemployment rate in 2002 was <u>equal to</u> the average between 1962 and 2002. Between 1976 and 2002, the male labour force participation rate <u>decreased</u> and the female labour force participation rate <u>increased</u>. Between 1977 and 2002, the percentage of workers who had part-time jobs <u>increased</u>. The unemployment that arises from normal labour market turnover is called <u>frictional</u> unemployment and the unemployment that fluctuates over the business cycle is called <u>cyclical</u> unemployment. When <u>cyclical</u> unemployment equals zero, the economy is experiencing <u>full</u> employment.

True or false

1. False; page 170
2. False; page 171
3. True; page 172
4. True; page 173
5. True; page 169

Multiple choice

1. b; page 167
2. a; page 167
3. c; page 172
4. a; page 172
5. a; page 172
6. b; page 169
7. d; page 173
8. b; page 169
9. c; page 170

Short answer

1. a. The unemployment rate rises; page 167.

   b. Cyclical unemployment increases; page 169.

   c. The number of involuntary part-time workers increases; page 173.

2. a. Unemployment rates in the 1960s were low, and dipped to 3.3 percent in 1966; page 167.

   b. During the 1970s, the unemployment rate rose persistently, mainly because a large number of baby boomers entered the labour force; page 167.

   c. The 1982 recession pushed the unemployment rate up to 11.9 percent in 1983, the highest since the 1930s. By the end of the 1980s, a period of expansion brought the unemployment rate down to below the long-term average by 1989; page 167.

■ **CHECKPOINT 7.3**

Fill in the blanks

The real GDP that the economy would produce at full employment is called potential GDP. If potential GDP exceeds real GDP, the output gap is negative and is called a deflationary gap. When the output gap is positive, the inflation rate speeds up.

True or false

1. False; page 175
2. False; page 175
3. False; page 175
4. False; page 176
5. True; page 177

Multiple choice

1. a; page 175
2. d; page 175
3. a; page 175
4. b; page 175
5. d; page 177
6. b; page 176
7. b; page 177
8. a; page 175

Short answer

1a. the economy was at full employment in 1995; page 175.

b. The output gap was positive in 1990, 1991, 1996, 1997, 1998, 1999, and 2000; page 175.

c. There was a deflationary gap in 1992, 1993, and 1994; page 175.

d. The inflation rate increased in 1990, 1991, 1996, 1997, 1998, 1999, and 2000; page 177.

e. There was an inflationary gap in 1990, 1991, 1996, 1997, 1998, 1999, and 2000; page 175.

f. The inflation rate slowed in 1992, 1993, and 1994; page 177.

Aggregate Supply and Aggregate Demand

Chapter 8

Chapter 8 uses the aggregate supply-aggregate demand model to study the business cycle.

■ **Explain the influences on aggregate supply.**

Along the aggregate supply (*AS*) curve, the only influence on production plans that changes is the price level. All other influences on production plans, which include the money wage rate and potential GDP, remain constant. Potential GDP is the level of real GDP that the economy would produce if it were at full employment. Potential GDP depends only on the economy's resources and not on the price level. Aggregate supply changes when potential GDP changes or the money wage rate changes. Anything that changes potential GDP changes aggregate supply and shifts the aggregate supply curve.

■ **Explain the influences on aggregate demand.**

The quantity of real GDP demanded is the total amount of final goods and services produced in Canada that people, businesses, governments, and foreigners plan to buy. A change in the price level changes the quantity of real GDP demanded and brings a movement along the aggregate demand curve. A change in the price level brings changes in the buying power of money, the real interest rate, and the real prices of exports and imports, which influence the quantity of real GDP demanded. The factors that change aggregate demand are expectations about the future, fiscal policy and monetary policy, and the state of the world economy. The aggregate demand multiplier is an effect that magnifies changes in expenditure plans and brings potentially large fluctuations in aggregate demand.

■ **Explain how aggregate supply and aggregate demand determine real GDP and the price level.**

Macroeconomic equilibrium occurs when the quantity of real GDP demanded equals the quantity of real GDP supplied at the point of intersection of the *AD* curve and the *AS* curve. The macroeconomic equilibrium can be a full-employment equilibrium, an above full-employment equilibrium, or a below full-employment equilibrium.

■ **Explain how changes in aggregate supply and aggregate demand bring economic growth, inflation, and the business cycle.**

Economic growth occurs because potential GDP increases. Inflation occurs because aggregate demand increases on the average at a faster pace than aggregate supply. Fluctuations in real GDP and the price level can result from changes in either aggregate demand or aggregate supply. When the economy is away from full employment, gradual adjustment of the money wage rate moves real GDP towards potential GDP.

EXPANDED CHAPTER CHECKLIST

When you have completed this chapter, you will be able to

1 **Explain the influences on aggregate supply.**

- Define aggregate supply.

- Draw an *AS* curve and list the influences on production plans that change and that remain constant along the *AS* curve.

- Explain why an increase in the price level increases the quantity of real GDP supplied.

- Discuss the factors that change aggregate supply and shift the *AS* curve.

2 **Explain the influences on aggregate demand.**

- Define aggregate demand.

- Discuss the influence of the price level on expenditure plans.

- Draw an *AD* curve and discuss the factors that change aggregate demand and shift the *AD* curve.

- Describe the aggregate demand multiplier.

3 **Explain how aggregate supply and aggregate demand determine real GDP and the price level.**

- Explain and illustrate macroeconomic equilibrium.

- Illustrate the three types of macroeconomic equilibrium: full-employment equilibrium, above full-employment equilibrium, and below full-employment equilibrium.

4 **Explain how changes in aggregate supply and aggregate demand bring economic growth, inflation, and the business cycle.**

- Describe and illustrate how fluctuations in aggregate supply change real GDP and the price level.

- Describe and illustrate how fluctuations in aggregate demand change real GDP and the price level.

- Describe how changes in the money wage rate gradually move real GDP toward potential GDP.

KEY TERMS

- Above full-employment equilibrium (page 197)

- Aggregate demand (page 190)

- Aggregate supply (page 184)

- Below full-employment equilibrium (page 197)

- Full-employment equilibrium (page 197)

- Macroeconomic equilibrium (page 196)

- Recession (page 198)

- Stagflation (page 199)

CHECKPOINT 8.1

■ **Explain the influences on aggregate supply.**
Practice Problem 8.1

In May 2000, armed men took over the Parliament in Fiji and held the Prime Minister and other people as hostages. This action led to many other events. Explain the effect of each of the following events on Fiji's aggregate supply:

a. Downtown Suva (the capital of Fiji) was heavily looted, and businesses were destroyed.

b. Dock workers in Australia refused to handle cargo to and from Fiji, including raw material going to Fiji's garment industry and clothing going to Australia.

c. The number of tourists fell and many hotels closed.

d. As unemployment increased, the workweek was shortened.

e. The fresh tuna industry boomed with increased sales to Japan and the United States.

f. With widespread shortages, suppose that the unionized workers demanded higher wages and got them.

Solution to Practice Problem 8.1

To answer this Practice Problem, remember that aggregate supply changes when any influence on production plans other than the price level changes.

Quick Review

*   *Factors that change aggregate supply* Aggregate supply changes when potential GDP changes OR the money wage rate changes.

a. **Downtown Suva (the capital of Fiji) was heavily looted, and businesses were destroyed.**

As businesses were destroyed, real GDP supplied at the current price level decreased. Aggregate supply decreased. In the figure, the *AS* curve shifts leftward from AS_0 to AS_1.

b. **Dock workers in Australia refused to handle cargo to and from Fiji, including raw material going to Fiji's garment industry and clothing going to Australia.**

The actions of the Australian dock workers decreased the resources available to Fiji's garment industry. Production in the garment industry decreased. The quantity of real GDP supplied at the current price level decreased. Aggregate supply decreased. In the figure, the *AS* curve shifts leftward from AS_0 to AS_1.

c. **The number of tourists fell and many hotels closed.**

As hotels close, the quantity of tourist services supplied decreased. The quantity of real GDP supplied at the current price level decreased. Aggregate supply decreased. In the figure, the *AS* curve shifts leftward from AS_0 to AS_1.

d. **As unemployment increased, the workweek was shortened.**

As the workweek was shortened, production decreased and the quantity of real GDP supplied at the current price level decreased. Aggregate supply decreased. In the figure, the *AS* curve shifts leftward from AS_0 to AS_1.

e. **The fresh tuna industry boomed with increased sales to Japan and the United States.**

As the tuna industry expanded, production increased. The expansion of the tuna industry considered apart from the other events increases aggregate supply. In the figure, the *AS* curve shifts rightward from AS_0 to AS_2.

f. **With widespread shortages, suppose that the unionized workers demanded higher wages and got them.**

As the money wage rate rises, for a given price level, the real wage rate rises. Some firms decreased production and others closed. The quantity of real GDP supplied at the current price level decreased. Aggregate supply decreased. In the figure, the *AS* curve shifts leftward from AS_0 to AS_1.

Additional Practice Problem 8.1a

Describe the effect of advances in computer software during the last decade on aggregate supply and the *AS* curve.

Solution to Additional Practice Problem 8.1a

Advances in computer software mean that the same quantity of output can be produced by fewer workers. Some workers who were formerly employed as typists or data entry clerks can now produce other goods and services. Aggregate supply increases and the *AS* curve shifts rightward.

■ Self Test 8.1

Fill in the blanks

Along the *AS* curve, as the price level rises, the quantity of real GDP supplied _____ (decreases; does not change; increases) because the real wage rate _____ (falls; rises). Potential GDP _____ (depends; does not depend) on the price level. When potential GDP increases, a _____ (movement along; shift of) the *AS* curve occurs. When the money wage rate changes, a _____ (movement along; shift of) the *AS* curve occurs.

True or false

1. Along the aggregate supply curve, a rise in the price level decreases the quantity of real GDP supplied.

2. A rise in the price level decreases potential GDP.

3. Anything that changes potential GDP shifts the aggregate supply curve.

4. An increase in the money wage rate shifts the aggregate supply curve leftward.

5. Aggregate supply is the relationship between the quantity of real GDP supplied and potential GDP when the price level remains constant.

Multiple choice

1. The potential GDP line is

a. upward sloping.

b. horizontal.

c. vertical.

d. downward sloping.

2. The aggregate supply curve is

a. upward sloping.

b. downward sloping.

c. a vertical line.

d. a horizontal line.

3. When the price level falls,

a. the *AS* curve shifts rightward.

b. there is a movement up along the *AS* curve.

c. the *AS* curve shifts leftward.

d. there is a movement down along the *AS* curve.

4. As the price level rises relative to costs and the real wage rate falls, profits _____ and the number of firms in business _____.

a. increase; increases

b. increase; decreases

c. decrease; increases

d. decrease; decreases

5. When potential GDP increases,

a. the *AS* curve shifts rightward.

b. there is a movement up along the *AS* curve.

c. the *AS* curve shifts leftward.

d. there is a movement down along the *AS* curve.

6. If the money wage rate rises

a. the *AS* curve shifts rightward.

b. there is a movement up along the *AS* curve.

c. the *AS* curve shifts leftward.

d. there is a movement down along the *AS* curve.

Complete the graph

1. The table gives the aggregate supply schedule and potential GDP schedule for a nation.

Price level (GDP deflator, 1997 = 100)	Quantity of real GDP supplied (billions of 1997 dollars)	Potential GDP (billions of 1997 dollars)
120	1,000	900
115	950	900
110	900	900
105	850	900
100	800	900

a. Label the axes and then plot the *AS* curve and potential GDP line in Figure 8.1.

b. Suppose the money wage rate falls. Show the effect of this change on aggregate supply and potential GDP in Figure 8.1.

■ **FIGURE 8.1**

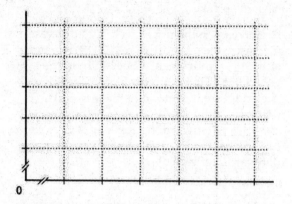

Short answer

1. Why does the *AS* curve slope upward?

2. Why does the aggregate supply curve shift when the money wage rate rises? Why doesn't the potential GDP line also shift?

3. Explain the change in the intersection of the *AS* curve and the potential GDP line if the money wage rate rises by 10 percent.

CHECKPOINT 8.2

■ **Explain the influences on aggregate demand.**

Practice Problem 8.2

Mexico has signed free trade agreements with many countries, including the United States, Canada, and the European Union. Explain the effect of each of the following events on Mexico's aggregate demand in the short run:

a. The price level in Mexico rises.

b. Mexico's real interest rate rises in the short run.

c. The United States and Canada experience strong economic growth.

d. The European Union goes into a recession.

e. The Mexican government sets new environmental standards that require factories to upgrade their production facilities.

f. Mexico adopts an expansionary monetary policy and increases the quantity of money.

Solution to Practice Problem 8.2

To answer this Practice Problem, remember that a change in any factor that influences expenditure plans other than the price level brings a change in aggregate demand.

Quick Review

• *Factors that change aggregate demand* Aggregate demand changes if expected future income, expected future inflation, or expected future profit change; fiscal policy or monetary policy changes; or the state of the world economy changes.

a. **The price level in Mexico rises.**

A rise in Mexico's price level means that Mexican exports become relatively more expensive. Mexico's trading partners want to buy fewer goods from Mexico. The quantity demanded of Mexican real GDP decreases. The figure shows that as the price rises, there is a movement up along the *AD* curve.

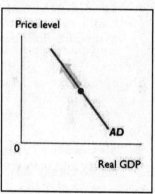

b. **Mexico's real interest rate rises in the short run.**

When the price level rises, the real interest rate rises and businesses and people delay plans to buy new capital and consumer durable goods. Spending decreases and the quantity of Mexican real GDP demanded decreases. The figure above shows that as the quantity of real GDP demanded decreases, there is a movement up along the *AD* curve.

c.   **The United States and Canada experience strong economic growth.**

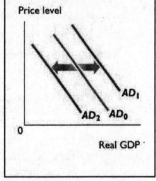

Strong economic growth in the United States and Canada increases demand for Mexican exports. Aggregate demand in Mexico increases. In the figure, the AD curve shifts rightward from AD_0 to AD_1.

d.   **The European Union goes into a recession.**

If the European Union goes into a recession, the demand for Mexican exports decreases. Aggregate demand in Mexico decreases. In the above figure, the AD curve shifts leftward from AD_0 to AD_2.

e.   **The Mexican government sets new environmental standards that require factories to upgrade their production facilities.**

As factories purchase the equipment to upgrade their production facilities, investment increases. Aggregate demand in Mexico increases. In the figure, the AD curve shifts rightward from AD_0 to AD_1.

f.   **Mexico adopts an expansionary monetary policy and increases the quantity of money.**

If Mexico increases the quantity of money, aggregate demand increases. In the figure, the AD curve shifts rightward from AD_0 to AD_1.

Additional Practice Problem 8.2a

If people think a tax cut is unlikely to occur, what is the effect on aggregate demand? If many people believe that the tax cut will occur, what is the effect on aggregate demand?

Solution to Additional Practice Problem 8.2a

If people think a large tax cut is unlikely to occur, there is no change in expected future income. Aggregate demand does not change. If many people believe that the tax cut will occur, there is

an increase in expected future income. Aggregate demand increases.

■ Self Test 8.2

Fill in the blanks

An increase in the price level _____ (decreases; increases) the quantity of real GDP demanded and a _____ (movement along; shift of) the aggregate demand curve occurs. An increase in expected future income shifts the AD curve _____ (leftward; rightward). A tax cut shifts the AD curve _____ (leftward; rightward). A decrease in real foreign income shifts the AD curve _____ (leftward; rightward).

True or false

1.   As the price level falls, other things remaining the same, the quantity of real GDP demanded increases.

2.   An increase in expected future income will not increase aggregate demand until the income actually increases.

3.   A decrease in government expenditure shifts the aggregate demand curve rightward.

4.   An increase in income in Mexico decreases aggregate demand in Canada because Mexicans will buy more Mexican-produced goods.

5.   Aggregate demand is the relationship between the quantity of real GDP demanded and the price level when all other influences on expenditure plans remain the same.

Multiple choice

1.   When the price level rises there is a _____ the aggregate demand curve.

a.   rightward shift of

b.   movement down along

c.   leftward shift of

d.   movement up along

2. A rise in the price level

a. raises the buying power of money.

b. decreases the real prices of exports.

c. lowers the buying power of money.

d. increases aggregate demand.

3. When the price level rises, the real interest rate ____ and the quantity of real GDP demanded ____.

a. rises; increases

b. rises; decreases

c. falls; increases

d. falls; decreases

4. A change in any of the following factors except ____ shifts the aggregate demand curve.

a. expectations about the future

b. the money wage rate

c. monetary and fiscal policy

d. the state of the world economy

5. Which of the following produce a leftward shift in the aggregate demand curve?

a. a decrease in expected future profit

b. an increase in the price level

c. a tax cut

d. an increase in real foreign income

6. When investment increases, the increase in aggregate demand is ____ the change in investment.

a. greater than

b. smaller than

c. the same as

d. unrelated to

Complete the graph

1. Figure 8.2 shows an aggregate demand curve.

a. In Figure 8.2, illustrate the effect of an increase in government expenditure.

b. In Figure 8.2, illustrate the effect of a decrease in the quantity of money.

■ **FIGURE 8.2**

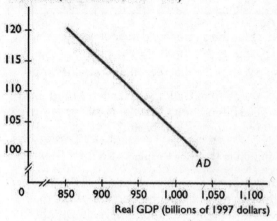

Price level (GDP deflator, 1997 = 100)

Short answer

1. Why does an increase in the price level decrease the quantity of real GDP demanded?

2. Expected future profit increases. What is the effect on aggregate demand?

3. The government cuts taxes. What is the effect on aggregate demand?

4. What is the aggregate demand multiplier?

CHECKPOINT 8.3

■ Explain how aggregate supply and aggregate demand determine real GDP and the price level.

Practice Problem 8.3

1. The table shows aggregate demand and aggregate supply schedules for the United Kingdom.

Price level (GDP deflator)	Real GDP demanded (billions of 1995 pounds)	Real GDP supplied (billions of 1995 pounds)
90	800	650
100	775	700
110	750	750
120	725	800
130	700	850

a. Plot the aggregate demand curve and the aggregate supply curve.

b. What is the macroeconomic equilibrium?

c. If potential GDP in the United Kingdom is 800 billion pounds, what is the type of macroeconomic equilibrium?

Solution to Practice Problems 8.3

Remember that macroeconomic equilibrium occurs where the aggregate demand curve intersects the aggregate supply curve. If equilibrium real GDP equals potential GDP, there is a full-employment equilibrium. If equilibrium real GDP exceeds potential GDP, there is an above full-employment equilibrium. And if equilibrium real GDP is less than potential GDP, there is a below full-employment equilibrium.

Quick Review

• *Macroeconomic equilibrium* When the quantity of real GDP demanded equals the quantity of real GDP supplied at the point of intersection of the *AD* curve and the *AS* curve.

a. **Plot the aggregate demand curve and the aggregate supply curve.**

The aggregate demand curve is the downward-sloping curve in the figure. Note that as the price level falls, the quantity of real GDP demanded increases. The aggregate supply curve is the upward-sloping curve in the

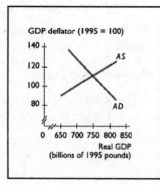

figure. Note that as the price level rises, the quantity of real GDP supplied increases.

b. **What is the macroeconomic equilibrium?**

The macroeconomic equilibrium is at a price level of 110 and real GDP of 750 billion pounds. The figure shows the macroeconomic equilibrium where the aggregate supply (*AS*) curve intersects the aggregate demand (*AD*) curve.

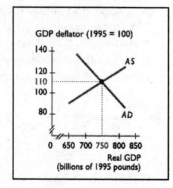

c. **If potential GDP in the United Kingdom is 800 billion pounds, what is the type of macroeconomic equilibrium?**

A below full-employment equilibrium occurs when potential GDP exceeds equilibrium real GDP. In the figure, potential GDP is 800 billion pounds and the

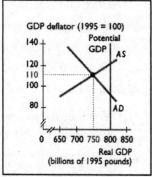

macroeconomic equilibrium is 750 billion pounds. The economy is in a below-full employment equilibrium. Equilibrium real GDP is less than potential GDP.

Additional Practice Problem 8.3a

Can real GDP ever exceed potential GDP?

Solution to Additional Practice Problem 8.3a

Yes, real GDP can exceed potential GDP. Equilibrium real GDP is determined at the intersection of the *AD* curve and the *AS* curve. Equilibrium real GDP is greater than potential GDP when these two curves intersect at a GDP that exceeds potential GDP. In this case, there is an above full-employment equilibrium.

■ Self Test 8.3

Fill in the blanks

Macroeconomic equilibrium occurs at the point of intersection of the *AD* curve and the _____ (*AS* curve; potential GDP line). When equilibrium real GDP exceeds potential GDP, there is _____ (an above; a below) full-employment equilibrium.

True or false

1. Macroeconomic equilibrium occurs at the point where aggregate demand equals potential GDP.

2. If the price level exceeds the equilibrium price level, firms are unable to sell all their output.

3. The only possible equilibrium is a full-employment equilibrium.

4. When real GDP exceeds potential GDP, there is a below full-employment equilibrium.

Multiple choice

1. Macroeconomic equilibrium occurs at the intersection of the _____ and the _____.

a. *AD* curve; potential GDP line

b. *AS* curve; potential GDP line

c. *AD* curve; *AS* curve

d. potential GDP line; potential price level line

2. If the price level is less than the equilibrium price level

a. inventories decrease.

b. inventories increase.

c. firms are unable to sell all their output.

d. potential GDP changes to restore the equilibrium price level.

3. If the quantity of real GDP supplied equals the quantity of real GDP demanded, then equilibrium real GDP

a. equals zero.

b. must equal potential GDP.

c. must be below potential GDP.

d. might be below, equal to, or above potential GDP.

4. If equilibrium real GDP is less than potential GDP, the economy is in _____ full-employment equilibrium; if equilibrium real GDP is greater than potential GDP, the economy is in _____ full-employment equilibrium.

a. an above; an above

b. an above; a below

c. a below; an above

d. a below; a below

Complete the graph

■ FIGURE 8.3

Price level (GDP deflator, 1997 = 100)

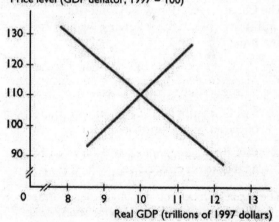

Real GDP (trillions of 1997 dollars)

1. In Figure 8.3, label the curves. What is the equilibrium price level and real GDP?

Short answer

1. The table gives the aggregate demand and aggregate supply schedules. What is the equilibrium price level and real GDP?

Price level (GDP deflator)	Quantity of real GDP demanded (trillions of 1997 dollars)	Quantity of real GDP supplied (trillions of 1997 dollars)
110	14	11
120	13	13
130	12	15
140	11	17

1. What is below full-employment equilibrium?
2. What is above full-employment equilibrium?

CHECKPOINT 8.4

■ Explain how changes in aggregate supply and aggregate demand bring economic growth, inflation, and the business cycle.

Practice Problem 8.4

The Canadian economy is in long-run equilibrium. Then the following events occur one at a time:

- A deep recession hits the world economy.
- Productivity growth slows.
- Canadian businesses expect future profits to fall.

a. Explain the effect of each event on aggregate demand and aggregate supply in Canada.

b. Explain the effect of each event separately on Canadian real GDP and price level.

c. Explain the combined effect of all the events together on Canadian real GDP and price level.

d. Which event, if any, brings stagflation?

Solution to Practice Problem 8.4

We use the *AS-AD* model to study the economic fluctuations that occur in a business cycle. This Practice Problem studies the effects of changes in aggregate demand and aggregate supply on the price level and real GDP.

Quick Review

- *Effect of decrease in aggregate demand* A decrease in aggregate demand, everything else remaining the same, lowers the price level and decreases real GDP.

- *Effect of decrease in aggregate supply* A decrease in aggregate supply, everything else remaining the same, raises the price level and decreases real GDP.

The Canadian economy is in long-run equilibrium. Then the following events occur one at a time:

- **A deep recession hits the world economy.**

- **Productivity growth slows.**

- **Canadian businesses expect future profits to fall.**

a. **Explain the effect of each event on aggregate demand and aggregate supply in Canada.**

When a recession in the world economy occurs, income in the rest of the world declines. People in the rest of the world decrease their demand for Canadian-produced goods. Canadian aggregate demand decreases. Canadian aggregate supply does not change.

A productivity growth slowdown decreases Canadian aggregate supply Aggregate demand does not change .

A decrease in expected future profits decreases investment. Aggregate demand decreases. Aggregate supply does not change.

b. **Explain the effect of each event separately on Canadian real GDP and price level.**

The world recession decreases aggregate demand. In the figure, the *AD* curve shifts leftward from AD_0 to AD_1. The price level falls from 110 to 105, and real GDP decreases from $1,000 billion to $900 billion.

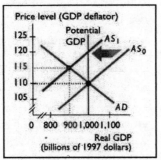

The productivity growth slowdown decreases aggregate supply. In the figure, the *AS* curve shifts leftward from AS_0 to AS_1. The price level rises from 110 to 115 and real GDP decreases from $1,000 billion to $900 billion.

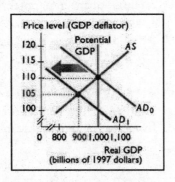

A decrease in expected future profits decreases the investment that firms plan to undertake. Aggregate demand decreases. In the figure, the aggregate demand curve shifts leftward from AD_0 to AD_1. The price level falls from 110 to 105, and real GDP decreases from $1,000 billion to $900 billion

c. **Explain the combined effect of all the events together on Canadian real GDP and price level.**

All three events decrease real GDP. The effect on the price level is ambiguous. If the productivity growth slowdown dominates, the price level rises, but if the other two effects dominate, the price level falls.

d. **Which event, if any, brings stagflation?**

Stagflation is the combination of recession and inflation. The productivity growth slowdown decreases GDP and raises the price level, so it brings stagflation.

Additional Practice Problem 8.4a

In the late 1990s, the French government passed a law decreasing the workweek. At the same time, the government also passed laws limiting the import of some genetically engineered foods. Explain the effect of each event separately on the equilibrium price and real GDP. Explain the combined effect of the events on real GDP and the price level.

Solution to Additional Practice Problem 8.4a

The decrease in the workweek decreases aggregate supply. The *AS* curve shifts leftward. The equilibrium price level rises and equilibrium real GDP decreases.

When food imports are limited, the French people buy more French-produced food. Aggregate demand increases and the *AD* curve shifts rightward. The equilibrium price level rises and equilibrium real GDP increases.

When the effects are combined, the price level rises because separately each event raises the price level. It is not possible to predict the total effect on real GDP because the first event decreases real GDP and the second event increases real GDP.

■ **Self Test 8.4**

Fill in the blanks

An increase in aggregate demand _____ (decreases; increases) real GDP. An increase in aggregate supply _____ (lowers; raises) the price level. Stagflation is a combination of _____ (expansion; recession) and a _____ (falling; rising) price level. When real GDP exceeds potential GDP, _____ (a deflationary; an inflationary) gap exists. When potential GDP exceeds real GDP, _____ (a deflationary; an inflationary) gap exists.

True or false

1. Starting from full employment, an increase in aggregate demand increases real GDP above potential GDP.

2. Starting from full employment, a decrease in aggregate demand shifts the aggregate demand curve leftward and creates an inflationary gap.

3. Starting from full employment, an increase in aggregate demand shifts the aggregate demand curve rightward and creates an inflationary gap.

4. A deflationary gap brings a rising price level to eliminate the gap.

5. A recession occurs whenever real GDP decreases.

Multiple choice

1. Which of the following statements is correct?

a. Changes in the price level shift the aggregate demand curve.

b. Aggregate supply cannot fluctuate.

c. The level of real GDP does not fluctuate.

d. Changes in aggregate demand and aggregate supply generate the business cycle.

2. An increase in investment _____ aggregate demand and shifts the aggregate demand _____. The economy is in _____.

a. decreases; rightward; an expansion

b. increases; rightward; an expansion

c. decreases; leftward; a recession

d. increases; rightward; a recession

3. If the wage rate rises, the

a. AD curve shifts rightward.

b. AS curve shifts leftward, the price level rises and real GDP decreases.

c. AD curve and the AS curve shift leftward, real GDP decreases and the price level rises.

d. AD curve and the AS curve shift rightward, the price level rises and real GDP decreases.

4. Stagflation is a combination of _____ real GDP and a _____ price level.

a. increasing; rising

b. increasing; falling

c. decreasing; rising

d. decreasing; falling

5. An inflationary gap is created when real GDP is _____ potential GDP.

a. greater than

b. equal to

c. less than

d. greater than, equal to, or less than

6. An economy is at full employment. If aggregate demand increases, _____ is created and _____.

a. an inflationary gap; the AS curve shifts leftward as the money wage rate rises

b. an inflationary gap; the AD curve shifts leftward

c. an inflationary gap; potential GDP increases to close the gap

d. a deflationary gap; the AS curve shifts leftward as the money wage rate falls

Complete the graph

1. Figure 8.4 shows an economy. Now suppose firms expect an increase in future profits.

■ FIGURE 8.4

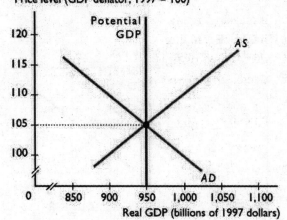

Price level (GDP deflator, 1997 = 100)

Real GDP (billions of 1997 dollars)

a. In Figure 8.4, show the effect an increase in expected future profits on the price level and real GDP.

b. In Figure 8.4, show how the economy returns to potential GDP.

2. Figure 8.5 shows an economy. Show the effect of a slowdown in productivity on the price level and real GDP. How does the economy return to full employment?

■ FIGURE 8.5

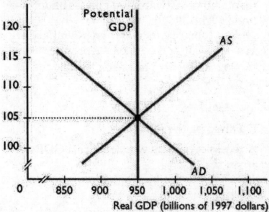

Price level (GDP deflator, 1997 = 100)

Real GDP (billions of 1997 dollars)

Short answer

1. What is stagflation? What creates stagflation?

2. Define inflationary gap and explain how it is eliminated.

3. How is the business cycle created?

SELF TEST ANSWERS

■ CHECKPOINT 8.1

Fill in the blanks

Along the *AS* curve, as the price level rises, the quantity of real GDP supplied <u>increases</u> because the real wage rate <u>falls</u>. Potential GDP <u>does not depend</u> on the price level. When potential GDP increases, a <u>shift of</u> the *AS* curve occurs. When the money wage rate changes, a <u>shift of</u> the *AS* curve occurs.

True or false

1. False; page 184
2. False; page 184
3. True; page 187
4. True; page 188
5. False; page 184

Multiple choice

1. c; page 184
2. a; page 185
3. d; page 184
4. a; page 186
5. a; page 187
6. c; page 188

Complete the graph

1. a. Figure 8.6 labels the axes. The aggregate supply curve is labelled *AS₀*; page 184.

   b. A fall in the money wage rate does not change potential GDP. The potential GDP line does not shift. When the money wage rate falls, aggregate supply increases. In Figure 8.6, the *AS* curve shifts rightward from *AS₀* to *AS₁*; page 188.

■ FIGURE 8.6

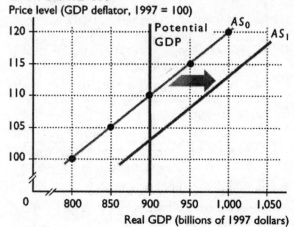

Price level (GDP deflator, 1997 = 100)

Short answer

1. The movement along the *AS* curve brings a change in the real wage rate. If the price level rises, the real wage rate falls.

   A fall in the real wage rate boosts a firm's profit. The number of firms in business increases.

   If the price level rises relative to costs, fewer firms will decide to shut down temporarily; so more firms operate.

   If the price level rises and the money wage rate doesn't change, an extra hour of labour that was previously unprofitable becomes profitable. So, the quantity of labour demanded increases and production increases.

   For the economy as a whole, as the price level rises, the quantity of real GDP supplied increases; pages 185-186.

2. An increase in the money wage rate increases firms' costs. The higher are firms' costs, the smaller is the quantity that firms are willing to supply at each price level. Aggregate supply decreases and the *AS* curve shifts leftward. A change in the money wage rate does not change potential GDP. Potential GDP depends only on the economy's real ability

to produce and on the full employment quantity of labour, which occurs at the equilibrium real wage rate. The equilibrium real wage rate can occur at any money wage rate; page 188.

3. Suppose that the economy is at full employment, the money wage rate is $20 an hour, and the price level is 100. Then the real wage rate is $20 an hour. If the money wage rate rises to $22 an hour, an increase of 10 percent but the full-employment equilibrium real wage rate remains at $20, real GDP now equals potential GDP when the price level is 110; page 188.

■ CHECKPOINT 8.2

Fill in the blanks

An increase in the price level <u>decreases</u> the quantity of real GDP demanded and a <u>movement along</u> the aggregate demand curve occurs. An increase in expected future income shifts the *AD* curve <u>rightward</u>. A tax cut shifts the *AD* curve <u>rightward</u>. A decrease in real foreign income shifts the *AD* curve <u>leftward</u>.

True or false

1. True; page 190

2. False; page 192

3. False; page 193

4. False; pages 193-194

5. True; page 190

Multiple choice

1. d; page 190

2. c; page 190

3. b; page 191

4. b; page 192

5. a; page 192

6. a; page 194

Complete the graph

1a. In Figure 8.7, an increase in government expenditure increases aggregate demand and shifts the *AD* curve rightward from AD_0 to AD_1; page 193.

b. In Figure 8.7, a decrease in the quantity of money decreases aggregate demand and shifts the *AD* curve leftward from AD_0 to AD_2; page 193.

■ FIGURE 8.7

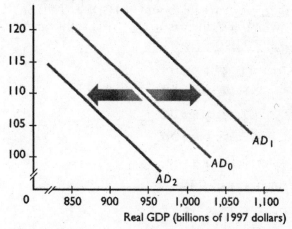

Price level (GDP deflator, 1997 = 100)

Short answer

1. An increase in the price level decreases the quantity of real GDP demanded because an increase in the price level lowers the buying power of money, raises the real interest rate, raises the real prices of exports, and lowers the real prices of imports; pages 190-192.

2. An increase in expected future profit increases the investment that firms plan to undertake now and increases aggregate demand; page 192.

3. The government can influence aggregate demand by changing taxes. When the government cuts taxes, aggregate demand increases; page 193.

4. The aggregate demand multiplier is an effect that magnifies changes in expenditure plans and brings potentially large fluctuations in aggregate demand. For example, an increase

in investment increases aggregate demand and increases income. The increase in income induces an increase in consumption expenditure so aggregate demand increases by more than the initial increase in investment; page 194.

■ CHECKPOINT 8.3

Fill in the blanks

Macroeconomic equilibrium occurs at the point of intersection of the *AD* curve and the <u>*AS* curve</u>. When equilibrium real GDP exceeds potential GDP, there is <u>an above</u> full-employment equilibrium.

True or false

1. False; page 196
2. True; page 196
3. False; page 197
4. False; page 197

Multiple choice

1. c; page 196
2. a; page 196
3. d; page 197
4. c; page 197

Complete the graph

Figure 8.8 labels the curves. The equilibrium price level is 110 and equilibrium real GDP is $10 trillion; page 196.

Short answer

1. The equilibrium price level is 120 and equilibrium real GDP is $13 trillion; page 196.

2. A below full-employment equilibrium occurs when potential GDP exceeds equilibrium real GDP; page 197.

3. An above full-employment equilibrium occurs when equilibrium real GDP exceeds potential GDP; page 197.

■ **FIGURE 8.8**

Price level (GDP deflator, 1997 = 100)

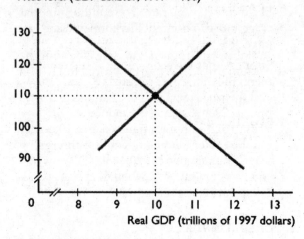

Real GDP (trillions of 1997 dollars)

■ CHECKPOINT 8.4

Fill in the blanks

An increase in aggregate demand <u>increases</u> real GDP. An increase in aggregate supply <u>lowers</u> the price level. Stagflation is a combination of <u>recession</u> and a <u>rising</u> price level. When real GDP exceeds potential GDP, <u>an inflationary</u> gap exists. When potential GDP exceeds real GDP, <u>a deflationary</u> gap exists.

True or false

1. True; page 200
2. False; pages 200-202
3. True; pages 200-202
4. False; page 202
5. False; page 198

Multiple choice

1. d; page 198
2. b; page 200
3. b; page 199
4. c; page 199
5. a; page 202
6. a; page 202

Complete the graph

1. a. An increase in expected future profit increases investment and aggregate demand. In Figure 8.9, the AD curve shifts rightward from AD_0 to AD_1. The equilibrium price level rises from 105 to 110 and equilibrium real GDP increases from $950 billion to $1,000 billion; page200.

■ FIGURE 8.9

Price level (GDP deflator, 1997 = 100)

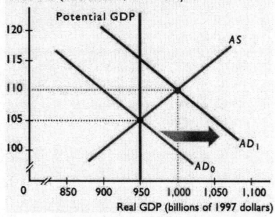

b. An inflationary gap now exists. The money wage rate rises and aggregate supply decreases. In Figure 8.10, the AS curve shifts leftward. Eventually the AS curve moves from AS_0 to AS_1. Real GDP returns to potential GDP and the price level rises to 115; page 202.

■ FIGURE 8.10

Price level (GDP deflator, 1997 = 100)

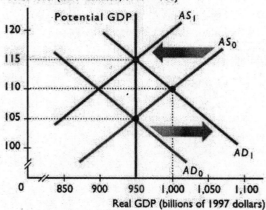

2. Figure 8.11 shows the effect of a productivity slowdown. Aggregate supply decreases and the AS curve shifts leftward from AS_0 to AS_1. The price level rises from 105 to 110 and real GDP decreases from, $950 billion to $900 billion. The economy now has a labour surplus. The money wage rate gradually falls and the aggregate supply curve shifts rightward. Eventually it reaches AS_0, where real GDP is back at potential GDP; page 202.

■ FIGURE 8.11

Price level (GDP deflator, 1997 = 100)

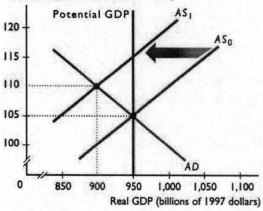

Short answer

1. Stagflation is a combination of recession (falling real GDP) and inflation (rising price level). Stagflation can be created by a decrease in aggregate supply; page 199.

2. An inflationary gap is a gap that exists when real GDP exceeds potential GDP and that brings a rising price level. Workers have experienced a fall in the buying power of their wages, and firms' profits have increased. Workers demand higher wages. As the money wage rate rises, aggregate supply decreases and the aggregate supply curve shifts leftward. Eventually, real GDP will return to potential GDP and the inflationary gap is eliminated; page 202.

3. The business cycle occurs because aggregate supply and aggregate demand fluctuate around their trends; page 198.

Economic Growth

Chapter 9

Chapter 9 discusses the factors that determine economic growth, studies different theories that explain economic growth, and examines possible government polices that can promote faster economic growth.

■ **Define and calculate the economic growth rate and explain the implications of sustained growth.**

Economic growth is a sustained expansion of production possibilities measured as the increase in real GDP over a given period. The economic growth rate is the annual percentage change of real GDP. The standard of living depends on real GDP per person, which is real GDP divided by the population. The Rule of 70 tells us that the number of years it takes for the level of any variable to double is approximately 70 divided by the annual percentage growth rate of the variable.

■ **Identify the main sources of economic growth.**

Real GDP grows when the quantities of the factors of production grow or when technology advances. Labour productivity is the quantity of real GDP produced by one hour of labour. When labour productivity grows, real GDP per person grows. The growth of labour productivity depends on saving and investment in physical capital, expansion of human capital, and discovery of new technologies. The productivity curve is a relationship that shows how labour productivity changes as the amount of physical capital per hour of labour changes with a given state of technology. The productivity curve shifts upward when technology advances or human capital increases. The one-third rule is the observation that on the average, with no change in human capital and technology, a *one percent* increase in capital per hour of labour brings a *one-third percent* increase in labour productivity.

■ **Review the theories of economic growth that explain why growth rates vary over time and across countries.**

The classical growth theory predicts that labour productivity rises and lifts real GDP per person above the subsistence level. A population explosion occurs, labour productivity falls, and real GDP per person returns to the subsistence level. Neoclassical growth theory is the theory that real GDP per person will increase as long as technology keeps advancing. New growth theory is the theory that our unlimited wants will lead us to ever greater productivity and perpetual economic growth.

■ **Describe policies that might promote faster economic growth.**

Governments can achieve faster economic growth by creating incentive mechanisms; by encouraging saving; by encouraging research and development; by encouraging international trade; and, by improving the quality of education.

EXPANDED CHAPTER CHECKLIST

When you have completed this chapter, you will be able to

1 Define and calculate the economic growth rate and explain the implications of sustained growth.

- Define economic growth rate.
- Calculate the growth rate of real GDP.
- Explain the relationship between the standard of living and real GDP per person.
- Calculate the growth rate of real GDP per person.
- Explain and be able to use the Rule of 70.

2 Identify the main sources of economic growth.

- Explain how growth in real GDP can be divided into growth in aggregate hours and growth in labour productivity.
- Tell how labour productivity is calculated, and discuss the importance of growth in labour productivity.
- List and explain the three sources of growth in labour productivity.
- Draw a productivity curve and distinguish between the factors that shift the curve from those that create a movement along the curve.
- Explain diminishing returns along the productivity curve.
- Use the one-third rule to identify the contribution of capital growth to labour productivity growth.

3 Review the theories of economic growth that explain why growth rates vary over time and across countries.

- Describe the classical growth theory and explain why it predicts a return to subsistence real income.

- Describe the neoclassical growth theory and explain why it predicts that national levels of real GDP and national growth rates will converge.
- Discuss the new growth theory and explain why it predicts national growth rates will not necessarily converge.
- Compare the predictions of each growth theory with the facts in the global economy.

4 Describe policies that might promote faster economic growth.

- List and explain the preconditions for economic growth and describe the five policies governments can implement to achieve faster economic growth.
- Discuss the extent to which government policy can affect economic growth.

KEY TERMS

- Classical growth theory (page 221)
- Economic freedom (page 231)
- Economic growth rate (page 210)
- Labour productivity (page 214)
- Malthusian theory (page 221)
- Neoclassical growth theory (page 223)
- New growth theory (page 225)
- One-third rule (page 219)
- Productivity curve (page 217)
- Property rights (page 231)
- Real GDP per person (page 210)
- Rule of 70 (page 211)

CHECKPOINT 9.1

■ **Define and calculate the economic growth rate and explain the implications of sustained growth.**

Practice Problem 9.1

Mexico's real GDP was 1,448 billion pesos in 1998 and 1,501 billion pesos in 1999. Mexico's population growth rate in 1999 was 1.8 percent. Calculate

a. Mexico's economic growth rate in 1999.

b. The growth rate of real GDP per person in Mexico in 1999.

c. The approximate number of years it takes for real GDP per person in Mexico to double if the 1999 economic growth rate and population growth rate are maintained.

d. The approximate number of years it takes for real GDP per person in Mexico to double if the 1999 economic growth rate is maintained but the population growth rate slows to 1 percent a year.

Solution to Practice Problem 9.1

This question uses three growth rate formulas. The first is the formula used to calculate the growth rate of real GDP; the second is the formula used to calculate the growth rate of real GDP per person; the third is the Rule of 70.

Quick Review

- *Growth rate of real GDP* The growth rate of real GDP equals

$$\frac{\left(\begin{array}{c}\text{Real GDP in}\\\text{current year}\end{array}\right) - \left(\begin{array}{c}\text{Real GDP in}\\\text{previous year}\end{array}\right)}{\text{Real GDP in previous year}} \times 100.$$

- *Growth rate of real GDP per person* The growth rate of real GDP per person equals the growth rate of real GDP minus the growth rate of the population.

- *Rule of 70* The number of years it takes for the level of any variable to double is approximately 70 divided by the annual percentage growth rate of the variable.

a. Mexico's economic growth rate in 1999.

The economic growth rate is annual percentage change of real GDP. Mexico's economic growth rate in 1999 equals [(Real GDP in 1999 – Real GDP in 1998) ÷ Real GDP in 1998] × 100. Real GDP in 1998 is 1,448 billion pesos and real GDP in 1999 is 1,501 billion pesos. So the economic growth rate is [(1,501 billion – 1,448 billion) ÷ 1,448 billion] × 100, which is 3.7 percent.

b. The growth rate of real GDP per person in Mexico in 1999.

The growth rate of real GDP per person equals the growth rate of real GDP minus the growth rate of the population. The growth rate of real GDP is 3.7 percent from part (a) and the population growth rate is 1.8 percent. The growth rate of real GDP per person is 3.7 percent – 1.8 percent, which equals 1.9 percent.

c. The approximate number of years it takes for real GDP per person in Mexico to double if the 1999 economic growth rate and population growth rate are maintained.

The number of years it takes for real GDP per person to double is given by the Rule of 70. The Rule of 70 tells us that the level of a variable that grows at 1.9 percent a year will double in 70 ÷ 1.9 years, which is approximately 37 years.

d. The approximate number of years it takes for real GDP per person in Mexico to double if the 1999 economic growth rate is maintained, but the population growth rate slows to 1 percent a year.

A change in the population growth rate, with all other things remaining the same, changes the growth rate of real GDP per person. The new growth rate of real GDP per person equals the growth rate of real GDP, 3.7 percent, minus the growth rate of population, 1 percent, which is 2.7 percent.

Next, use the Rule of 70. The Rule of 70 tells us that the level of a variable that grows at 2.7 percent a year will double in 70 ÷ 2.7 years, which is approximately 26 years.

Additional Practice Problem 9.1a

In the nation of Transylvania in 1999, real GDP was $3.0 million and the population was 1,000. In 2000, real GDP was $3.3 million and the population was 1,050.

a. What is Transylvania's economic growth rate in 2000?

b. What is the population growth rate?

c. What is Transylvania's growth rate of real GDP per person?

d. Did Transylvania's standard of living rise in 2000?

e. Calculate how many years it takes for real GDP per person to double.

Solution to Additional Practice Problem 9.1a

a. What is Transylvania's economic growth rate in 2000?

Transylvania's economic growth rate in 2000 equals [(Real GDP in 2000 – Real GDP in 1999) ÷ Real GDP in 1999] × 100. Real GDP in 1999 is $3 million and real GDP in 2000 is $3.3 million. So Transylvania's economic growth rate is [($3.3 million – $3.0 million) ÷ $3.0 million] × 100, which is 10 percent.

b. What is the population growth rate?

Transylvania's population growth rate in 2000 equals [(Population in 2000 – Population in 1999) ÷ Population in 1999] × 100. Population in 1999 is 1,000 and population in 2000 is 1,050. So Transylvania's population growth rate is [(1,050 – 1,000) ÷ 1,000] × 100, which is 5 percent.

c. What is Transylvania's growth rate of real GDP per person?

Transylvania's growth rate of real GDP per person equals the growth rate of real GDP minus the growth rate of the population. The growth rate of

real GDP per person is 10 percent – 5 percent, which is 5 percent.

d. Did Transylvania's standard of living rise in 2000?

The standard of living depends on real GDP per person. Real GDP per person increased in 2000 and so Transylvania's standard of living rose.

e. Calculate how many years it takes for real GDP per person to double.

Transylvania's real GDP per person is growing at 5 percent a year. According to the Rule of 70, the number of years for the level of any variable to double is approximately 70 divided by the annual percentage growth rate of the variable. So real GDP per person in Transylvania will double in 70 ÷ 5 years, which is 14 years.

■ Self Test 9.1

Fill in the blanks

The growth rate of real GDP equals real GDP in the current year minus real GDP in the previous year divided by real GDP in the ____ (current; previous) year all multiplied by 100. The growth rate of real GDP per person equals the growth rate of real GDP ____ (minus; plus) the growth rate of the population. The number of years it takes for the level of any variable to double is approximately ____ divided by the annual percentage growth rate of the variable.

True or false

1. If real GDP last year was $1.00 trillion and real GDP this year is $1.05 trillion, the growth rate of real GDP this year is 5 percent.

2. Real GDP per person equals real GDP divided by the population.

3. If a nation's population grows at 2 percent a year and its real GDP grows at 4 percent a year, then the growth rate of real GDP per person is 2 percent a year.

4. If real GDP is growing at 2 percent a year, it will take 70 years for real GDP to double.

Multiple choice

1. The economic growth rate is the
   a. annual percentage change of real GDP.
   b. annual percentage change of employment.
   c. level of real GDP.
   d. annual percentage change of the population.

2. Real GDP is $9 trillion in the current year and $8.6 trillion in the previous year. The economic growth rate in the current year is
   a. 10.31 percent.
   b. 4.65 percent.
   c. 5.67 percent.
   d. 7.67 percent.

3. The standard of living depends on
   a. real GDP.
   b. employment.
   c. employment per person.
   d. real GDP per person.

4. If the growth rate of the population is greater than a nation's growth rate of real GDP, then the growth rate of real GDP per person
   a. is negative.
   b. is positive.
   c. does not change.
   d. may rise or fall.

5. If during a year real GDP increases by 3 percent and the population increases by 1 percent, then real GDP per person grows by
   a. 4 percent a year.
   b. 2 percent a year.
   c. 3 percent a year.
   d. some amount that cannot be determined without more information.

6. If a country experiences a real GDP growth rate of 4 percent a year, real GDP will double in
   a. 14 years.
   b. 17.5 years.
   c. 23.3 years.
   d. 35 years.

Short answer

1. The table gives real GDP of a nation.

Year	Real GDP (billions of 1997 dollars)
2000	100.0
2001	110.0
2002	121.0
2003	133.1

   What is the growth rate of real GDP in 2001? In 2002? In 2003?

2. The table gives the growth rate of real GDP and the growth rate of the population for a nation.

Year	Real GDP growth rate (percent)	Population growth rate (percent)
2000	3	2
2001	4	2
2002	1	2
2003	4	4

   a. What is the growth rate of real GDP per person for each year?

   b. In what years did the standard of living improve?

3. If a nation's real GDP grows at 4 percent a year, how many years does it take for real GDP to double? If the growth rate is 5 percent how many years does it take for real GDP to double?

CHECKPOINT 9.2

■ **Identify the main sources of economic growth.**

Practice Problem 9.2

The table provides some data on the Canadian economy in 1995 and 1996.

Item	1995	1996
Aggregate hours (billions)	22.7	23.0
Real GDP (billions of 1997 dollars)	834.5	848.7
Capital per hour of labour (1997 dollars)	80.25	80.62

a. Calculate the growth rate of real GDP in 1996.

b. Calculate labour productivity in 1995 and 1996.

c. Calculate the growth rate of labour productivity in 1996.

d. If the one-third rule applies in Canada, what were the sources of labour productivity growth in 1996? Explain your answer.

Solution to Practice Problem 9.2

This question focuses on growth rates, labour productivity, and the one-third rule.

Quick Review

- *Labour productivity* The quantity of real GDP produced by one hour of labour. When labour productivity grows, real GDP per person grows.

- *One-third rule* The observation that on the average, with no change in human capital and technology, a *one percent* increase in capital per hour of labour brings a *one-third percent* increase in labour productivity.

a. **Calculate the growth rate of real GDP in 1996.**

Canada's economic growth rate in 1996 equals [(Real GDP in 1996 – Real GDP in 1995) ÷ Real GDP in 1995] × 100. Real GDP in 1995 is $834.5 billion and real GDP in 1996 is $848.7 billion. So the growth rate of real GDP in 1996 is [($848.7

billion – $834.5 billion) ÷ $834.5 billion] × 100, which is 1.7 percent.

b. **Calculate labour productivity in 1995 and 1996.**

Labour productivity is real GDP divided by aggregate hours. Labour productivity in 1995 is $834.5 billion ÷ 22.7 billion hours, which is $36.76 per hour of labour. Labour productivity in 1996 is $848.7 billion ÷ 23.0 billion hours, which is $36.90 per hour of labour.

c. **Calculate the growth rate of labour productivity in 1996.**

The growth rate of labour productivity in 1996 is labour productivity in 1996 minus labour productivity in 1995, divided by labour productivity in 1995 and all multiplied by 100. The growth rate of labour productivity in 1996 is [($36.90 – $36.76) ÷ $36.76] × 100, which is 0.38 percent.

d. **If the one-third rule applies in Canada, what were the sources of labour productivity growth in 1996? Explain your answer.**

The one-third rule identifies the contribution of capital growth to labour productivity growth. In 1996 capital per hour of labour grew by [($80.62 – $80.25) ÷ $80.25] × 100, which is 0.46 percent. The one-third rule tells us that (1/3) × 0.46 percent, which is 0.15 percent growth in labour productivity comes from capital growth. The remaining labour productivity growth, 0.38 percent minus 0.15 percent, which is 0.23 percent comes from technological advance and human capital growth.

Additional Practice Problem 9.2a

The table gives data on capital per hour of labour and real GDP per hour of labour for a small nation.

Capital per hour of labour (1997 dollars)	Real GDP per hour of labour (1997 dollars)
0	0
30	20.00
45	23.33
60	25.92

Label the axes in Figure 9.1 and plot this nation's productivity curve.

■ FIGURE 9.1

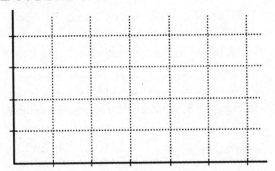

b.   When capital per hour of labour equals $30 or more, does this nation's productivity curve agree with the one-third rule?

Solution to Additional Practice Problem 9.2a

a.   The productivity curve is shown in Figure 9.2.

■ FIGURE 9.2

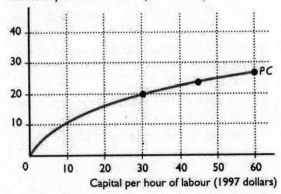

b.   Yes, the productivity curve agrees with the one-third rule. When capital per hour of labour grows by 50 percent, from $30 to $45, real GDP per hour of labour grows one third

of 50 percent, or 16.67 percent from $20 to $23.33. Similarly, when capital per hour of labour grows by 33.3 percent, from $45 to $60, real GDP per hour of labour grows one third of 33 percent, or 11.1 percent from $23.33 to $25.92.

■ Self Test 9.2

Fill in the blanks

All influences on real GDP growth can be divided into those that increase aggregate hours and those that increase _____ (labour productivity; population). Education and training, and job experience increase ____ (investment in physical capital; human capital). The ____ is a relationship that shows how labour productivity changes as the amount of physical capital per hour of labour changes with a given state of technology. A change in capital per hour of labour creates a ____ (movement along; shift of) the productivity curve and a technological advance creates a ____ (movement along; shift of) the productivity curve. The one-third rule tells us that a ____ (one; one-third) percent increase in capital per hour of labour brings a ____ (one; one-third) percent increase in labour productivity.

True or false

1.   Real GDP increases if aggregate hours increase or labour productivity increases.

2.   If labour productivity increases and aggregate hours do not change, then real GDP per person increases.

3.   Higher wages are a source of growth in labour productivity.

4.   A technological advance shifts the productivity curve upward.

5.   A productivity curve displays increasing returns.

Multiple choice

1. The only source of growth in aggregate labour hours that is sustainable over long periods of time is
   a. an increase in the labour force participation rate.
   b. population growth.
   c. a decrease in labour productivity.
   d. a decrease in the unemployment rate.

2. Real GDP equals aggregate hours
   a. divided by labour productivity.
   b. minus labour productivity.
   c. plus labour productivity.
   d. multiplied by labour productivity.

3. If real GDP is $1,200 billion, the population is 60 million, and aggregate hours are 80 billion, labour productivity is
   a. $5.00 an hour.
   b. $6.67 an hour.
   c. $15.00 an hour.
   d. $20,000.

4. Which of the following lists gives factors that increase labour productivity?
   a. saving and investment in physical capital, a rising wage rate, and discovery of new technologies
   b. expansion of human capital, labour force growth, and discovery of new technologies
   c. expansion of human capital, population growth, and discovery of new technologies
   d. saving and investment in physical capital, expansion of human capital, and discovery of new technologies

5. An increase in the amount of capital per hour of labour leads to ____ the productivity curve.
   a. a movement down along
   b. a movement up along
   c. an upward shift of
   d. a downward shift of

6. If capital per hour of labour grows by 6 percent with no growth in technology, labour productivity increases by
   a. 6 percent.
   b. 3 percent.
   c. 2 percent.
   d. 4 percent.

Complete the graph

1. In Figure 9.3, label the axes and draw a productivity curve.
   a. What factor causes a movement along the curve?
   b. What factors cause a shift of the curve?
   c. In Figure 9.3, illustrate the effect of a technological advance.

■ **FIGURE 9.3**

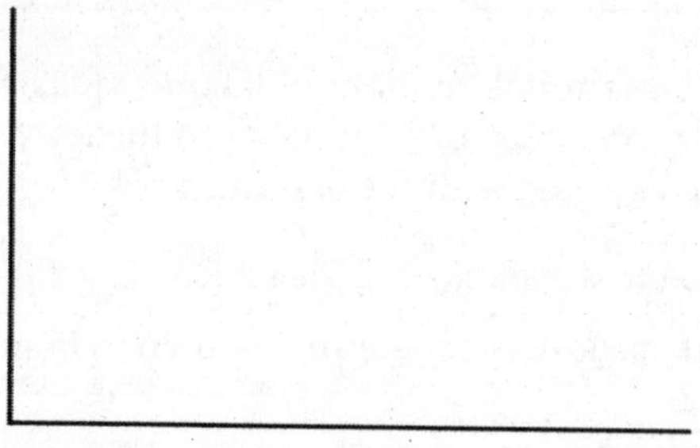

Short answer

1. Real GDP is $9 trillion and aggregate hours are 200 billion. What is labour productivity?

2. Aggregate hours are 200 billion and labour productivity is $45 an hour. What is real GDP?

3. What three factors increase labour productivity?

4. Last year, capital per hour of labour grew 6 percent and labour productivity increased 3 percent.
   a. How much did growth in capital per hour of labour contribute to the increase in labour productivity?
   b. How much did human capital growth or technological change contribute to the increase in labour productivity?

CHECKPOINT 9.3

■ Review the theories of economic growth that explain why growth rates vary over time and across countries.

Practice Problems 9.3

1. What does classical growth theory say will eventually end economic growth? Does the evidence of history support the prediction of the classical growth theory?

2. What does neoclassical growth theory say about the source of persistent growth in real GDP per person?

3. Why does neoclassical growth theory predict that national levels of real GDP and national growth rates will converge?

4. What is the driving force of growth, according to new growth theory?

5. What does new growth theory imply about growth in the global economy?

Solutions to Practice Problems 9.3

These questions focus on the three growth theories. You need to know how each theory differs from the others and each theory's conclusion about the persistence of economic growth.

Quick Review

*   *Classical growth theory* The theory that the clash between an exploding population and limited resources will eventually bring economic growth to an end.

*   *Neoclassical growth theory* The theory that real GDP per person will increase as long as technology keeps advancing.

*   *New growth theory* The theory that our unlimited wants will lead us to ever greater productivity and perpetual economic growth.

1. **What does classical growth theory say will eventually end economic growth? Does the evidence of history support the prediction of the classical growth theory?**

According to classical growth theory, when real GDP per person exceeds the subsistence level, population growth increases and real GDP per person decreases until it returns to the subsistence level. History does not support this prediction of the classical theory.

2. **What does neoclassical growth theory say about the source of persistent growth in real GDP per person?**

In neoclassical theory, technological advance is the source of persistent growth of real GDP per person. Technological advances increase the quantity of capital per hour of labour and real GDP per hour of labour.

3. **Why does neoclassical growth theory predict that national levels of real GDP and national growth rates will converge?**

All economies have access to the same technologies and capital is free to roam the globe seeking the highest available profits. So neoclassical theory predicts that national levels of real GDP and national growth rates will converge.

4. **What is the driving force of growth, according to new growth theory?**

The driving force of growth in the new growth theory is the incentive to innovate and an absence of diminishing returns to new knowledge.

5. **What does new growth theory imply about growth in the global economy?**

National growth rates are determined by national incentives to save, invest, and innovate. Because these incentives depend on factors that are special to each country, national growth rates will not necessarily converge.

Additional Practice Problem 9.3a

How does each of the growth theories reflect the period during which they were developed?

Solution to Additional Practice Problem 9.3a

The classical growth theory was developed during the Industrial Revolution. Observers, such as Thomas Malthus, saw some technological advances and rapid population growth. They combined these two observations into the classical growth theory, which predicts return to subsistence real income.

The neoclassical growth theory was developed in the 1960s, when rapid population growth was no longer a concern and when technological growth and capital per hour of labour were starting to grow more rapidly. The neoclassical growth theory assigned a key role to these two factors and concluded that growth would persist as long as technology advanced.

The new growth theory was developed in the 1980s, when technological growth exploded. The new growth theory assigns importance to technological growth. Based on the observation that technological growth has persisted during the past 200 years, the new growth theory concludes that technology and real GDP will grow forever.

■ Self Test 9.3

Fill in the blanks

The classical growth theory is the same as the ____ (Malthusian; new growth) theory. Classical growth theory says that an increase in real GDP per person leads to ____ (capital; population) growth. Neoclassical growth theory says that economic growth continues as long as ____ (the population grows; technology advances). New growth theory predicts that economic growth will persist ____ (temporarily; indefinitely). The ____ (neoclassical; new) growth theory predicts that levels of GDP in different nations will converge; ____ (neoclassical; new) growth theory predicts that gaps between rich and poor nations can persist.

True or false

1. The classical growth theory concludes that eventually real GDP per person returns to the subsistence level.

2. According to the neoclassical theory, the rate of technological change does not influence the rate of economic growth.

3. The new growth theory predicts that economic growth can persist indefinitely.

4. Economic growth in the real world suggests that the new growth theory fits the facts more closely than the classical growth theory or the neoclassical growth theory.

Multiple choice

1. Classical growth theory predicts that increases in
   a. real GDP per person are permanent and sustainable.
   b. real GDP per person are temporary and not sustainable.
   c. resources permanently increase labour productivity.
   d. resources permanently increase real GDP per person.

2. If real GDP per person is above the subsistence level, then according to classical growth theory,
   a. the population will increase.
   b. the population will decrease.
   c. the standard of living will continue to improve.
   d. labour productivity will increase.

3. Neoclassical growth theory predicts that economic growth is
   a. only temporary due to overpopulation.
   b. the result of technological advances.
   c. impossible due to extremes in weather.
   d. caused by women entering the labour force.

4. The new growth theory states that

a. technological advances are the result of random chance.

b. technological advances are the result of discoveries and choices.

c. technological advances are the responsibility of the government.

d. the subsistence income level leads to technological advances.

5. The theory that suggests that our unlimited wants will lead to perpetual economic growth is the

a. classical growth theory.

b. sustained growth theory.

c. neoclassical growth theory.

d. new growth theory.

6. New growth theory predicts that

a. national growth rates will not necessarily converge over time.

b. national growth rates will slowly converge over time.

c. countries with the highest real GDP per person are likely to be the first to experience a slowing economy.

d. national growth rates will rise and fall as population rates change.

Short answer

1. What role do technological advances play in each of the three growth theories?

2. What role does population growth play in each of the three growth theories?

3. What role do diminishing returns play in the new growth theory?

4. Which growth theory is most pessimistic about the prospects for persistent economic growth? Which is most optimistic?

CHECKPOINT 9.4

■ **Describe the policies that might promote faster economic growth.**

Practice Problems 9.4

1. What are the preconditions for economic growth?

2. Why does much of Africa experience slow economic growth?

3. Why is economic freedom crucial for achieving economic growth?

4. What role do property rights play in encouraging economic growth?

5. Explain why, other things remaining the same, a country with a well-educated population has a faster economic growth rate than a country that has a poorly educated population.

Solution to Practice Problems 9.4

These questions emphasize the role that the government can play to encourage economic growth by providing the necessary preconditions and by conducting the proper policies.

Quick Review

*   *Preconditions for economic growth* The three preconditions are economic freedom, property rights, and markets.

*   *Actions to achieve faster growth* The main actions that governments can take to achieve faster economic growth are to create the incentive mechanisms; encourage saving; encourage research and development; encourage international trade; and improve the quality of education.

1. **What are the preconditions for economic growth?**

Economic freedom, property rights, and markets are the preconditions for economic growth. Economic freedom is a condition in which people are able to make personal choices, their private property is protected, and they are free to buy and sell in markets. Property rights are the social arrangements that govern the protection of private property. Markets enable people to trade and to save and invest.

2. **Why does much of Africa experience slow economic growth?**

Much of Africa lacks economic freedom, property rights are not enforced, and markets do not function well. These African countries do not have the preconditions for economic growth, so people have little incentive to specialize and trade or to accumulate physical and human capital.

3. **Why is economic freedom crucial for achieving economic growth?**

Individuals know more about their own skills and preferences than can the government, or anyone else. Economic freedom allows people to make their own choices and gives incentives to pursue growth-producing activities.

4. **What role do property rights play in encouraging economic growth?**

Property rights and a legal system to enforce them encourage people to work, save, invest, and accumulate human capital.

5. **Explain why, other things remaining the same, a country with a well-educated population has a faster economic growth rate than a country that has a poorly educated population.**

A well-educated population has more skills and greater labour productivity, is more likely to create new technology, adapts faster to new innovations, and can implement new technology faster.

Additional Practice Problem 9.4a

In 1949 East Germany and West Germany had about the same real GDP per person. By 1989 West Germany had a real GDP per person more than twice the level of East Germany. Why did East Germany grow so much more slowly than West Germany over those 40 years?

Solution to Additional Practice Problem 9.4a

In 1949, East Germany was formed with state ownership of capital and land, and virtually no economic freedom. West Germany was formed with private ownership of most capital and land, and significant economic freedom.

West Germany had the preconditions for economic growth; East Germany did not. When East Germany collapsed in 1989, West Germany had more human capital, more capital per hour of labour, and better technology. The different incentives had given West German workers the incentive to acquire human capital, West German investors the incentive to acquire physical capital, and West German entrepreneurs the incentive to innovate new and better technology.

■ Self Test 9.4

Fill in the blanks

____, ____, and ____ are preconditions for economic growth. Policies the government can take to encourage faster economic growth are to ____ (create; discourage) incentive mechanisms; ____ (encourage; discourage) saving; ____ (encourage; discourage) research and development; ____ (encourage; discourage) international trade; and, improve the quality of ____ (education; pollution control).

True or false

1. To achieve economic growth, economic freedom must be coupled with a democratic political system.

2. Markets slow specialization and economic growth.

3. Encouraging saving can increase the growth of capital and stimulate economic growth.

4. Limiting international trade will increase economic growth.

Multiple choice

1. Economic freedom means that

a. firms are regulated by the government.

b. some goods and services are free.

c. people are able to make personal choices and their private property is protected.

d. the rule of law does not apply.

2. Property rights protect

a. only the rights to physical property.

b. only the rights to financial property.

c. all rights except rights to intellectual property.

d. rights to physical property, financial property, and intellectual property.

3. Which of the following statements is FALSE?

a. Saving helps create economic growth.

b. Improvements in quality of education are important for economic growth.

c. Free international trade helps create economic growth.

d. Faster population growth is the key to growth in real GDP per person.

4. Saving

a. slows growth because it decreases consumption.

b. finances investment, which brings capital accumulation.

c. has no impact on economic growth.

d. is very low in most East Asian nations.

5. The fastest-growing nations today are those with

a. barriers that significantly limit international trade.

b. the fastest-growing exports and imports.

c. government intervention in markets to ensure high prices.

d. few funds spent on research and development.

6. Economic growth is encouraged by

a. free international trade.

b. limiting international trade so that the domestic economy can prosper.

c. discouraging saving because increased saving means less spending.

d. None of the above.

Short answer

1. Does persistent economic growth necessarily occur when a nation meets all the preconditions for growth?

2. What role does specialization and trade play in determining economic growth?

3. Is it possible for the government to create a large increase in the economic growth rate in a year?

SELF TEST ANSWERS

■ CHECKPOINT 9.1

Fill in the blanks

The growth rate of real GDP equals real GDP in the current year minus real GDP in the previous year divided by real GDP in the <u>previous</u> year, all multiplied by 100. The growth rate of real GDP per person equals the growth rate of real GDP <u>minus</u> the growth rate of the population. The number of years it takes for the level of any variable to double is approximately <u>70</u> divided by the annual percentage growth rate of the variable.

True or false

1. True; page 210
2. True; page 210
3. True; page 211
4. False; page 211

Multiple choice

1. a; page 210
2. b; page 210
3. d; page 210
4. a; page 211
5. b; page 211
6. b; page 211

Short answer

1. 10 percent; 10 percent; 10 percent; page 210.
2a. In 2000, the growth rate of real GDP per person is 1 percent; in 2001, the growth rate of real GDP per person is 2 percent; in 2002, the growth rate of real GDP per person is –1 percent; and in 2003, the growth rate of real GDP per person is zero; page 211
b. 2000 and 2001; page 210
3. 70 ÷ 4 = 17.5 years; 70 ÷ 5 = 14 years; page 211.

■ CHECKPOINT 9.2

Fill in the blanks

All influences on real GDP growth can be divided into those that increase aggregate hours and those that increase <u>labour productivity</u>. Education and training, and job experience increase <u>human capital</u>. The <u>productivity curve</u> is a relationship that shows how labour productivity changes as the amount of physical capital per hour of labour changes with a given state of technology. A change in capital per hour of labour creates a <u>movement along</u> the productivity curve and a technological advance creates a <u>shift of</u> the productivity curve. The one-third rule tells us that a <u>one</u> percent increase in capital per hour of labour brings a <u>one-third</u> percent increase in labour productivity.

True or false

1. True; page 214
2. True; page 214
3. False; page 215
4. True; page 217
5. False; page 218

Multiple choice

1. b; page 214
2. d; page 214
3. c; page 214
4. d; page 215
5. b; page 217
6. c; page 219

Complete the graph

1. The productivity curve is illustrated in Figure 9.4, labelled PC_0.

■ FIGURE 9.4
Real GDP per hour of labour (1997 dollars)

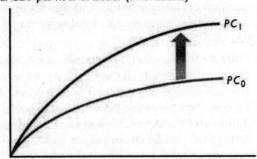

Capital per hour of labour (1997 dollars)

a. A change in capital per hour of labour; page 217.

b. A change in human capital or a technological advance; pages 217.

c. In Figure 9.4, a technological advance shifts the productivity curve upward from PC_0 to PC_1; page 217.

Short answer

1. Labour productivity is $45 an hour; page 214.

2. Real GDP is $9 trillion; page 214.

3. Saving and investment in physical capital; expansion of human capital; discovery of new technologies; page 215.

4a. 1/3 of 6 percent, which is 2 percent; page 219.

 b. 1 percent; page 219.

■ CHECKPOINT 9.3

Fill in the blanks

The classical growth theory is the same as the Malthusian theory. Classical growth theory says that an increase in real GDP per person leads to population growth. Neoclassical growth theory says that economic growth continues as long as technology advances. New growth theory predicts that economic growth will persist indefinitely. The neoclassical growth theory predicts that levels of GDP in different nations will converge; new growth theory predicts that gaps between rich and poor nations can persist.

True or false

1. True; page 221

2. False; page 223

3. True; page 225

4. True; page 228

Multiple choice

1. b; page 221

2. a; page 221

3. b; page 223

4. b; page 225

5. d; pages 226-227

6. a; page 228

Short answer

1. In the classical growth theory, advances in technology start a temporary period of economic growth; in the neoclassical growth theory, economic growth continues as long as technology advances; and in the new growth theory, economic growth continues indefinitely, in part because technology grows indefinitely; pages 221-222, 224, 227.

2. Population growth plays a crucial role only in the classical growth theory because in that theory population growth leads the economy back to subsistence real income; page 222.

3. The new growth theory assumes that the economy does not experience diminishing returns. As capital accumulates, labour productivity grows indefinitely; page 226.

4. The most optimistic theory is the new growth theory, which concludes that economic growth can continue forever. The

most pessimistic theory is the classical growth theory, which concludes that real GDP per person will return to the subsistence level; pages 221, 225.

■ CHECKPOINT 9.4

Fill in the blanks

Economic freedom, property rights, and markets are preconditions for economic growth. Policies the government can take to encourage faster economic growth are to create incentive mechanisms; encourage saving; encourage research and development; encourage international trade; and, improve the quality of education.

True or false

1. False; page 231
2. False; page 231
3. True; page 232
4. False; page 233

Multiple choice

1. c; page 231
2. d; page 231
3. d; pages 232-233
4. b; page 232
5. b; page 233
6. a; page 233

Short answer

1. No. The preconditions for growth are necessary for growth to occur. But for growth to be persistent, people must face incentives that encourage saving and investment, expansion of human capital, and the discovery and application of new technologies; pages 231-232.

2. Growth begins when people can specialize in the activities in which they have a comparative advantage and trade with each other. As an economy reaps the benefits from specialization and trade, production and consumption grow, real GDP per person increases, and the standard of living rises; page 232.

3. No, the government cannot create a large increase in the economic growth rate in a year. The government can pursue policies that will nudge the growth rate upward. Over time the benefits from these policies will be large; page 233.

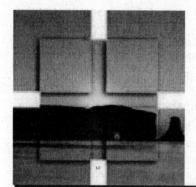

Money and the Monetary System

CHAPTER IN PERSPECTIVE

Chapter 10 defines money, describes the monetary system in Canada, and describes the functions of the Bank of Canada.

■ **Define money and describe its functions.**

Money is any commodity or token that is generally accepted as a means of payment. Money performs three vital functions. It serves as a medium of exchange, which is an object that is generally accepted in return for goods and services; a unit of account, which is an agreed-upon measure for stating the prices of goods and services; and a store of value, which is any commodity or token that can be held and exchanged later for goods and services. Money today consists of currency and deposits at banks and other financial institutions. Currency in a bank is not money. Deposits are money but cheques are not money. Credit cards, debit cards, and electronic cheques are not money. Electronic cash is not sufficiently widely accepted to serve as money today. M1 and M2+ are the two official measures of money in Canada today. M1 is currency outside the banks plus chequable deposits owned by individuals and businesses at chartered banks. M2+ is M1 plus personal savings deposits and nonpersonal notice deposits at banks plus deposits at credit unions, caisses populaires, and other depository institutions. All of M1 is money, but only part of M2+ is money.

■ **Describe the monetary system and explain the functions of banks and other monetary institutions.**

The monetary system consists of the Bank of Canada and the banks and other institutions that accept deposits and provide the services that enable people and businesses to make and receive payments. Three types of monetary institutions are chartered banks, credit unions and caisses populaires, and other depository institutions. A bank makes loans at a higher interest rate than the interest rate it pays on deposits. To achieve security for its depositors, a bank divides its assets into three parts: cash assets, bonds, and loans. Monetary institutions create liquidity, lower the costs of lending and borrowing, pool risks, and make payments.

■ **Describe the functions of the Bank of Canada.**

The Bank of Canada is the central bank of Canada. The Bank of Canada conducts the nation's monetary policy. The Bank of Canada's ultimate monetary policy objective is to keep the inflation rate inside a target range of between 1 percent and 3 percent a year. A daily monetary policy target is a target that the Bank of Canada sets and achieves each day in pursuit of its ultimate inflation target. The Bank of Canada can use four policy tools to achieve its objectives: the bank rate and the bankers' deposit rate, open market operations, government deposit shifting, and required reserve ratios. The monetary base is the sum of chartered banks' deposits at the Bank of Canada plus coins and Bank of Canada notes.

EXPANDED CHAPTER CHECKLIST

When you have completed this chapter, you will be able to

1 Define money and describe its functions.

- Define money and discuss how money serves as a medium of exchange, a unit of account, and a store of value.
- Categorize currency in a bank, cheques, credit cards, debit cards, e-cheques and e-cash as money or not money.
- Define M1 and M2+.

2 Describe the monetary system and explain the functions of banks and other monetary institutions.

- Describe the different types of monetary institutions.
- Explain how a chartered bank achieves its goal of maximizing its stockholders' long-term wealth.
- Explain the four economic functions of monetary institutions.

3 Describe the functions of the Bank of Canada.

- Describe the monetary policy goals of the Bank of Canada.
- Describe the Bank of Canada's policy tools and briefly summarize how each works.
- Define monetary base.

KEY TERMS

- Bank of Canada (page 255)
- Bank rate (page 257)
- Bankers' deposit rate (page 257)
- Barter (page 241)
- Caisse populaire (page 250)
- Central bank (page 255)
- Chartered bank (page 248)
- Credit union (page 250)
- Currency (page 242)
- Daily monetary policy target (page 255)
- Electronic cash (e-cash) (page 244)
- Electronic cheque (e-cheque) (page 244)
- Fiat money (page 242)
- Large Value Transfer System (page 256)
- Liquid asset (page 252)
- M1 (page 245)
- M2+ (page 245)
- Means of payment (page 240)
- Medium of exchange (page 241)
- Monetary base (page 258)
- Monetary policy (page 255)
- Monetary system (page 248)
- Money (page 240)
- Money market mutual fund (page 250)
- Open market operation (page 258)
- Overnight rate (page 249)
- Reserves (page 249)
- Store of value (page 241)
- Trust and mortgage loan company (page 251)
- Ultimate monetary policy objective (page 255)
- Unit of account (page 241)

CHECKPOINT 10.1

■ Define money and describe its functions.

Practice Problems 10.1

1. In Canada today, money includes which of the following items?
a. Your Visa card

b. The quarters inside public phones

c. The $20 bills in your wallet

d. The cheque that you have just written to pay for your rent

e. The loan you took out last August to pay for your school fees

2. In July 2001, currency held outside the banks was $36 billion; chequable deposits owned by individuals and businesses at chartered banks were $80 billion; personal savings deposits at banks were $345 billion; nonpersonal notice deposits at banks were $50 billion; and deposits at institutions other than banks were $223 billion.

a. What was M1 in July 2001?

b. What was M2+ in July 2001?

Solution to Practice Problems 10.1

In the first problem, remember that money is a means of payment. In the second problem remember the definitions of M1 and M2+.

Quick Review

- *M1* Currency outside the banks plus chequable deposits owned by individuals and businesses at chartered banks.

- *M2+* M1 plus personal savings deposits and nonpersonal notice deposits at banks plus deposits at credit unions, caisses populaires, and other depository institutions.

1. **In Canada today, money includes which of the following items?**

a. **Your Visa card**

Your Visa card is a credit card and a credit card is not money. It is an ID card that allows for an instant loan.

b. **The quarters inside public phones**

Coins in a public phone are currency outside the banks, so they are money.

c. **The $20 bills in your wallet**

Dollar bills in your wallet are currency outside the banks, so they are money.

d. **The cheque that you have just written to pay for your rent**

Cheques are not money. A cheque instructs the bank to transfer money from one person to another. In this case, the cheque is an instruction to transfer money from your account to the account of your landlord.

e. **The loan you took out last August to pay for your school fees**

A loan isn't money. When you received the loan you probably received a cheque, which you turned over to the school. But the cheque wasn't money. When the school cashed the cheque it received a deposit from the bank and that deposit was money.

2. **In July 2001, currency held outside the banks was $36 billion; chequable deposits owned by individuals and businesses at chartered banks were $80 billion; personal savings deposits at banks were $345 billion; nonpersonal notice deposits at banks were $50 billion; and deposits at institutions other than banks were $223 billion.**

a. **What was M1 in July 2001?**

M1 consists of currency held outside the banks plus chequable deposits owned by individuals and businesses at chartered banks. M1 in July 2001 equals $36 billion + $80 billion, which is $116 billion.

b. **What was M2+ in July 2001?**

M2+ consists of M1 plus personal savings deposits and nonpersonal notice deposits at chartered banks plus deposits at credit unions, caisses populaires, and other depository institutions. M2+ in July 2001 equals $116 billion + $345 billion + $50 billion + $223 billion, which is $734 billion.

Additional Practice Problem 10.1a

You go to the bank and withdraw $200 from your chequing account. You keep $100 in cash and deposit the other $100 in your savings account. What is the change in M1? What is the change in M2+?

Solution to Additional Practice Problem 10.1a

M1, which includes currency outside the banks and chequable deposits owned by individuals and businesses at chartered banks, changes by the $200 decrease in the chequing account and by the $100 increase in currency. So M1 decreases by $100. M2+, which includes currency outside the banks, chequable deposits, and personal savings deposits, does not change. Your chequing account decreases by $200, but your currency increases by $100 and your savings account increases by $100. These changes offset each other so there is no change to M2+.

■ **Self Test 10.1**

Fill in the blanks

Any commodity or token that is generally accepted as a means of payment is ____ (currency; money). A ____ (unit of account; store of value; medium of exchange) is an object that is generally accepted in return for goods and services. A ____ (unit of account; store of value; medium of exchange) is an agreed-upon measure for stating the prices of goods and services. A ____ (unit of account; store of value; medium of exchange) is any commodity or token that can be held and exchanged later for goods and services. Currency inside the banks ____ (is; is not) money and currency outside the banks ____ (is; is not) money. A credit card ____ (is; is not) money. M1 is ____ (more; less) than M2+. Chequable deposits ____ (are; are not) part of M1 and personal savings deposits ____ (are; are not) part of M1.

True or false

1. Using money as a medium of exchange is called barter.

2. Prices in terms of money reflect money's role as a unit of account.

3. Currency is money but chequable deposits at banks are not money.

4. A debit card is not money.

5. M1 and M2+ are money.

Multiple choice

1. Which of the following best defines what money is now and what it has been in the past?
   a. currency
   b. currency plus chequing deposits
   c. currency plus credit cards
   d. anything accepted as a means of payment

2. For something to be a "means of payment" means that it
   a. is valuable and backed by gold.
   b. is valuable and backed by a commodity.
   c. can be used to settle a debt.
   d. requires a double coincidence of wants.

3. Which of the following is not a function of money?
   a. unit of account
   b. store of value
   c. unit of debt
   d. medium of exchange

4. Barter is
   a. the exchange of goods and services for money.
   b. the pricing of goods and services with one agreed-upon standard.
   c. the exchange of goods and services directly for other goods and services.
   d. a generally accepted means of payment.

5. If someone buries money in a tin can beneath a tree, the money is functioning as a
   a. medium of exchange.
   b. unit of account.
   c. means of payment.
   d. store of value.

6. Credit cards, debit cards, and e-cheques are

a. always counted as money.

b. not money.

c. counted as M1.

d. counted as M2+.

7. Which of the following counts as part of M1?

a. $5,000 worth of gold

b. $5,000 worth of government bonds

c. $5,000 in a chequing account at a chartered bank

d. $5,000 credit line on a credit card

8. M2+ equals

a. M1 and is just another name for currency.

b. M1 plus personal savings deposits and non-personal notice deposits at banks plus deposits at credit unions, caisses populaires, and other depository institutions.

c. M1 plus chequable deposits at banks.

d. M1 plus currency outside the banks.

Short answer

1. Why was it possible at one time to use whales' teeth as money?

2. What are the functions of money?

3. Why is currency money?

4. Why are e-cheques not money?

5. Some parts of M2+ are not money. Why are these parts included in M2+?

CHECKPOINT 10.2

■ **Describe the monetary system and explain the functions of banks and other monetary institutions.**

Practice Problems 10.2

1. What are the institutions that make up Canada's monetary system?

2. What is a bank's "balancing act"?

3. A bank has the following deposits and assets: $320 in chequable deposits, $896 in savings deposits, $840 in term deposits, $990 in loans to businesses, $400 in outstanding credit card balances, $634 in government bonds and Treasury bills, $2 in currency, and $30 in its deposit account at the Bank of Canada. Calculate the bank's

a. Total deposits

b. Deposits that are part of M1

c. Deposits that are part of M2+

d. Loans

e. Securities

f. Reserves

Solution to Practice Problems 10.2

A bank accepts deposits and then uses the deposits to make loans. A bank maximizes its stockholders' long-term wealth by making loans at a higher interest rate than the interest rate it pays on deposits. But banks must keep enough funds as reserves to meet depositors' withdrawals. In Canada, the banks on the average keep reserves of less than 1 percent of total deposits.

Quick Review

• *Reserves* The currency in a bank's vaults plus its deposit at the Bank of Canada.

1. **What are the institutions that make up the monetary system?**

The monetary system consists of the Bank of Canada, chartered banks, credit unions and caisses populaires, and other depository institutions.

2. **What is a bank's "balancing act"?**

To maximize stockholders' long-term wealth, a bank makes loans at a higher interest rate than the interest rate it pays on deposits. The bank must hold enough reserves to meet depositors' withdrawals. The bank's "balancing act" is to balance the profit for its stockholders against security for its depositors.

3. **A bank has the following deposits and assets: $320 in chequable deposits, $896 in savings deposits, $840 in term deposits, $990 in loans to businesses, $400 in outstanding credit card balances, $634 in government bonds and Treasury bills, $2 in currency, and $30 in its deposit account at the Bank of Canada. Calculate the bank's**

a. **Total deposits**

Total deposits are the sum of chequable deposits, $320, savings deposits, $896, and term deposits, $840, which equals $2,056.

b. **Deposits that are part of M1**

The only deposits that are part of M1 are chequable deposits, which are $320.

c. **Deposits that are part of M2+**

All of the bank's deposits, which equal $2,056 are part of M2+.

d. **Loans**

Total loans include loans to businesses and credit card balances. Credit card balances are the amount lent to the cardholder to pay for purchases. Total loans are $990 + $400, which is $1,390.

e. **Securities**

Securities are the government bonds and Treasury bills, which equal $634.

f. **Reserves**

Reserves are the currency in the bank's vaults, $2, plus its deposit at the Bank of Canada, $30, which equals $32.

Additional Practice Problem 10.2a

The Acme Bank just sold $100 in securities in exchange for a $100 bill. It made a $50 loan, and the borrower left with the cash. It also accepted a $60 cash deposit. How have the bank's reserves changed as a result of all these actions? How have its deposits changed?

Solution to Additional Practice Problem 10.2a

The $100 sale of securities adds $100 to reserves. The $50 loan removes $50 from the bank and from its reserves, and the $60 deposit adds to reserves. Acme now has $110 more in reserves than before. The $60 deposit is the only transaction that affects deposits, so deposits rise by $60.

■ **Self Test 10.2**

Fill in the blanks

The currency in a bank's vaults is part of the bank's ____ (reserves; loans). The interest rate on overnight loans between banks and other large financial institutions is the _____ (monetary; overnight) rate. At chartered banks in Canada, the majority of deposits ____ (are; are not) chequable deposits. An asset that can easily, and with certainty, be converted into money is a ____ (current; liquid) asset. Banks ____ (lower; raise) the costs of lending and borrowing.

True or false

1. A chartered bank accepts chequable deposits, savings deposits, and term deposits.

2. A chartered bank achieves its goal by refusing to make any risky loans.

3. When a credit union makes loans to its members, the interest rate it charges is the overnight rate.

4. Credit unions and caisses populaires have most of Canada's bank deposits.

5. By lending to a large number of businesses and individuals, a bank lowers the average risk it faces.

Multiple choice

1. A chartered bank's goal is to

a. provide loans to its customers.

b. maximize the long-term wealth of its stockholders.

c. help the government when it needs money.

d. lend money to the Bank of Canada.

2. A chartered bank divides its assets into three parts:

a. cash assets, bonds, and loans.

b. reserves, securities, and bonds.

c. reserves, cash assets, and bonds.

d. securities, reserves, and debts.

3. A chartered bank's reserves are

a. bonds issued by the Canadian government that are very safe.

b. the provision of funds to businesses and individuals.

c. currency in its vaults plus its deposit at the Bank of Canada.

d. savings and term deposits.

4. A bank has $220 in chequable deposits, $796 in savings deposits, $740 in term deposits, $890 in loans to businesses, $300 in outstanding credit card balances, $534 in government bonds and Treasury bills, $3 in currency in its vaults, and $20 in its deposit account at the Bank of Canada. The bank's deposits that are part of M1 are equal to

a. $1,016.

b. $220.

c. $796.

d. $221.

5. All of the following institutions accept deposits from the public EXCEPT

a. caisses populaires.

b. credit unions.

c. the Bank of Canada.

d. chartered banks.

6. Banks on the average keep reserves of

a. less than 1 percent of total deposits.

b. 8 percent of cash assets.

c. 28 percent of total deposits.

d. 63 percent of total deposits.

7. Banks and other monetary institutions perform which of the following functions?

a. create liquidity

b. lower costs of borrowing

c. pool the risks of lending

d. All of the above answers are correct.

8. A liquid asset is

a. any deposit held at a chartered bank.

b. bank loans made to low-risk borrowers.

c. any asset than can be converted into money easily and with certainty.

d. any deposit held at the Bank of Canada.

Short answer

1. What are a bank's reserves? How does a bank use its reserve account at the Bank of Canada?

2. Which is a larger percentage of M2+: chartered bank deposits or credit union and caisses populaires deposits?

3. What economic functions are performed by the nation's monetary institutions?

4. What does it mean for banks to "pool risk"?

5. What is the overnight rate?

CHECKPOINT 10.3

■ **Describe the functions of the Bank of Canada.**

Practice Problems 10.3

1. What is the Bank of Canada?

2. What is monetary policy?

3. What is the ultimate monetary policy objective?

4. What is the daily monetary policy target?

5. What are the Bank of Canada's policy tools?

6. What is the monetary base?

7. Suppose that at the end of December 2006, the monetary base in Canada is $70 billion, Bank of Canada notes are $65 billion, and banks' reserves at the Bank of Canada are $2 billion. Calculate the quantity of coins.

Solution to Practice Problems 10.3

These Practice Problems study the Bank of Canada and the role it plays in the Canadian economy. Knowledge of the Bank of Canada and its policies will help you to understand a significant part of the ongoing debate about macroeconomic policy.

Quick Review

- *Bank of Canada* The Bank of Canada's is Canada's central bank.
- *Central bank* A public authority that provides banking services to banks and regulates financial institutions and markets.

1. What is the Bank of Canada?

The Bank of Canada is Canada's central bank. A central bank is a public authority that regulates financial institutions and markets and provides banking services to banks. A central bank does not provide banking services to businesses and individual citizens.

2. What is monetary policy?

Monetary policy is the adjustment of the quantity of money in the economy.

3. What is the ultimate monetary policy objective?

An ultimate monetary policy objective is a final goal of monetary policy. The Bank of Canada's ultimate monetary policy objective is to keep the inflation rate inside a target range of between 1 percent and 3 percent a year. By keeping the inflation rate steady and low, the Bank seeks to maintain full employment, moderate the business cycle, and contribute towards achieving faster and sustained economic growth.

4. What is the daily monetary policy target?

A daily monetary policy target is a target that the Bank of Canada sets and achieves each day in pursuit of its ultimate inflation target. The daily monetary policy target has changed over the years, and today it is the overnight rate. The overnight rate is the interest rate on overnight loans between banks and other large financial institutions.

5. What are the Bank of Canada's policy tools?

The Bank of Canada can use four policy tools to achieve its objectives: the bank rate and the bankers' deposit rate, open market operations, government deposit shifting, and required reserve ratios. Today, the Bank of Canada does not use required reserve ratios as a monetary policy tool. The required reserve ratio is zero.

6. What is the monetary base?

The monetary base is the sum of chartered banks' deposits at the Bank of Canada plus coins and Bank of Canada notes.

6. Suppose that at the end of December 2006, the monetary base in Canada is $70 billion, Bank of Canada notes are $65 billion, and banks' reserves at the Bank of Canada are $2 billion. Calculate the quantity of coins.

The monetary base is the sum of chartered banks' deposits at the Bank of Canada plus coins and Bank of Canada notes. So the quantity of coins equals the monetary base minus chartered banks' deposits at the Bank of Canada minus Bank of Canada notes. The quantity of coins is $70 billion – $65 billion – $2 billion, which is $3 billion.

Additional Practice Problem 10.3a

What is the relationship between open market operations and the overnight rate?

Solution to Additional Practice Problem 10.3a

An open market operation is the purchase or sale of government securities—government of Canada Treasury bills and bonds—in the open market by the Bank of Canada. These transactions by the Bank of Canada change the reserves of the banks. A change in reserves immediately impacts the amount of overnight borrowing and lending and enables the Bank to hit its overnight rate target.

■ Self Test 10.3

Fill in the blanks

The Bank of Canada is a _____ (central; chartered) bank. The Bank of Canada's ultimate monetary policy objective is to keep the inflation rate inside a target range of between _____ (1 and 3; 2 and 4; 3 and 5) percent a year. The _____ (bank; bankers' deposit) rate is the interest rate at which the Bank of Canada stands ready to lend reserves to chartered banks. An open market operation is the _____ (purchase; sale; purchase or sale) of government securities in the open market by the Bank of Canada. The _____ (monetary base; quantity of money) is the sum of chartered banks' deposits at the Bank of Canada plus coins and Bank of Canada notes.

True or false

1. The Bank of Ottawa is the central bank of Canada.

2. The Bank of Canada's ultimate monetary policy objective is to keep the unemployment rate between 1 percent and 3 percent.

3. An open market operation is the purchase or sale of government securities in the open market by the government of Canada.

4. If bank deposits fall by $10 million and banks use $1 million of reserves to buy $1 million worth of newly printed notes from the Bank of Canada, the monetary base does not change.

5. Bank of Canada notes are an asset of the Bank of Canada.

Multiple choice

1. The daily monetary policy target of the Bank of Canada is an interest rate called the

a. bank rate.

b. bankers' deposit rate.

c. treasury rate.

d. overnight rate.

2. The policy tools that the Bank of Canada can use include

a. open market operations.

b. government deposit shifting and required reserve ratios.

c. the bank rate and the bankers' deposit rate.

d. all of the above.

3. The required reserve ratio in Canada today is

a. zero.

b. 1 percent of total deposits.

c. 2 percent of total deposits.

d. 3 percent of total deposits.

4. The bankers' deposit rate is the interest rate that

a. chartered banks charge on loans.

b. the Bank of Canada pays banks on their deposits at the Bank of Canada.

c. the Bank of Canada pays the government on its deposits at the Bank of Canada.

d. the Bank of Canada charges chartered banks on loans.

5. The monetary base is the

a. minimum reserves banks must hold to cover any losses from unpaid loans.

b. sum of chartered banks' deposits at the Bank of Canada plus coins and Bank of Canada notes.

c. sum of gold and foreign exchange held by the Bank of Canada.

d. sum of government securities and loans held by the Bank of Canada.

Short answer

1. What is the Large Value Transfer System?

2. What is the Bank of Canada's ultimate monetary policy objective?

3. What is an open market operation?

SELF TEST ANSWERS

■ CHECKPOINT 10.1

Fill in the blanks

Any commodity or token that is generally accepted as a means of payment is <u>money</u>. A <u>medium of exchange</u> is an object that is generally accepted in return for goods and services. A <u>unit of account</u> is an agreed-upon measure for stating the prices of goods and services. A <u>store of value</u> is any commodity or token that can be held and exchanged later for goods and services. Currency inside the banks <u>is not</u> money and currency outside the banks <u>is</u> money. A credit card <u>is not</u> money. M1 is <u>less</u> than M2+. Chequable deposits <u>are</u> part of M1 and personal savings deposits <u>are not</u> part of M1.

True or false

1. False; page 241
2. True; page 241
3. False; page 242
4. True; page 244
5. False; page 245

Multiple choice

1. d; page 240
2. c; page 240
3. c; pages 240-241
4. c; page 241
5. d; page 241
6. b; pages 243-244
7. c; page 245
8. b; page 245

Short answer

1. It was possible to use whales' teeth as money because whales' teeth were generally accepted as a means of payment. At one time, most people were willing to trade goods and services in exchange for whales' teeth; page 240.

2. Money has three functions. It is a medium of exchange, an object that is generally accepted in return for goods and services. It is a unit of account, an agreed-upon measure for stating the prices of goods and services. And it is a store of value, a commodity or token that can be held and exchanged at a later date for goods and services; page 241.

3. Currency is money because it is generally accepted as a means of payment. It is generally accepted because the government has declared that currency is money; page 242.

4. E-cheques are not money because they are instructions to transfer money from one person's deposit account to another person's deposit account; page 244.

5. Some savings deposits in M2+ are just as much a means of payment as the chequable deposits in M1. You can use the ATM to transfer funds from your savings accounts to pay for your purchases. But other savings deposits such as term deposits, cannot be transferred in this manner, so they are not means of payment. These other savings deposits are included in M2+ because although they are not money, they are very easily converted into money; page 245.

■ CHECKPOINT 10.2

Fill in the blanks

The currency in a bank's vault is part of the bank's <u>reserves</u>. The interest rate on overnight loans between banks and other large financial institutions is the <u>overnight</u> rate. At chartered banks in Canada, the majority of deposits <u>are not</u> chequable deposits. An asset that can easily, and with certainty, be converted into money is a <u>liquid</u> asset. Banks <u>lower</u> the costs of lending and borrowing.

True or false

1. True; page 248

2. False; page 249

3. False; pages 249-250

4. False; page 251

5. True; page 252

Multiple choice

1. b; page 249

2. a; page 249

3. c; page 249

4. b; page 249

5. c; page 248

6. a; page 249

7. d; page 252

8. c; page 252

Short answer

1. A bank's reserves are the currency in its vaults plus its deposit at the Bank of Canada. Chartered banks use their reserve accounts at the Bank of Canada to make payments and receive payments and to obtain currency; page 249.

2. Chartered bank deposits are a larger percentage of M2+ than credit union and caisses populaires deposits. Personal savings deposits and nonpersonal notice deposits at chartered banks account for 53 percent of M2+. Deposits at credit unions and caisses populaires account for about 15 percent of M2+; page 251.

3. The nation's monetary institutions perform four economic functions: They create liquidity, they lower the costs of lending and borrowing, they pool risks, and they make payments; pages 252-253.

4. Making loans is risky because the borrower might not repay the loan. If a lender has loaned to only one borrower who does not repay the loan, the lender suffers a large loss.

Banks make loans to many different borrowers and pool or gather together the risk of the loans. Although some loans will not be repaid, the majority will be repaid and the average risk from failure to be repaid is lower; page 252.

■ **CHECKPOINT 10.3**

Fill in the blanks

The Bank of Canada is a <u>central</u> bank. The Bank of Canada's ultimate monetary policy objective is to keep the inflation rate inside a target range of between <u>1 and 3</u> percent a year. The <u>bank</u> rate is the interest rate at which the Bank of Canada stands ready to lend reserves to chartered banks. An open market operation is the <u>purchase or sale</u> of government securities in the open market by the Bank of Canada. The <u>monetary base</u> is the sum of chartered banks' deposits at the Bank of Canada plus coins and Bank of Canada notes.

True or false

1. False; page 255

2. False; page 255

3. False; page 258

4. True; page 258

5. False; page 258

Multiple choice

1. d; page 255

2. d; page 257

3. a; page 258

4. b; page 257

5. b; page 258

Short answer

1. The Large Value Transfer System is Canada's national electronic payments system for very large transactions between the chartered banks, the Bank of Canada, and a few other big financial institutions; page 256.

2. An ultimate monetary policy objective is a final goal of monetary policy. The Bank of Canada's ultimate monetary policy objective is to keep the inflation rate inside a target range of between 1 percent and 3 percent a year; page 255

3. An open market operation is the purchase or sale of government securities—Government of Canada Treasury bills and bonds—in the open market by the Bank of Canada; page 258.

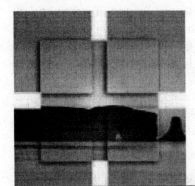

Money Creation and Control

Chapter 11

CHAPTER IN PERSPECTIVE

Chapter 11 explains how banks create money by studying the link between the banks' reserves, the quantity of loans that banks make, and the quantity of deposits they create. Chapter 11 also explains how the Bank of Canada uses open market operations to influence the quantity of money.

■ **Explain how banks create money by making loans.**

Banks accept deposits, hold some deposits as reserves, buy government securities and make loans. Deposits are a liability of the bank; reserves, government securities, and loans are assets of the bank. The desired reserve ratio is the ratio of reserves to deposits that banks wish to hold so that they are sure to have enough cash to cover withdrawals by their customers. Excess reserves are actual reserves minus desired reserves. Banks use excess reserves to buy government securities and make loans. When a bank makes loans, it places the amount loaned in the chequable deposit accounts of the borrowers. The bank has now created some money. To spend their loans, the borrowers write cheques on their chequable deposits. If the people who receive the cheques deposit them at a different bank, this bank's reserves and deposits increase. Now the banks that received the deposits have excess reserves, so they can make some loans. And these loans will create some more money. This process continues until there are no excess reserves in the banking system. The deposit multiplier is the number by which an increase in bank reserves is multiplied to find the resulting increase in bank deposits. The deposit multiplier equals (1 ÷ desired reserve ratio).

■ **Explain how the Bank of Canada influences the quantity of money.**

The Bank of Canada uses three monetary policy tools to influence the quantity of money in the economy: changes in the bank rate and the bankers' deposit rate, government deposit shifting, and open market operations. An increase in the bank rate and the overnight rate makes the banks pay a higher price for borrowed reserves, makes them less wiling to borrow reserves, and decreases the quantity of money. If the Bank of Canada shifts government funds from itself to the banks, the banks' reserves and ability to make loans increase. When the Bank of Canada makes an open market purchase, banks' reserves increase and excess reserves increase. Banks lend the excess reserves, new deposits are created, and the quantity of money increases. The monetary base changes by the amount of the open market purchase. A currency drain is an increase in currency held outside the banks. The money multiplier is the number by which a change in the monetary base is multiplied to find the resulting change in the quantity of money. The larger the currency drain and the larger the desired reserve ratio, the smaller is the money multiplier.

EXPANDED CHAPTER CHECKLIST

When you have completed this chapter, you will be able to

1 Explain how banks create money by making loans.

- Describe the assets and liabilities that appear on a bank's balance sheet.

- Calculate a bank's excess reserves.

- Explain how loans made by the banking system create money.

- Define and calculate the deposit multiplier and use it to compute the change in deposits that results from a change in reserves.

2 Explain how the Bank of Canada influences the quantity of money.

- Explain how the Bank of Canada can influence the quantity of money by changes in the bank rate and the bankers' deposit rate.

- Explain how the Bank of Canada can influence the quantity of money by government deposit shifting.

- Describe the multiplier effect of an open market operation.

- Define currency drain and money multiplier.

- Calculate the money multiplier and explain the effects of the currency drain and the desired reserve ratio on the money multiplier.

KEY TERMS

- Balance sheet (page 266)

- Currency drain (page 280)

- Deposit multiplier (page 274)

- Desired reserve ratio (page 268)

- Excess reserves (page 269)

- Money multiplier (page 282)

- Reserve ratio (page 268)

CHECKPOINT 11.1

■ **Explain how banks create money by making loans.**

Practice Problems 11.1

1. How do banks create new deposits by making loans, and what factors limit the amount of deposits and loans they can create?

2. The desired reserve ratio is 0.1, and banks have no excess reserves. Jamie deposits $100 in his bank. Calculate:

a. The bank's excess reserves as soon as Jamie makes the deposit.

b. The deposit multiplier.

c. The maximum increase in deposits.

Solution to Practice Problems 11.1

These Practice Problems concentrate on the role that banks play in creating money.

Quick Review

- *Excess reserves* Actual reserves minus desired reserves.

- *Deposit multiplier* The number by which an increase in bank reserves is multiplied to find the resulting increase in bank deposits. The deposit multiplier equals 1 ÷ (desired reserve ratio) and is greater than 1.

1. **How do banks create new deposits by making loans, and what factors limit the amount of deposits and loans they can create?**

Banks can make loans when they have excess reserves—actual reserves in excess of desired reserves. So when a bank makes a loan, it uses its excess reserves. The bank creates a new deposit for the person who receives the loan. The amount of loans the bank makes, and the amount of deposits the bank makes, is limited by the bank's excess reserves and by the desired reserve ratio.

2. **The desired reserve ratio is 0.1 and banks have no excess reserves. Jamie deposits $100 in his bank. Calculate:**

a. **The bank's excess reserves as soon as Jamie makes the deposit.**

The new deposit of $100 increases the bank's actual reserves by $100. The bank desires to keep 10 percent of deposits as reserves. So desired reserves are $10 and excess reserves, which are actual reserves minus desired reserves, equal $100 − $10, which is $90.

b. **The deposit multiplier.**

The deposit multiplier equals (1 ÷ desired reserve ratio). The deposit multiplier is (1 ÷ 0.10), which is 10.

c. **The maximum increase in deposits.**

The deposit multiplier is the number by which an increase in bank reserves is multiplied to find the resulting increase in bank deposits. When reserves increase by $100 and the deposit multiplier is 10, the increase in deposits is 10 x $100, which is $1,000.

Additional Practice Problem 11.1a

In Practice Problem 2, how much can Jamie's bank loan in the first round of the process? What was the amount of new money created by Jamie's bank in the first round?

Solution to Additional Practice Problem 11.1a

Jamie's bank can loan the amount of its excess reserves. When Jamie deposits $100, her bank has $90 of excess reserves. So Jamie's bank can loan $90. In making this loan, Jamie's bank creates a deposit, which is new money equal to $90.

■ **Self Test 11.1**

Fill in the blanks

Assets on a bank's balance sheet include ____ (cash; chequable deposits) and ____ (loans; owner's equity). A liability on a bank's balance sheet is ____ (reserves; chequable deposits). Banks ____ (create; do not create) money when they make loans. A bank ____ (can; cannot) create unlimited amounts of money. The deposit multiplier is the number by which an increase in bank _____ (deposits; reserves) is multiplied to find the resulting increase in bank _____ (deposits; reserves).

True or false

1. The first step in creating a bank is to accept deposits.

2. Chequable deposits are an asset on a bank's balance sheet.

3. A chartered bank's cash and its reserves at the Bank of Canada are assets on its balance sheet.

4. Excess reserves increase when the desired reserve ratio increases, all other things remaining the same.

5. When banks clear cheques, they create money.

6. When a bank increases its loans, it creates money.

7. The deposit multiplier equals the desired reserve ratio.

8. Sandy, an immigrant, comes to Canada and deposits $190,000 into a bank. The desired reserve ratio is 5 percent. If banks loan all of their excess reserves, Sandy's deposit leads to a total increase in deposits of $3.8 million.

Multiple choice

1. Which of the following is not an action of a chartered bank?

a. buying government securities
b. clearing cheques
c. making loans
d. printing money

2. A bank's balance sheet is a statement that summarizes

a. only the bank's loans.
b. only the bank's reserves.
c. the bank's assets and liabilities.
d. the number of banks in a community.

3. Cash in a bank is part of the bank's

a. owner's equity.
b. liabilities.
c. assets.
d. government securities.

4. Which of the following is a bank liability?

a. chequable deposits
b. government securities
c. equipment
d. loans

5. If the desired reserve ratio is 20 percent, then for every dollar that is deposited in the bank, the bank

a. keeps 20 cents as reserves.
b. keeps 80 cents as reserves.
c. loans 80 cents.
d. loans 20 cents.

6. A bank has chequable deposits of $500,000, loans of $300,000, and government securities of $200,000. If the desired reserve ratio is 10 percent, the amount of desired reserves is

a. $20,000.
b. $30,000.
c. $50,000.
d. $500,000.

7. Excess reserves are the

a. same as the desired reserves.
b. amount of reserves the Bank of Canada desires banks to hold.
c. amount of reserves held above what is desired.
d. amount of reserves a bank holds at the Bank of Canada.

8. Scott writes a $500 cheque to Larry drawn on the Bank of Montreal. Larry deposits the $500 cheque in his chequing account at the Royal Bank. When the cheque clears both banks, the _____ by $500.

a. Bank of Montreal's assets decrease
b. Bank of Montreal's assets increase
c. Bank of Montreal's liabilities increase
d. Royal Bank's assets decrease

9. Banks can make loans up to an amount equal to their

a. total deposits.
b. total reserves.
c. desired reserves.
d. excess reserves.

10. The banking system can create more money than an initial increase in excess reserves because

a. banks are sneaky.
b. the Bank of Canada lends money to the chartered banks.
c. excess reserves are loaned and then deposited in other banks.
d. banks charge more interest than they pay out.

11. The deposit multiplier equals

a. 1 ÷ (desired reserves).
b. 1 ÷ (desired reserve ratio).
c. the desired reserve ratio.
d. 1 ÷ (excess reserve ratio).

12. If the desired reserve ratio is 15 percent and banks loan all of their excess reserves, a new deposit of $20,000 leads to a total increase in deposits of

a. $3,000.

b. $20,000.

c. $133,333.

d. $200,000.

Short answer

1. The First Bank of Townsville has reserves at the Bank of Canada of $100, owner's equity of $200, loans of $800, chequable deposits of $1,000, cash of $200, and government securities of $100. Arrange these entries in the balance sheet below.

Assets	Liabilities

2. The Bank of Saskatchewan has deposits of $500 million and reserves of $60 million. If the desired reserve ratio is 10 percent, calculate the bank's excess reserves. How much can the bank loan? If the desired reserve ratio is 8 percent, calculate the bank's excess reserves. Now how much can the bank loan?

3. How does making a loan create a deposit?

4. Meg tutors 10 students during the final week of term and is paid $500 in cash. She deposits the $500 in her bank. The desired reserve ratio is 10 percent and banks always loan the maximum possible.

a. Starting with Meg's $500 deposit, complete the following table.

Round	Increase in deposits (dollars)	Increase in reserves (dollars)	Increase in excess reserves (dollars)	Loan (dollars)
1	____	____	____	____
2	____	____	____	____
3	____	____	____	____
4	____	____	____	____

b. After the first four rounds, what is the total increase in deposits?

c. What will be the total increase in deposits?

5. If the desired reserve ratio is 10 percent, what is the deposit multiplier? If the desired reserve ratio is 5 percent, what is the deposit multiplier? What is the relationship between the desired reserve ratio and the deposit multiplier?

CHECKPOINT 11.2

■ **Explain how the Bank of Canada influences the quantity of money.**

Practice Problems 11.2

1. What are the Bank of Canada's policy tools?

2. What is the money multiplier? What determines its magnitude?

3. If the Bank of Canada makes an open market purchase of $1 million:

a. Who can sell the securities to the Bank of Canada in an open market operation? Does it matter from whom the Bank of Canada buys the securities?

b. What initial changes occur in the economy if the Bank of Canada buys from a bank?

c. What is the process by which the quantity of money changes?

d. What determines how much the quantity of money changes?

Solution to Practice Problems 11.2

These Practice Problems are designed to help you understand how the Bank of Canada operates to influence the quantity of money in Canada.

Quick Review

- *Open market operation* The purchase of government securities by the Bank of Canada from a chartered bank or the non-bank public or the sale of government securities by the Bank of Canada to a chartered bank or the non-bank public.

- *Money multiplier* The number by which a change in the monetary base is multiplied to find the resulting change in the quantity of money.

1. What are the Bank of Canada's policy tools?

The Bank of Canada's policy tools are government deposit shifting, changes in the bank rate and the bankers' deposit rate, and open market operations.

2. What is the money multiplier? What determines its magnitude?

The money multiplier is the number by which a change in the monetary base is multiplied to find the resulting change in the quantity of money. The two factors that determine the magnitude of the money multiplier are the desired reserve ratio and the currency drain. If the desired reserve ratio or currency drain increase, the money multiplier will be smaller.

3. If the Bank of Canada makes an open market purchase of $1 million:

a. Who can sell the securities to the Bank of Canada in an open market operation? Does it matter from whom the Bank of Canada buys the securities?

The Bank of Canada buys government securities from banks and the public. The Bank of Canada does not buy securities from the Canadian government. It does not matter whether the Bank of Canada buys the securities from banks or the public. If it buys from a bank, the bank's reserves increase by the amount of the purchase when the Bank of Canada pays for the securities. If the Bank of Canada buys from the public, the Bank of Canada pays by cheque and the bank's reserves increase by the amount of the purchase as soon as the cheque is deposited. The change in the monetary base is the same.

b. What initial changes occur in the economy if the Bank of Canada buys from a bank?

When the Bank of Canada buys securities from a bank, the monetary base increases by $1 million. Ownership of the securities passes from the bank to the Bank of Canada and the Bank of Canada's assets increase by $1 million. The Bank of Canada pays for the securities by increasing the bank's deposit with the Bank of Canada by $1 million. So the Bank of Canada's liabilities increase by $1 million. The composition of the bank's assets changes, but the value of the bank's total assets does not change. The bank now has $1 million more in reserves and $1 million less in securities.

c. What is the process by which the quantity of money changes?

The bank's reserves have increased by $1 million and its deposits have not changed. The bank has $1 million in excess reserves. It will loan these excess reserves and create new deposits, which are new money. The borrower writes a cheque, which is deposited in another bank. This bank now has excess reserves, which it can loan. This loan creates another new deposit, which is new money. The process of depositing, loaning, and creating new deposits continues and the quantity of money increases.

d. What determines how much the quantity of money changes?

Anything that affects the size of the money multiplier affects the change in the quantity of money that will result from this open market operation. The two factors that affect the size of the money multiplier are the desired reserve ratio and the currency drain. If the desired reserve ratio increases or if the currency drain increases, the money multiplier decreases in magnitude and there is a smaller change in the quantity of money from an open market operation.

Additional Practice Problem 11.2a

If the Bank of Canada makes an open market sale of $1 million of government securities to CIBC, what initial changes occur on the Bank of Canada's balance sheet and on CIBC's balance sheet? Be sure to tell if each change affects an asset or a liability.

Solution to Additional Practice Problem 11.2a

When the Bank of Canada sells $1 million of government securities, the Bank of Canada's holding of government securities decreases by $1 million. The Bank of Canada decreases CIBC's reserves at the Bank of Canada by $1 million. One of the Bank of Canada's assets, government securities, and one of its liabilities, reserves, decrease by $1 million. For CIBC, its holdings of government securities increase by $1 million and its reserves at the Bank of Canada decrease by $1 million. For CIBC, one of its assets, government securities, increases by $1 million, and another of its assets, reserves at the Bank of Canada, decreases by $1 million.

■ Self Test 11.2

Fill in the blanks

If the Bank of Canada shifts government funds from itself to the banks, the banks' ability to make loans _____ (decreases; increases). If the Bank of Canada raises the bank rate and the bankers' deposit rate, the banks _____ (decrease; increase) their reserves. When the Bank of Canada purchases government securities, it _____ (decreases; increases) the quantity of money. An open market sale of government securities by the Bank of Canada _____ (decreases; increases) the monetary base and _____ (decreases; increases) banks' excess reserves. An increase in currency held outside the banks is called _____ (an excess currency removal; a currency drain; multiplier reserve). If the money multiplier is 2.0, a $4 million increase in the monetary base will create an increase of _____ ($2; $8) million in the quantity of money.

True or false

1. If the Bank of Canada shifts government funds from the banks to itself, the banks' reserves and ability to make loans increase.

2. When the Bank of Canada lowers the bank rate and the bankers' deposit rate, the banks decrease their reserves and increase loans.

3. The overnight rate is greater than the bank rate and greater than the bankers' deposit rate.

4. When the Bank of Canada sells government securities, it decreases the quantity of banks' reserves.

5. The effect on the quantity of money when the Bank of Canada buys government securities depends on whether the Bank of Canada buys the securities from a bank or the non-bank public.

6. When the Bank of Canada buys government securities from a bank, the bank has fewer securities and more reserves.

7. The larger the currency drain, the larger the money multiplier.

8. If the currency drain is 0.25 and the desired reserve ratio is 0.1, the money multiplier is 0.675.

Multiple choice

1. The Bank of Canada's policy tools are

a. the excess reserve ratio, the desired reserve ratio, and the bank rate.

b. government deposit shifting, changes in the bank rate and the bankers' deposit rate, and open market operations.

c. open market operations, excess reserves, and desired reserves.

d. open market operations, closed market operations, and desired reserves.

2. If the Bank of Canada shifts government funds from itself to the banks, the banks' reserves _____ and the banks ability to make loans _____.

a. increase; increase
b. increase; decrease
c. decrease; increase
d. decrease; decrease

3. The bankers' deposit rate is set at _____ the bank rate

a. one-half of a percentage point below
b. one-half of a percentage point above
c. one percentage point above
d. one percentage point below

4. When the Bank of Canada buys or sells securities, it is conducting _____ operation.

a. a closed door
b. an open market
c. a multiplier
d. a deposit

5. If the Bank of Canada buys securities from a chartered bank, the effect on the quantity of money

a. is larger than when the Bank of Canada buys securities from the non-bank public.
b. is less than when the Bank of Canada buys securities from the non-bank public.
c. is the same as when the Bank of Canada buys securities from the non-bank public.
d. depends on whether the bank was borrowing reserves from another bank.

6. If the Bank of Canada buys government securities, then

a. the quantity of money is not changed, just its composition.
b. new bank reserves are created.
c. the quantity of money decreases.
d. old bank reserves are destroyed.

7. The Bank of Montreal sells $100,000 of government securities to the Bank of Canada. This sale will lead to

a. a decrease in the quantity of money.
b. a decrease in the bank's deposits.
c. an increase in the desired reserve ratio.
d. an increase in the quantity of money.

8. The Bank of Canada sells $10 million of government of Canada securities to the Royal Bank. The Royal Bank's balance sheet shows this transaction as a $10 million _____ in government securities and a $10 million _____ in reserves.

a. increase; increase
b. increase; decrease
c. decrease; increase
d. decrease; decrease

9. A currency drain is

a. cash lost in the drain.
b. cash draining into the banks.
c. an increase in currency held outside the banks.
d. cash held at the Bank of Canada.

10. If the currency drain increases,

a. the monetary base increases.
b. the money multiplier decreases.
c. the quantity of money increases.
d. banks' reserves increase.

11. The money multiplier is used to determine how much the

a. monetary base increases when the Bank of Canada purchases government securities.
b. quantity of money increases when the monetary base increases.
c. monetary base increases when the quantity of money increases.
d. quantity of money increases when the desired reserve ratio increases.

12. The Bank of Canada makes an open market purchase of $200,000 of government securities. The currency drain is 0.33 and the desired reserve ratio is 0.10. By how much does the quantity of money increase?

a. $250,000

b. $333,333

c. $2,000,000

d. $500,000

Short answer

1. Name the three monetary policy tools used by the Bank of Canada and describe how each works.

2. The Bank of Canada buys $1,000 of government securities from CIBC. The desired reserve ratio is 0.10 and the currency drain is 0.20. All banks loan all of their excess reserves. Complete the following table. Calculate the total increase in deposits, currency, and the quantity of money following the first four rounds of the multiplier process.

Round	Increase in reserves (dollars)	Increase in excess reserves (dollars)	Increase in currency (dollars)	Increase in deposits (dollars)
1	1,000	1,000	___	___
2	___	___	___	___
3	___	___	___	___
4	___	___	___	___

3. The Bank of Canada buys $1,000 of government securities from the Bank of Montreal. The desired reserve ratio is 0.10 and the currency drain is 0.50. All banks loan all of their excess reserves. Complete the following table. Calculate the total increase in deposits, currency, and the quantity of money following the first four rounds of the multiplier process.

Round	Increase in reserves (dollars)	Increase in excess reserves (dollars)	Increase in currency (dollars)	Increase in deposits (dollars)
1	1,000	1,000	___	___
2	___	___	___	___
3	___	___	___	___
4	___	___	___	___

4. In which question, 2 or 3, was the increase in the quantity of money largest after four rounds?

5. Calculate the money multiplier when the desired reserve ratio is 0.10 and the currency drain is 0.25. Calculate the money multiplier when the desired reserve ratio is 0.10 and the currency drain is 0.60. As the currency drain increases, what happens to the magnitude of the money multiplier?

6. Why does an increase in the desired reserve ratio or in the currency drain decrease the magnitude of the money multiplier?

SELF TEST ANSWERS

■ CHECKPOINT 11.1

Fill in the blanks

Assets on a bank's balance sheet include <u>cash</u> and <u>loans</u>. A liability on a bank's balance sheet is <u>chequable deposits</u>. Banks <u>create</u> money when they make loans. A bank <u>cannot</u> create unlimited amounts of money. The deposit multiplier is the number by which an increase in bank <u>reserves</u> is multiplied to find the resulting increase in bank <u>deposits</u>.

True or false

1. False; page 266

2. False; page 268

3. True; page 268

4. False; pages 268- 269

5. False; pages 269-270

6. True; pages 271-272

7. False; page 274

8. True; page 274

Multiple choice

1. d; page 266

2. c; page 266

3. c; page 266

4. a; page 268

5. a; page 268

6. c; page 268

7. c; page 269

8. a; page 269

9. d; page 271

10. c; page 272

11. b; page 274

12. c; page 274

Short answer

1. The completed balance sheet is below; page 271.

Assets		Liabilities	
Cash	$200		
Reserves at the Bank of Canada	$100	Chequable deposits	$1,000
Loans	$800	Owner's equity	$200
Government securities	$100		
Total assets	$1,200	Total liabilities	$1,200

2. The Bank of Saskatchewan's desired reserves are (0.10) × ($500 million), which is $50 million. The bank has excess reserves of $60 million – $50 million, which is $10 million. It can loan the amount of its excess reserves, $10 million.

   If the desired reserve ratio is 8 percent, the bank's desired reserves are $40 million and the bank has $60 million – $40 million, which is $20 million of excess reserves. It can loan the amount of its excess reserves, $20 million.

   When the desired reserve ratio decreases, the amount the bank can loan increases; pages 268-269.

3. When a bank makes a loan, the bank deposits the amount of the loan in the borrowers' chequable deposit account. When a loan is made, an equal sized deposit is created; page 271.

4. a. The completed table is below; page 273.

Round	Increase in deposits (dollars)	Increase in reserves (dollars)	Increase in excess reserves (dollars)	Loan (dollars)
A	500.00	500.00	450.00	450.00
B	450.00	450.00	405.00	405.00
C	405.00	405.00	364.50	364.50
D	364.50	364.50	328.05	328.05

   b. The total increase in deposits after the first four rounds is $1,719.50.

c. The deposit multiplier equals (1 ÷ desired reserve ratio) so the deposit multiplier is (1 ÷ 0.10), which equals 10. The total increase in deposits equals the deposit multiplier, 10, multiplied by the increase in reserves, $500. So the total increase in deposits is $5,000; page 274.

5. The deposit multiplier equals 1 ÷ (desired reserve ratio). When the desired reserve ratio is 10 percent, the deposit multiplier is 1 ÷ 0.10, which is 10. When the desired reserve ratio is 5 percent, the deposit multiplier is 1 ÷ 0.05, which is 20. When the desired reserve ratio is smaller, the deposit multiplier is larger; page 274.

■ **CHECKPOINT 11.2**

Fill in the blanks

If the Bank of Canada shifts government funds from itself to the banks, the banks' ability to make loans increases. If the Bank of Canada raises the bank rate and the bankers' deposit rate, the banks increase their reserves. When the Bank of Canada purchases government securities, it increases the quantity of money. An open market sale of government securities by the Bank of Canada decreases the monetary base and decreases banks' excess reserves. An increase in currency held outside the banks is called a currency drain. If the money multiplier is 2.0, a $4 million increase in the monetary base will create an increase of $8 million in the quantity of money.

True or false

1. False; page 276
2. True; page 276
3. False; page 276
4. True; page 276
5. False; page 277
6. True; page 277
7. False; pages 282-283
8. False; pages 282-283

Multiple choice

1. b; page 276
2. a; page 276
3. a; page 276
4. b; page 276
5. c; pages 277-279
6. b; page 277
7. d; page 277
8. b; page 279
9. c; page 280
10. b; page 280
11. b; pages 282-283
12. d; pages 282-283

Short answer

1. The Bank of Canada uses three monetary policy tools, which are government deposit shifting, changes in the bank rate and the bankers' deposit rate, and open market operations.

   If the Bank of Canada shifts government funds from itself to the banks, the banks' reserves and ability to make loans increase. If the Bank of Canada shifts government funds from the banks to itself, the banks' reserves and ability to make loans decrease.

   If the Bank of Canada raises the bank rate and the bankers' deposit rate, the banks increase their reserves and decrease loans. And if the Bank of Canada lowers these interest rates, the banks decrease their reserves and increase loans.

   An open market purchase of government securities by the Bank of Canada increases banks' excess reserves and increases the quantity of money. An open market sale of government securities by the Bank of Canada decreases banks' excess reserves and decreases the quantity of money; page 276.

2. The completed table is below.

Round	Increase in reserves (dollars)	Increase in excess reserves (dollars)	Increase in currency (dollars)	Increase in deposits (dollars)
1	1,000.00	1,000.00	200.00	800.00
2	800.00	720.00	144.00	576.00
3	576.00	518.40	103.68	414.72
4	414.72	373.25	74.65	298.60

After four rounds, currency increases by $522.33, deposits increase by $2,089.32, and the quantity of money increases by the sum of the increase in currency and the increase in deposits, which is $2,611.65; page 281.

3. The completed table is below.

Round	Increase in reserves (dollars)	Increase in excess reserves (dollars)	Increase in currency (dollars)	Increase in deposits (dollars)
1	1,000.00	1,000.00	500.00	500.00
2	500.00	450.00	225.00	225.00
3	225.00	202.50	101.25	101.25
4	101.25	91.13	45.57	45.57

After four rounds, currency increases by $871.82, deposits increase by $871.82, and the quantity of money increases by the sum of the increase in currency and the increase in deposits, which is $1,743.64; page 281.

4. The increase in the quantity of money is greater when the currency drain is smaller, in question 2; page 283.

5. To answer this question, use two formulas. First use $L = (1 - C) \times (1 - R)$ where C is the currency drain and R is the desired reserve ratio. Then calculate the money multiplier, which equals $1 \div (1 - L)$.

When $R = 0.10$ and $C = 0.25$, $L = 0.675$, and the money multiplier equals 3.08.

When $R = 0.10$ and $C = 0.60$, $L = 0.360$, and the money multiplier equals 1.56.

As the currency drain increases, the magnitude of the money multiplier decreases; pages 282-283.

6. The money multiplier exists because of the process of loaning, depositing the proceeds in another bank, and then making another loan. The more each bank loans, the greater the final increase in the quantity of money and the larger the money multiplier. If the desired reserve ratio increases, banks will be able to loan less of any additional deposit they receive. And if the currency drain increases, less is deposited in a bank and the bank will be able to loan less. Because an increase in the desired reserve ratio and an increase in the currency drain decrease the amount that can be loaned, both decrease the size of the money multiplier; page 282.

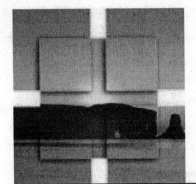

Money, Interest, and Inflation

Chapter 12

Chapter 12 discusses how the quantity of money determines the nominal interest rate. It also studies the relationships between the quantity of money and the price level, and money growth and inflation.

■ **Explain what determines the demand for money and how the demand for money and the supply of money determine the nominal interest rate.**

The amount of money that households and firms choose to hold is the quantity of money demanded. The nominal interest rate is the opportunity cost of holding money. The demand for money curve shows the relationship between quantity of money demanded and the nominal interest rate, when all other influences on the amount of money that people wish to hold remain the same. A change in the price level, real GDP or financial technology shifts the demand for money curve. The supply of money is a fixed quantity on any given day. Equilibrium in the money market determines the nominal interest rate. When the Bank of Canada increases the quantity of money, the nominal interest rate falls and when the Bank of Canada decreases the quantity of money, the nominal interest rate rises.

■ **Explain how in the long run, the quantity of money determines the price level and money growth brings inflation.**

An increase in the quantity of money lowers the nominal interest rate in the short run. In the long run, an increase in the quantity of money brings an equal percentage increase in the price level and the nominal interest rate returns to its initial value. The quantity theory of money is the proposition that when real GDP equals potential GDP, an increase in the quantity of money brings an equal percentage increase in the price level. The equation of exchange states that the quantity of money multiplied by the velocity of circulation equals the price level multiplied by real GDP. In rates of change or growth rates, money growth plus velocity growth equals the inflation rate plus real GDP growth.

■ **Identify the costs of inflation and the benefits of a stable value of money.**

The four costs of inflation are tax costs, shoe-leather costs, confusion costs, and uncertainty costs. Inflation is a tax. The inflation tax interacts with the income tax to lower saving and investment. Shoe-leather costs are costs that arise from an increase in the velocity of circulation of money and an increase in the amount of running around that people do to try to avoid incurring losses from the falling value of money. Confusion costs are costs of making errors because of rapidly changing prices. Uncertainty costs arise because long-term planning is difficult, people have a shorter-term focus, investment falls, and the growth rate of real GDP slows.

EXPANDED CHAPTER CHECKLIST

When you have completed this chapter, you will be able to

1 Explain what determines the demand for money and how the demand for money and the supply of money determine the nominal interest rate.

- Discuss the factors that influence the demand for money.

- Explain the relationship between the nominal interest rate, the real interest rate, and the expected inflation rate.

- Draw a figure to illustrate the money market and indicate the money market equilibrium.

- Explain how the nominal interest rate changes when the Bank of Canada changes the quantity of money.

2 Explain how in the long run, the quantity of money determines the price level and money growth brings inflation.

- Describe the money market in the long run.

- Explain the relationship between a change in the quantity of money and the nominal interest rate in the short run and in the long run.

- Explain the quantity theory of money and the equation of exchange.

3 Identify the costs of inflation and the benefits of a stable value of money.

- List and discuss the four costs of inflation.

- Discuss the relationship between the rate and predictability of inflation and its cost.

KEY TERMS

- Demand for money (page 292)
- Equation of exchange (page 303)
- Hyperinflation (page 307)
- Quantity of money demanded (page 291)
- Quantity theory of money (page 303)
- Supply of money (page 296)
- Velocity of circulation (page 303)

CHECKPOINT 12.1

■ Explain what determines the demand for money and how the demand for money and the supply of money determine the nominal interest rate.

Practice Problems 12.1

1. The figure shows the demand for money curve.

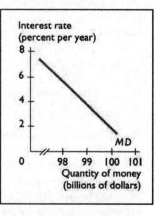

a. If the quantity of money is $99 billion, what is the nominal interest rate?

b. If real GDP increases, how will the interest rate change? Explain the process that brings about the change in the interest rate.

c. In part (a), the Bank of Canada decreases the quantity of money to $98 billion. Will bond prices rise or fall? Why? What happens to the nominal interest rate?

2. Suppose that banks increase the fee they charge for credit cards, introduce a user fee on every credit card purchase, and increase the interest rate on outstanding credit card balances.

a. How would the demand for money change?

b. How would the nominal interest rate change?

Solution to Practice Problems 12.1

These problems show how the nominal interest rate is determined in the money market.

Quick Review

*   *Shifts in the demand for money curve* When real GDP, the price level, and financial technology change, the demand for money curve shifts.

1a. If the quantity of money is $99 billion, what is the nominal interest rate?

The nominal interest rate is 4 percent a year at the intersection of the demand for money curve and the supply of money curve. The figure shows the nominal interest rate at the intersection of MD and MS.

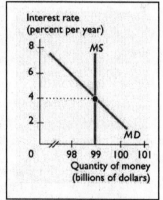

1b. If real GDP increases, how will the interest rate change? Explain the process that brings about the change in the interest rate.

When real GDP increases, the demand for money increases. In the figure, the demand for money curve shifts rightward from MD_0 to MD_1. At an interest rate of 4 percent a year, people want to hold more money. They sell bonds. The price of a bond falls and the interest rate rises.

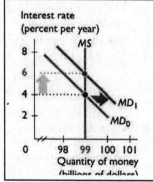

1c. In part (a), the Bank of Canada decreases the quantity of money to $98 billion. Will bond prices rise or fall? Why? What happens to the nominal interest rate?

At an interest rate of 4 percent a year, people want to hold $99 billion. Only $98 billion is available, so they sell bonds. The price of a bond falls and the interest rate rises. The figure shows that the supply of money curve shifts leftward from MS_0 to MS_1 and the interest rate rises to 6 percent a year.

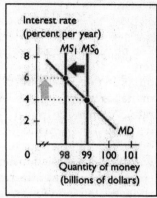

2. Suppose that banks increase the fee they charge for credit cards, introduce a user fee on every credit card purchase, and increase the interest rate on outstanding credit card balances.

a. How would the demand for money change?

People will use their credit cards less. The demand for money increases as people use money for more transactions.

b. How would the nominal interest rate change?

An increase in the demand for money raises the nominal interest rate.

Additional Practice Problem 12.1a

Tomorrow all stores will install retinal scanner identification machines, which make it easier for people to make purchases on credit. What effect will this have on the demand for money and on the nominal interest rate?

Solution to Additional Practice Problem 12.1a

This change in technology increases credit purchases and decreases the number of purchases made with money. The demand for money decreases. People want to hold less money than they are actually holding. They buy bonds. The price of a bond rises and the interest rate falls.

■ Self Test 12.1

Fill in the blanks

The nominal interest rate equals the real interest rate ____ (plus; minus; divided by) the expected inflation rate. The opportunity cost of holding money is the ____ (price level; nominal interest rate). An increase in real GDP ____ (increases; decreases) the demand for money and shifts the demand for money curve ____ (rightward; leftward). An increase in the price level ____ (increases; decreases) the demand for money and shifts the demand for money curve ____ (rightward; leftward). If the nominal interest rate is above the equilibrium level people ____ (buy; sell) bonds, the price of a bond _____ (falls; rises), and the interest rate _____ (falls; rises). If the Bank of Canada decreases the quantity of money, the nominal interest rate ____ (rises; falls).

True or false

1. The real interest rate is the opportunity cost of holding money.

2. An increase in real GDP shifts the demand for money curve leftward.

3. If the price of a government bond rises, the interest rate on the bond rises.

4. When the interest rate is above its equilibrium level, people buy bonds and the interest rate falls.

5. An increase in the quantity of money lowers the interest rate.

6. ATMs have increased the marginal benefit of money and increased the demand for money.

Multiple choice

1. The quantity of money demanded
   a. is infinite.
   b. has no opportunity cost.
   c. is the quantity that balances the benefit of holding an additional dollar of money against the opportunity cost of doing so.
   d. is directly controlled by the Bank of Canada.

2. The nominal interest rate equals the
   a. real interest rate minus the expected inflation rate.
   b. real interest rate plus the expected inflation rate.
   c. expected inflation rate minus the real interest rate.
   d. expected inflation rate plus the price index.

3. The opportunity cost of holding money is the
   a. real interest rate.
   b. nominal interest rate.
   c. inflation rate.
   d. time it takes to go to the ATM or bank.

4. The demand for money curve shows the relationship between the quantity of money demanded and _____, when all other influences on the amount of money that people wish to hold remain the same.
   a. the nominal interest rate
   b. the real interest rate
   c. the inflation rate
   d. real GDP

5. The demand for money ____ when the price level rises.
   a. increases
   b. decreases
   c. remains constant
   d. None of the above answers is correct.

6. Every day _____ adjusts to make the quantity of money demanded equal the quantity of money supplied.

a. the inflation rate

b. the nominal interest rate

c. the quantity of money

d. potential GDP

7. If the nominal interest rate is above its equilibrium level, then

a. people sell bonds and the interest rate falls.

b. people buy bonds and the interest rate falls.

c. the demand for money curve shifts rightward and the interest rate rises.

d. the supply of money curve shifts leftward and the interest rate rises.

8. When the Bank of Canada increases the quantity of money, the

a. equilibrium interest rate falls.

b. equilibrium interest rate rises.

c. demand for money curve shifts rightward.

d. supply of money curve shifts leftward.

Complete the graph

1. The table has data on the nominal interest rate and the quantity of money demanded.

Nominal interest rate (percent per year)	Quantity of money demanded (billions of dollars)
2.5	110
3.0	108
3.5	106
4.0	104
4.5	102
5.0	100

a. Using the data, label the axes and plot the demand for money curve in Figure 12.1.

b. Suppose the Bank of Canada sets the quantity of money at $104 billion. Plot this quantity in Figure 12.1. What is the equilibrium nominal interest rate?

c. Suppose the Bank of Canada wants the nominal interest rate to equal 3 percent a year. What action must the Bank of Canada take?

■ **FIGURE 12.1**

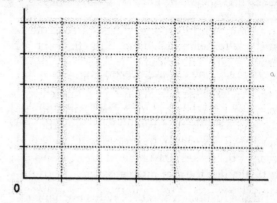

Short answer

1. What is the opportunity cost of holding money and why is this the opportunity cost?

2. What effect will an increase in real GDP have on the demand for money curve?

3. Suppose a government bond pays $100 in interest each year. If you buy the bond for $1,000, what is the interest rate? If you buy the bond for $2,000 dollars, what is the interest rate? As the price of the bond increases, what happens to the interest rate?

4. If the nominal interest rate is less than the equilibrium nominal interest rate, what happens to restore the money market to equilibrium?

5. How can the Bank of Canada lower the nominal interest rate?

CHECKPOINT 12.2

■ Explain how in the long run, the quantity of money determines the price level and money growth brings inflation.

Practice Problems 12.2

1. In 1999, the Canadian economy was at full employment. Real GDP was $886 billion, nominal GDP was $975 billion, the nominal interest rate was around 6 percent per year, the inflation rate was 2 percent a year, and the price level was 110.

a. Calculate the real interest rate.

b. If the real interest rate remains unchanged when the inflation rate increases to 4 percent a year, explain how the nominal interest rate changes.

c. If the velocity of circulation was 10, what was the quantity of money in Canada?

2. If the quantity of money grows at a rate of 10 percent a year and potential GDP grows at 3 percent a year, what is the inflation rate in the long run?

Solution to Practice Problems 12.2

Remember that in the long run, the inflation rate equals the growth rate of the quantity of money minus the growth rate of potential GDP. Also in the long run, an increase in the inflation rate leads to an increase in the nominal interest rate.

Quick Review

• *Inflation rate in the long run* In the long run, the inflation rate equals the growth rate of the quantity of money minus the growth rate of potential GDP.

• *Quantity theory of money* The proposition that when real GDP equals potential GDP, an increase in the quantity of money brings an equal percentage increase in the price level.

• *Equation of exchange* An equation that states that the quantity of money multiplied by the velocity of circulation equals nominal GDP.

1. **In 1999, the Canadian economy was at full employment. Real GDP was $886 billion, nominal GDP was $975 billion, the nominal interest rate was around 6 percent per year, the inflation rate was 2 percent a year, and the price level was 110.**

a. **Calculate the real interest rate.**

The real interest rate equals the nominal interest rate minus the inflation rate. The real interest rate equals 6 percent a year minus 2 a year percent, which is 4 percent a year.

b. **If the real interest rate remains unchanged when the inflation rate increases to 4 percent a year, explain how the nominal interest rate changes.**

The nominal interest rate equals the real interest rate plus the inflation rate. When the inflation rate is 4 percent a year and the real interest rate is 4 percent a year, the nominal interest rate is 4 percent a year plus 4 percent a year, which is 8 percent a year.

c. **If the velocity of circulation was 10, what was the quantity of money in Canada?**

The equation of exchange is $M \times V = P \times Y$. Nominal GDP, which is $P \times Y$ is $975 billion, and velocity, V, is 10. Rewriting the equation, $M = P \times Y \div V = \$975$ billion $\div 10 = \$97.5$ billion. So the quantity of money in Canada is $97.5 billion.

2. **If the quantity of money grows at a rate of 10 percent a year and potential GDP grows at 3 percent a year, what is the inflation rate in the long run?**

With velocity constant, velocity growth is zero. So in the long run, the inflation rate equals the growth rate of the quantity of money minus the real GDP growth rate. The inflation rate equals 10 percent a year minus 3 percent a year, which is 7 percent a year.

Additional Practice Problem 12.2a

The quantity of money is $90 billion, nominal GDP is $990 billion, and the price level is 105. Find the velocity of circulation.

Solution to Additional Practice Problem 12.2a

The equation of exchange is $M \times V = P \times Y$. Rearrange the equation of exchange to give $V = P \times Y \div M$. Nominal GDP is $990 billion, which equals $P \times Y$. So velocity equals $990 \div 90$, which is 11.

■ **Self Test 12.2**

Fill in the blanks

The equilibrium real interest rate depends on the _____ (productivity of capital; quantity of money). In the long run, other things remaining the same, a given percentage change in the quantity of money brings an equal percentage change in the _____ (inflation rate; price level). The number of times in a year that the average dollar of money gets used to buy final goods and services is the _____ (velocity of circulation; velocity of GDP). Money growth plus velocity growth equals _____ (inflation rate plus real GDP growth; inflation rate minus real GDP growth; real GDP growth).

True or false

1. In the long run, other things remaining the same, a given percentage increase in the quantity of money brings an equal percentage decrease in the price level.

2. In the long run, an increase in the quantity of money raises the price level and leaves the nominal interest rate unchanged.

3. Money growth + Velocity growth = Inflation rate + Real GDP growth.

4. According to the quantity theory of money, in the long run an increase in the quantity of money brings an equal percentage increase in real GDP.

5. $M \times P = V \times Y$ is the equation of exchange.

6. On any given day, the value of the real interest rate is equal in all countries and the value of the nominal interest rate is equal in all countries.

Multiple choice

1. In the long run, the price level adjusts to achieve

a. equality of the real interest rate and the nominal interest rate.

b. an inflation rate equal to zero.

c. money market equilibrium at the long-run equilibrium interest rate.

d. equality of nominal GDP and real GDP.

2. Other things remaining the same, if the quantity of money increases by a given percentage, then in the long run the ____ by the same percentage.

a. price level rises

b. price level falls

c. real interest rate rises

d. real interest rate falls

3. In the long run, an increase in the quantity of money _____ the price level and _____ the nominal interest rate.

a. raises; raises

b. raises; does not change

c. raises; lowers

d. does not change; raises

4. If the quantity of money grows at 3 percent a year, velocity is constant, and real GDP grows at 2 percent a year, then the inflation rate equals

a. 6 percent a year.

b. 5 percent a year.

c. 1 percent a year.

d. −1 percent a year.

5. The quantity theory of money is a proposition about the

a. Bank of Canada's operating procedures to change the quantity of money.

b. relationship between nominal and real interest rates.

c. relationship between a change in the quantity of money and the change in the price level in the long run.

d. relationship between financial assets and currency demanded in the long run.

6. Suppose that nominal GDP is $5,000 billion and the quantity of money is $500 billion. Then the velocity of circulation is

a. 50.

b. 500.

c. 10.

d. 20.

7. Hyperinflation is

a. inflation caused by negative growth in the quantity of money.

b. inflation at a rate that exceeds 50 percent a month.

c. inflation caused by excessive growth in the demand for money.

d. inflation at a rate that exceeds 5 percent a month.

Short answer

1. In the long run, what is the effect of a 5 percent increase in the quantity of money other things remaining the same?

2. In the long run, if real GDP grows at 3 percent a year, velocity does not change, and the quantity of money grows at 5 percent a year, what is the inflation rate?

3. The table gives data for Quantoland, a small nation to the south. In 2001, 2002, and 2003, real GDP equals potential GDP.

Year	Quantity of money (billions of 1997 dollars)	Velocity of circulation	Price level (1997 = 100)	Real GDP (billions of 1997 dollars)
2001	100	11	____	1,000
2002	110	11	____	1,000
2003	121	11	____	1,000

a. Complete the table.

b. Calculate the percentage change in the quantity of money and the percentage change in the price level in 2002 and in 2003.

c. What key proposition is illustrated in your answer to part (b)?

4. What is a hyperinflation? What leads to hyperinflation?

CHECKPOINT 12.3

■ **Identify the costs of inflation and the benefits of a stable value of money.**

Practice Problem 12.3

Suppose that you have $1,000 in your savings account and the bank pays an interest rate of 5 percent a year. The inflation rate is 3 percent a year. The government taxes the interest you earn on your deposit at 20 percent.

a. Calculate the nominal after-tax interest rate that you earn.

b. Calculate the real after-tax interest rate you earn.

Solution to Practice Problem 12.3

The interaction of income tax and inflation is an important real world cost of inflation.

Quick Review

• *The inflation rate and income tax* Inflation increases the nominal interest rate, and because income taxes are paid on nominal interest income, the true income tax rate rises with inflation.

Suppose that you have $1,000 in your savings account and the bank pays an interest rate of 5 percent a year. The inflation rate is 3 percent a year. The government taxes the interest you earn on your deposit at 20 percent.

a. Calculate the nominal after-tax interest rate that you earn.

In a year, you earn interest income of 5 percent of $1,000, which is $50. You pay the government 20 percent of your $50 interest income, which is $10. The interest income you earn after tax is $40. The nominal after-tax interest rate is ($40 ÷ $1,000) x 100, which is 4 percent a year.

b. Calculate the real after-tax interest rate you earn.

The real after-tax interest rate equals the nominal after-tax interest rate, 4 percent a year, minus the inflation rate, 3 percent a year. So the real after-tax interest rate is 4 percent a year – 3 percent a year, which equals 1 percent a year.

Additional Practice Problem 12.3a

In recent years in the island nation of Atlantis where you live, the inflation rate has been varying between 3 percent a year and 10 percent a year. You are willing to lend money if you are guaranteed a real interest rate of at least 2 percent a year. There are potential borrowers, but they will borrow only if they are guaranteed a real interest rate of not more than 5 percent a year.

a. Can you successfully make a loan if everyone can accurately predict the inflation rate?

b. Can you successfully make a loan if neither you nor the borrowers can accurately predict the inflation rate?

Solution to Additional Practice Problem 12.3a

a. Can you successfully make a loan if everyone can accurately predict the inflation rate?

If you and the potential borrowers can accurately predict the inflation rate, it is possible to make a loan. If everyone knows the inflation rate is 10 percent a year, you are willing to lend as long as

you receive a nominal interest rate of at least 12 percent a year. Borrowers are willing to pay a real interest rate of no more than 5 percent a year, so borrowers are willing to agree to a loan as long as the nominal rate is no more than 15 percent a year. Because they are willing to pay up to 15 percent a year and you are willing to take as little as 12 percent a year, you can make a loan and charge a nominal interest rate between 12 percent a year and 15 percent a year. Similarly, if everyone knows the inflation rate is 3 percent a year, a loan can be made with a nominal interest rate between 5 percent a year and 8 percent a year.

b. Can you successfully make a loan if neither you nor the borrowers can accurately predict the inflation rate?

To receive a real interest rate of at least 2 percent a year you must receive a nominal rate of at least 12 percent a year in case inflation is 10 percent a year. If borrowers pay a nominal interest rate of 12 percent a year and inflation is 3 percent a year, they are paying a real interest rate of 9 percent a year. Because the inflation rate could be as low as 3 percent a year, borrowers are not willing to take a loan at a nominal interest rate of more than 8 percent a year (inflation of 3 percent a year plus a real interest rate of 5 percent a year). Because of the uncertainty about the inflation rate you don't make the loan.

■ **Self Test 12.3**
Fill in the blanks

Inflation _____ (is; is not) a tax. The higher the inflation rate, the _____ (lower; higher) the true income tax rate on income from capital. Costs that arise from an increase in the velocity of circulation of money and an increase in the amount of running around to avoid incurring losses from the falling value of money are _____ (shoe-leather; confusion) costs. Increased uncertainty about inflation leads to a _____ (fall; rise) in investment.

True or false

1. Inflation is a tax.

2. The "shoe-leather costs" of inflation arise from an increase in the velocity of circulation when inflation increases.

3. One of the benefits of inflation is that it makes the value of money change, which benefits both borrowers and lenders.

4. When there is a high inflation rate, the growth rate of real GDP slows.

5. No country in the world has experienced hyperinflation since the end of the 1950s.

Multiple choice

1. All of the following are costs of inflation EX-CEPT
   a. tax costs.
   b. confusion costs.
   c. uncertainty costs.
   d. government spending costs.

2. Becky holds $30,000 as money. If inflation is 5 percent a year, the inflation tax after one year is
   a. $500.
   b. $1,000.
   c. $1,500.
   d. $3,000.

3. Suppose a country has a real interest rate of 4 percent a year and an inflation rate of 3 percent a year. If the income tax rate is 20 percent, then the real after-tax interest rate is
   a. 2.6 percent.
   b. 4.0 percent.
   c. 5.6 percent.
   d. 7.0 percent.

4. Shoe-leather costs arise from inflation because the velocity of circulation of money ____ as the inflation rate ____.
   a. increases; falls
   b. decreases; rises
   c. increases; rises
   d. None of the above answers is correct.

5. A consequence of hyperinflation is that people
   a. who make fixed-payment loans to others receive higher payments as inflation increases.
   b. spend time trying to keep their money holdings near zero.
   c. receive higher nominal raises, which increases their purchasing power for goods and services.
   d. want to lend funds because interest rates are so high.

6. The uncertainty costs of inflation cause people to
   a. increase long-run investment.
   b. increase investment causing real GDP growth to decrease.
   c. focus on the short run, which decreases investment and slows real GDP growth.
   d. focus on the long run, which increases investment and increases real GDP growth.

7. The costs of inflation ____ when inflation is more rapid and ____ when inflation is more unpredictable.
   a. increase; increase
   b. increase; decrease
   c. decrease; increase
   d. increase; do not change

8. It is estimated that if the inflation rate is lowered from 3 percent a year to zero, the growth rate of real GDP will rise by _____ percentage points a year.

a. 0.06 to 0.09

b. zero to 3

c. 2.3

d. 3.2

Short answer

1. Jose holds $600 of money. If the inflation rate is 5 percent a year, calculate Jose's inflation tax.

2. The real interest rate is 2 percent a year and the inflation rate is zero. If the income tax rate is 25 percent, what is the real after-tax interest rate? If the inflation rate rises to 6 percent a year, what is the real after-tax interest rate? If the inflation rate rises to 10 percent a year, what is the real after-tax interest rate?

3. Why does the velocity of circulation increase in a hyperinflation?

4. On what factors does the cost of inflation depend?

SELF TEST ANSWERS

■ CHECKPOINT 12.1

Fill in the blanks

The nominal interest rate equals the real interest rate <u>plus</u> the expected inflation rate. The opportunity cost of holding money is the <u>nominal interest rate</u>. An increase in real GDP <u>increases</u> the demand for money and shifts the demand for money curve <u>rightward</u>. An increase in the price level <u>increases</u> the demand for money and shifts the demand for money curve <u>rightward</u>. If the nominal interest rate is above the equilibrium level people <u>buy</u> bonds, the price of a bond <u>rises</u>, and the interest rate <u>falls</u>. If the Bank of Canada decreases the quantity of money, the nominal interest rate <u>rises</u>.

True or false

1. False; page 292
2. False; page 293
3. False; page 295
4. True; page 296
5. True; page 297
6. True; page 294

Multiple choice

1. c; page 291
2. b; page 292
3. b; page 292
4. a; page 292
5. a; page 293
6. b; page 296
7. b; page 296
8. a; page 297

Complete the graph

1. a. Figure 12.2 plots the demand for money curve; page 292.

b. Figure 12.2 shows the supply of money curve when the Bank of Canada sets the quantity of money at $104 billion. The equilibrium nominal interest rate is 4 percent a year at the intersection of MD and MS; page 296.

■ FIGURE 12.2

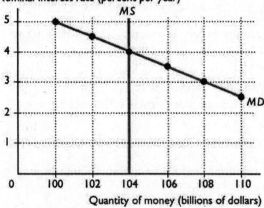

c. If the Bank of Canada wants to lower the interest rate to 3 percent a year, it increases the quantity of money to $108 billion. In Figure 12.3, the supply of money curve shifts rightward from MS_0 to MS_1; page 297.

■ FIGURE 12.3

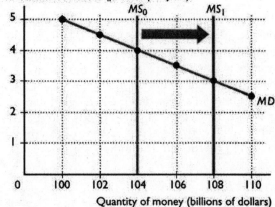

Short answer

1. The opportunity cost of holding money is the nominal interest rate. By holding money rather than an alternative asset, the nominal interest rate is forgone; page 291.

2. An increase in real GDP increases the demand for money and shifts the demand for money curve rightward; page 293.

3. When the price of the bond is $1,000, the interest rate equals ($100 ÷ $1,000) × 100, which is 10 percent a year. When the price of the bond is $2,000, the interest rate equals ($100 ÷ $2,000) × 100, which is 5 percent a year. When the price of the bond increases, the interest rate falls; page 295.

4. If the nominal interest rate is less than the equilibrium interest rate, people would like to hold more money than they are actually holding. People sell bonds. The price of bonds falls and the interest rate rises. The interest rate continues to rise until the quantity of money that people want to hold decreases to equal the quantity of money supplied; page 296.

5. The Bank of Canada lowers the nominal interest rate by increasing the quantity of money; page 297.

■ **CHECKPOINT 12.2**

Fill in the blanks

The equilibrium real interest rate depends on the productivity of capital. In the long run, other things remaining the same, a given percentage change in the quantity of money brings an equal percentage change in the price level. The number of times in a year that the average dollar of money gets used to buy final goods and services is the velocity of circulation. Money growth plus velocity growth equals inflation rate plus real GDP growth.

True or false

1. False; page 301

2. True; page 301

3. True; page 305

4. False; page 303

5. False; page 303

6. False; page 300

Multiple choice

1. c; page 301

2. a; page 301

3. b; page 301

4. c; page 305

5. c; page 303

6. c; page 303

7. b; page 307

Short answer

1. If nothing else changes, in the long run a 5 percent increase in the quantity of money leads to a 5 percent increase in the price level; page 301.

2. From the equation of exchange, Money growth + Velocity growth = Inflation rate + Real GDP growth. Velocity growth is zero, so Inflation rate = Money growth − Real GDP growth, which is 5 percent a year − 3 percent a year = 2 percent a year; page 305.

3. The completed table is below.

Year	Quantity of money (billions of 1997 dollars)	Velocity of circulation	Price level (1997 = 100)	Real GDP (billions of 1997 dollars)
2001	100	11	110.0	1,000
2002	110	11	121.0	1,000
2003	121	11	133.1	1,000

a. Use the equation of exchange to solve for the price level; page 303.

b. In 2002, the percentage change in the quantity of money is [($110 billion − $100 billion) ÷ $100 billion] × 100, which is 10 percent.

In 2003, the percentage change in the quantity of money is [($121 billion – $110 billion) ÷ $110 billion] x 100, which is 10 percent. Similarly, in 2002, the percentage change in the price level is [(121.0 – 110.0) ÷ 110.0] x 100, which is 10 percent.

In 2003, the percentage change in the price level is [(133.1 – 121.0) ÷ 121.0] x 100, which is 10 percent.

c. The answer to part (b) illustrates the quantity of theory of money, which is the proposition that when real GDP equals potential GDP, an increase in the quantity of money brings an equal percentage increase in the price level; page 303

4. A hyperinflation is inflation at a rate that exceeds 50 percent a month. Hyperinflation occurs when a government's payments exceed the sum of what it can collect in tax receipts and borrow. The government prints money and the quantity of money increases at an extraordinarily rapid rate; page 307.

■ **CHECKPOINT 12.3**
Fill in the blanks

Inflation is a tax. The higher the inflation rate, the higher the true income tax rate on income from capital. Costs that arise from an increase in the velocity of circulation of money and an increase in the amount of running around to avoid incurring losses from the falling value of money are shoe-leather costs. Increased uncertainty about inflation leads to a fall in investment.

True or false

1. True; page 309
2. True; page 310
3. False; page 310
4. True; page 311
5. False; page 312

Multiple choice

1. d; page 309

2. c; page 309
3. a; page 309
4. c; page 310
5. b; page 310
6. c; page 311
7. a; page 312
8. a; page 312

Short answer

1. With an inflation rate of 5 percent a year, Jose's money will buy only $570 of goods and services. He losses ($600 x .05) = $30. Jose pays an inflation tax of $30; page 309.

2. The real after-tax interest rate equals the nominal after-tax interest rate minus the inflation rate. When inflation is zero, the nominal interest rate equals the real interest rate, which is 2 percent. With a 25 percent income tax, the nominal after-tax interest rate equals 1.5 percent a year, so the real after-tax interest rate is 1.5 percent.

When the inflation rate is 6 percent a year, the nominal interest rate equals the real interest rate, 2 percent a year, plus the inflation rate, 6 percent a year, which is 8 percent. The nominal after-tax interest rate is 6 percent a year, so the real after-tax interest rate equals 6 percent a year minus the inflation rate, 6 percent a year, which is zero.

When the inflation rate equals 10 percent a year, the nominal interest rate is 12 percent a year, so the nominal after-tax interest rate is 9 percent a year. The real after-tax interest rate is 9 percent a year – 10 percent a year, which is –1 percent a year; page 317.

3. The velocity of circulation increases because people try to spend their money as rapidly as possible to avoid incurring losses from the falling value of money; page 310.

4. The costs of an inflation depend on its rate and its predictability. The higher the rate, the greater is the cost, and the more unpredictable the rate, the greater is the cost; page 312.

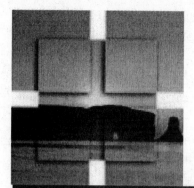

Aggregate Expenditure

Chapter

13

CHAPTER IN PERSPECTIVE

Chapter 13 explores the business cycle by studying the aggregate expenditure model.

■ **Distinguish between autonomous expenditure and induced expenditure and explain how real GDP influences expenditure plans.**

Aggregate planned expenditure is the sum of planned consumption expenditure, planned investment, planned government expenditure, and planned exports minus planned imports. Induced expenditure is the part of aggregate expenditure that changes in response to a change in real GDP; autonomous expenditure is the part of aggregate expenditure that does not respond to changes in real GDP. The consumption function is the relationship between consumption expenditure and disposable income, other things remaining the same. The marginal propensity to consume, *MPC*, is the fraction of a change in disposable income that is spent on consumption. The marginal propensity to import is the fraction of an increase in real GDP that is spent on imports.

■ **Explain how real GDP adjusts to achieve equilibrium expenditure.**

Equilibrium expenditure occurs when aggregate *planned* expenditure equals real GDP at the point where the *AE* curve intersects the 45° line. If aggregate planned expenditure is less than real GDP, an unplanned increase in inventories occurs. Firms decrease production and real GDP decreases until real GDP equals aggregate planned expenditure and the economy is at equilibrium expenditure. If aggregate planned expenditure exceeds real GDP, an unplanned decrease in inventories occurs. Firms increase production and real GDP increases until real GDP equals aggregate planned expenditure and the economy is at equilibrium expenditure.

■ **Describe and explain the expenditure multiplier.**

The multiplier is the amount by which a change in any component of autonomous expenditure is magnified or multiplied to determine the change that it generates in equilibrium expenditure and real GDP. If we ignore income taxes and imports, the multiplier equals 1 ÷ (1 – *MPC*). Imports and income taxes reduce the size of the multiplier. In general, the multiplier equals 1 ÷ (1 – slope of *AE* curve).

■ **Derive the *AD* curve from equilibrium expenditure.**

When the price level rises, aggregate planned expenditure decreases, the *AE* curve shifts downward, and equilibrium expenditure decreases. When the price level falls, aggregate planned expenditure increases, the *AE* curve shifts upward, and equilibrium expenditure increases. Each point of equilibrium expenditure corresponds to a point on the *AD* curve.

EXPANDED CHAPTER CHECKLIST

When you have completed this chapter, you will be able to

1 **Distinguish between autonomous expenditure and induced expenditure and explain how real GDP influences expenditure plans.**

- Define aggregate planned expenditure and explain why aggregate planned expenditure does not always equal real GDP.

- Compare autonomous expenditure and induced expenditure.

- Describe the consumption function and define the marginal propensity to consume.

- List and explain the factors that influence planned consumption expenditure.

- Define the marginal propensity to import.

2 **Explain how real GDP adjusts to achieve equilibrium expenditure.**

- Describe the relationship between aggregate planned expenditure and real GDP and draw an *AE* curve.

- Discuss how equilibrium expenditure is determined and illustrate equilibrium expenditure using the *AE* curve and a 45° line.

- Describe the convergence to equilibrium when aggregate planned expenditure does not equal real GDP.

3 **Describe and explain the expenditure multiplier.**

- Define the multiplier.

- Explain the relationship between the *MPC* and the multiplier.

- Discuss why income taxes and imports reduce the size of the multiplier.

- State the general formula for the multiplier.

- Describe what triggers a business cycle expansion or recession and discuss the impact of the multiplier in creating expansions and recessions.

4 **Derive the *AD* curve from equilibrium expenditure.**

- Discuss the differences between the *AE* curve and the *AD* curve.

- Explain the effect of a change in the price level on aggregate planned expenditure, the *AE* curve, and equilibrium expenditure.

- Derive the *AD* curve.

KEY TERMS

- Aggregate planned expenditure (page 319)

- Autonomous expenditure (page 320)

- Consumption function (page 320)

- Disposable income (page 320)

- Equilibrium expenditure (page 328)

- Induced expenditure (page 320)

- Marginal propensity to consume (page 322)

- Marginal propensity to import (page 324)

- Marginal tax rate (page 335)

- Multiplier (page 332)

- Saving (page 320)

CHECKPOINT 13.1

■ **Distinguish between autonomous expenditure and induced expenditure and explain how real GDP influences expenditure plans.**

Practice Problems 13.1

1. If the marginal propensity to consume is 0.8 and if disposable income increases by $50

billion, by how much will consumption expenditure change?

2. If Canadians decrease the fraction of each dollar of disposable income they spend on consumption, how will the Canadian consumption function change?

3. If Canadians decide to decrease consumption expenditure by a fixed number of dollars, how will the Canadian consumption function change?

4. Suppose that expected future disposable income increases. Explain how this change in expectation will influence the consumption function.

5. The figure illustrates a consumption function. Calculate the marginal propensity to consume and autonomous consumption.

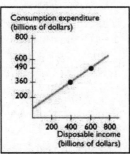

Solution to Practice Problems 13.1

These problems study the consumption function, its slope, and the influences that create a movement along the consumption function or a shift of the consumption function.

Quick Review

- *Autonomous expenditure* The components of aggregate expenditure that do not change when real GDP changes.

- *Induced expenditure* The components of aggregate expenditure that change when real GDP changes.

- *Consumption function* The relationship between consumption expenditure and disposable income, other things remaining the same.

- *Marginal propensity to consume* The fraction of a change in disposable income that is spent on consumption—the change in consump-

tion expenditure divided by the change in disposable income that brought it about.

1. If the marginal propensity to consume is 0.8 and if disposable income increases by $50 billion, by how much will consumption expenditure change?

The change in consumption expenditure equals the change in disposable income multiplied by the marginal propensity to consume, which is ($50 billion) × (0.8) = $40 billion.

2. If Canadians decrease the fraction of each dollar of disposable income they spend on consumption, how will the Canadian consumption function change?

When the fraction of each dollar of disposable income spent on consumption decreases, the *MPC* decreases. The *MPC* equals the slope of the consumption function. The consumption function becomes less steep.

3. If Canadians decide to decrease consumption expenditure by a fixed number of dollars, how will the Canadian consumption function change?

The decrease in consumption expenditure by a fixed number of dollars is a decrease in autonomous consumption. The consumption function shifts downward.

4. Suppose that expected future disposable income increases. Explain how this change in expectation will influence the consumption function.

When expected future disposable income increases, people increase their consumption expenditure today. The consumption function shifts upward.

5. The figure illustrates a consumption function. Calculate the marginal propensity to consume and autonomous consumption.

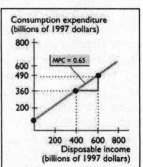

The *MPC* is calculated as the change in consumption expenditure divided by the change in disposable income that brought it about. The figure shows that when disposable income increases from $400 billion to $600 billion, an increase of $200 billion, consumption expenditure increases from $360 billion to $490 billion, an increase of $130 billion. The *MPC* equals $130 billion ÷ $200 billion, which is 0.65. Autonomous consumption is the amount of consumption when disposable income is zero and equals the *y*-axis intercept, $100 billion.

Additional Practice Problem 13.1a

If disposable income increases by $15 billion and the *MPC* is 0.8, what is the change in consumption expenditure? If the *MPC* equals 0.6, what is the change in consumption expenditure?

Solution to Additional Practice Problem 13.1a

The change in consumption expenditure equals the *MPC* times the change in disposable income. When the *MPC* is 0.8, the change in consumption expenditure equals $15 billion × 0.8, which is $12 billion. When the *MPC* is 0.6, the change in consumption expenditure is $15 billion × 0.6, which is $9 billion.

■ Self Test 13.1

Fill in the blanks

Aggregate planned expenditure ____ (does not always equal; always equals) GDP. The components of aggregate expenditure that change when real GDP changes are ____ (induced; autonomous) expenditure. The ____ (consumption; induced consumption) function is the relationship between consumption expenditure and disposable income, other things remaining the same. The marginal propensity to consume equals the change in consumption expenditure ____ (plus; multiplied by; divided by) the change in disposable income that brought it about. The slope of the consumption function equals ____ (the *MPC*; 1 minus the *MPC*). A change in disposable income is shown by a ____ (shift of; movement along) the consumption function and a change in the buying power of money is shown by a ____ (shift of; movement along) the consumption function.

True or false

1. Induced expenditure increases as real GDP increases.

2. The slope of the consumption function is less than the slope of the 45° line.

3. Dissaving occurs when consumption expenditure exceeds saving.

4. The marginal propensity to consume is greater than 1.

5. The marginal propensity to consume equals consumption expenditure divided by disposable income.

Multiple choice

1. The aggregate expenditure model explains

a. changes in the price level while holding the level of real GDP constant.

b. changes in real GDP and the price level simultaneously.

c. the quantity of real GDP demanded and changes in that quantity at a given price level.

d. total spending in the context of falling prices.

2. The four components of aggregate expenditure are

a. consumption expenditure, interest, gross spending, and net spending.

b. consumption expenditure, investment, government expenditure on goods and services, and net income.

c. consumption expenditure, interest, government expenditure on goods and services, and net exports.

d. consumption expenditure, investment, government expenditure on goods and services, and net exports.

3. Which of the following is true?

a. Actual aggregate expenditure does not always equal real GDP.

b. Aggregate planned expenditure always equals real GDP.

c. Actual aggregate expenditure always equals real GDP.

d. Aggregate planned expenditure and actual aggregate expenditure always equal real GDP.

4. Autonomous expenditure is the component of

a. aggregate expenditure that changes when real GDP changes.

b. induced expenditure that changes when real GDP changes.

c. aggregate planned expenditure that changes when government expenditure changes.

d. aggregate expenditure that does not change when real GDP changes.

5. The components of aggregate expenditure that change when real GDP changes are

a. unplanned expenditure.

b. induced expenditure.

c. planned expenditure.

d. autonomous expenditure.

6. The consumption function is the relationship between _____, other things remaining the same.

a. consumption expenditure and saving

b. real GDP and net taxes

c. consumption expenditure and disposable income

d. net taxes and disposable income

7. When disposable income increases from $900 billion to $1,000 billion, consumption expenditure increases from $600 billion to $680 billion. The *MPC* is

a. 1.0.

b. 0.8.

c. 0.67

d. 0.68.

8. A decrease in the buying power of money ____ consumption expenditure and the consumption function shifts ____.

a. increases; upward

b. decreases; downward

c. increases; downward

d. decreases; upward

Complete the graph

1. The table gives data on consumption expenditure and disposable income.

Disposable income (trillions of 1997 dollars)	Consumption expenditure (trillions of 1997 dollars)
0.0	0.4
1.0	1.2
2.0	2.0
3.0	2.8
4.0	3.6
5.0	4.4

a. Using the data, label the axes and plot the consumption function in Figure 13.1.

b. Indicate the amount of autonomous consumption expenditure in Figure 13.1.

c. What is the amount of saving if disposable income equals $1.0 trillion? $4.0 trillion?

d. Calculate the marginal propensity to consume.

e. Suppose the real interest rate falls and consumers increase their consumption by $0.6 trillion at every level of disposable income. Draw the new consumption function in Figure 13.1. What is the amount of autonomous consumption now?

■ **FIGURE 13.1**

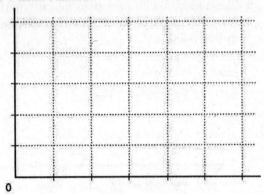

Short answer

1. What is the relationship between actual aggregate expenditure and real GDP? Between aggregate planned expenditure and real GDP?

2. What is autonomous expenditure? What is induced expenditure?

3. What is the relationship between the consumption function and the *MPC*? At what point on the consumption function is consumption expenditure equal to autonomous consumption?

4. Complete the following table.

Change in disposable income (trillions of 1997 dollars)	Change in consumption expenditure (trillions of 1997 dollars)	Marginal propensity to consume, *MPC*
2	1.8	____
1	0.9	____
4	3.0	____

■ Explain how real GDP adjusts to achieve equilibrium expenditure.

Practice Problem 13.2

1. The table is a spreadsheet that gives the components of real GDP in billions of dollars.

	Y	C	I	G	X	M
A	100	110	50	60	60	15
B	200	170	50	60	60	30
C	300	230	50	60	60	45
D	400	290	50	60	60	60
E	500	350	50	60	60	75
F	600	410	50	60	60	90

a. Calculate aggregate planned expenditure when real GDP is $200 billion.

b. Calculate aggregate planned expenditure when real GDP is $600 billion.

c. Calculate equilibrium expenditure.

d. If real GDP is $200 billion, explain the process that moves the economy towards equilibrium expenditure.

e. If real GDP is $600 billion, explain the process that moves the economy towards equilibrium expenditure.

Solution to Practice Problem 13.2

This Practice Problem calculates equilibrium expenditure and studies the forces that move aggregate expenditure towards equilibrium expenditure. If aggregate planned expenditure exceeds real GDP, firms increase production and real GDP increases. If aggregate planned expenditure is less than real GDP, firms decrease production and real GDP decreases.

Quick Review

•   *Equilibrium expenditure* The level of aggregate expenditure that occurs when aggregate planned expenditure equals real GDP.

a. **Calculate aggregate planned expenditure when real GDP is $200 billion.**

Aggregate planned expenditure equals $C + I + G + X - M$. When real GDP is $200 billion, aggregate planned expenditure equals $170 billion + $50 billion + $60 billion + $60 billion – $30 billion, which is $310 billion.

b. **Calculate aggregate planned expenditure when real GDP is $600 billion.**

When real GDP is $600 billion, aggregate planned expenditure equals $410 billion + $50 billion + $60 billion + $60 billion – $90 billion, which is $490 billion.

c. **Calculate equilibrium expenditure.**

Equilibrium expenditure occurs when real GDP equals aggregate planned expenditure. When real GDP equals $400 billion, aggregate planned expenditure equals $290 billion + $50 billion + $60 billion + $60 billion – $60 billion, which is $400 billion. Equilibrium expenditure occurs when real GDP is $400 billion.

d. **If real GDP is $200 billion, explain the process that moves the economy towards equilibrium expenditure.**

When GDP is $200 billion, aggregate planned expenditure exceeds real GDP. An unplanned decrease in inventories occurs. Firms increase production to restore their inventories. Real GDP increases. Firms continue to increase production as long as aggregate planned expenditure exceeds real GDP. When real GDP reaches $400 billion, aggregate planned expenditure equals real GDP. The economy is at equilibrium expenditure. The unplanned inventory change is zero and firms have no reason to change production.

e. **If real GDP is $600 billion, explain the process that moves the economy towards equilibrium expenditure.**

When GDP is $600 billion, aggregate planned expenditure is less than real GDP. An unplanned increase in inventories occurs. Firms decrease production to reduce their inventories. Real GDP decreases. Firms continue to decrease production as long as aggregate planned expenditure is less than real GDP. When real GDP reaches $400 billion, aggregate planned expenditure equals real GDP. The economy is at equilibrium expenditure. The unplanned inventory change is zero and firms have no reason to change production.

Additional Practice Problem 13.2a

The table is a spreadsheet that gives the components of real GDP in billions of 1997 dollars.

Y	C	I	G	X	M
50	50	20	25	25	10
100	85	20	25	25	15
150	120	20	25	25	20
200	155	20	25	25	25
250	190	20	25	25	30
300	225	20	25	25	35

In Figure 13.2, label the axes, draw the aggregate expenditure curve and find the equilibrium level of real GDP.

■ **FIGURE 13.2**

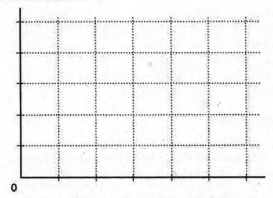

Solution to Additional Practice Problem 13.2a

To construct the *AE* curve add the components of aggregate planned expenditure together for each level of real GDP. The *AE* curve is illustrated in Figure 13.3. Equilibrium expenditure occurs at the level of real GDP where the *AE* curve intersects the 45° line, which is $200 billion.

■ **FIGURE 13.3**

Aggregate planned expenditure (billions of 1997 dollars)

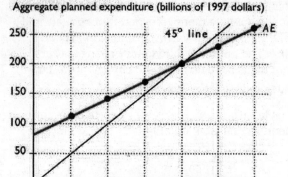

■ **Self Test 13.2**

Fill in the blanks

As real GDP increases, aggregate planned expenditure ____ (increases; does not change; decreases). Equilibrium expenditure is the level of aggregate expenditure that occurs when aggregate planned expenditure equals ____ (autonomous; real) GDP. If aggregate planned expenditure exceeds real GDP, an unplanned _____ (decrease; increase) in inventories occurs and firms ____ (increase; decrease) production.

True or false

1. Equilibrium expenditure occurs at the intersection of the aggregate expenditure curve and the 45° line.

2. Inventories increase when aggregate planned expenditure exceeds real GDP.

3. If aggregate planned expenditure is less than real GDP, inventories increase.

4. If aggregate planned expenditure exceeds real GDP, inventories decrease and firms decrease production.

5. If unplanned investment occurs, then aggregate expenditure is not at its equilibrium level.

Multiple choice

1. Aggregate planned expenditure decreases if
   a. government expenditure increases.
   b. exports increase.
   c. real GDP decreases.
   d. investment increases.

2. The *AE* curve illustrates the relationship between
   a. aggregate planned expenditure and real GDP.
   b. real GDP and actual expenditure.
   c. real GDP and the interest rate.
   d. the interest rate and actual expenditure.

3. Equilibrium expenditure occurs when
   a. aggregate planned expenditure equals real GDP.
   b. disposable income equals real GDP.
   c. disposable income equals consumption expenditures plus imports.
   d. real GDP plus net taxes equals disposable income.

4. When aggregate planned expenditure exceeds real GDP, there is _____ in inventory.
   a. a planned decrease
   b. a planned increase
   c. an unplanned decrease
   d. an unplanned increase

5. If aggregate planned expenditure is greater than real GDP
   a. an unplanned decrease in inventories leads to an increase in production.
   b. an unplanned increase in inventories leads to a decrease in production.
   c. a planned decrease in inventories leads to a decrease in production.
   d. a planned increase in inventories leads to an increase in production.

6. If real GDP equals aggregate planned expenditure, then

a. inventories rise above their target levels.

b. inventories fall below their target levels.

c. inventories equal their target levels.

d. None of the above .

7. Equilibrium expenditure is the level of expenditure at which

a. firm's inventories are zero.

b. firm's inventories are at the desired level.

c. firms produce more output than they sell.

d. None of the above answers is correct.

8. If planned expenditure is less than actual expenditure, firms

a. increase production.

b. cut production.

c. stop production.

d. do not change production.

Complete the graph

1. The table is a spreadsheet that gives the components of real GDP in trillions of 1997 dollars.

GDP	C	I	G	X	M	AE
0.0	0.6	0.4	0.2	0.2	0.2	—
1.0	1.2	0.4	0.2	0.2	0.4	—
2.0	1.8	0.4	0.2	0.2	0.6	—
3.0	2.4	0.4	0.2	0.2	0.8	—
4.0	3.0	0.4	0.2	0.2	1.0	—
5.0	3.6	0.4	0.2	0.2	1.2	—

a. Complete the table.

b. Label the axes in Figure 13.4 and then plot the *AE* curve.

c. Show the equilibrium expenditure in Figure 13.4.

d. Over what range of GDP is there an unplanned increase in inventories? An unplanned decrease in inventories?

e. What is the amount of planned and actual investment when GDP equals $3.0 trillion?

■ FIGURE 13.4

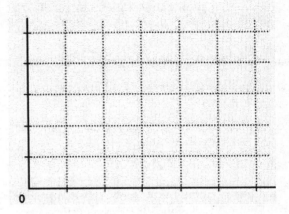

Short answer

1. What is the relationship between aggregate planned expenditure and real GDP? Explain the relationship.

2. In a diagram with an aggregate expenditure curve, what does the 45° line represent? Why is equilibrium expenditure determined by the intersection of the aggregate expenditure curve and the 45° line?

3. If aggregate planned expenditure is less than real GDP, what forces drive the economy to equilibrium expenditure?

CHECKPOINT 13.3

■ **Describe and explain the expenditure multiplier.**

Practice Problems 13.3

1. An economy has no imports or taxes, the *MPC* is 0.80, and real GDP is $150 billion. If businesses increase investment by $5 billion,

a. Calculate the multiplier.

b. Calculate the change in real GDP.

c. Calculate the new level of real GDP.

d. Explain why real GDP increases by more than $5 billion.

2. An economy has no imports or taxes. An increase in autonomous expenditure of $2 trillion increases equilibrium expenditure by $8 trillion.

a. Calculate the multiplier.

b. Calculate the marginal propensity to consume.

c. What happens to the multiplier if an income tax is introduced?

Solution to Practice Problems 13.3

The Practice Problems give you valuable practice working with the multiplier. To solve the Practice Problems remember the definition of the multiplier and the formulas you use to calculate it.

Quick Review

- *Multiplier* The multiplier is the amount by which a change in any component of autonomous expenditure is magnified or multiplied to determine the change that it generates in equilibrium expenditure and real GDP.

$$\text{Multiplier} = \frac{\text{Change in equilibrium expenditure}}{\text{Change in autonomous expenditure}}.$$

- *Multiplier and the MPC* With no imports or income taxes,

$$\text{Multiplier} = \frac{1}{(1 - MPC)}.$$

- *Multiplier with imports and income taxes* With imports and income taxes

$$\text{Multiplier} = \frac{1}{(1 - \text{Slope of the } AE \text{ curve})}.$$

1. **An economy has no imports or taxes, the *MPC* is 0.80, and real GDP is $150 billion. If businesses increase investment by $5 billion,**

a. **Calculate the multiplier.**

With no taxes or imports, the multiplier equals $1/(1 - MPC)$. The *MPC* is 0.8, so the multiplier equals $1 \div (1 - 0.8)$, which is 5.0.

b. **Calculate the change in real GDP.**

The change in real GDP is equal to the multiplier times the change in investment, which is $5 \times \$5$ billion = $25 billion.

c. **Calculate the new level of real GDP.**

Real GDP increases by $25 billion from $150 billion to $175 billion.

d. **Explain why real GDP increases by more than $5 billion.**

The increase in investment increases real GDP, which, in turn, increases income and induces an additional increase in consumption expenditure. So real GDP increases because of the increase in investment and the increase in consumption expenditure.

2. **An economy has no imports or taxes. An increase in autonomous expenditure of $2 trillion increases equilibrium expenditure by $8 trillion.**

a. **Calculate the multiplier.**

The multiplier equals the change in equilibrium expenditure divided by the change in autonomous expenditure. The multiplier equals $8 trillion ÷$2 trillion, which is 4.

b. **Calculate the marginal propensity to consume.**

The multiplier equals $1/(1 - MPC)$. The multiplier is 4, so set $1/(1 - MPC)$ equal to 4 and solve. The *MPC* is 0.75.

c. **What happens to the multiplier if an income tax is introduced?**

When an income tax is introduced, the smaller are the changes in disposable income and real

GDP that result from a given change in autonomous expenditure. The slope of the *AE* curve becomes smaller and the multiplier, which equals $1/(1 - \text{Slope of the } AE \text{ curve})$ becomes smaller.

Additional Practice Problem 13.3a

Suppose there are no income taxes or imports. How would the following events affect equilibrium expenditure and real GDP?

a. Investment increases by $40 billion and the *MPC* equals 0.6.

b. Parliament increases military spending by $100 million and the *MPC* is 0.8.

Solution to Additional Practice Problem 13.3a

a. The increase in investment is an increase in autonomous expenditure. The change in equilibrium expenditure and real GDP equals the multiplier times the change in autonomous expenditure. The multiplier equals $1/(1 - MPC)$, which is 2.5. The change in equilibrium expenditure and real GDP equals $2.5 \times \$40$ billion, which is $100 billion.

b. The increase in military spending is an increase in government expenditure and is an increase in autonomous expenditure. The change in equilibrium expenditure and real GDP equals the multiplier times the change in autonomous expenditure. The multiplier equals $1/(1 - MPC)$, which is 5.0. The change in equilibrium expenditure and real GDP equals $5.0 \times \$100$ million, which is $500 million.

■ Self Test 13.3

Fill in the blanks

The multiplier equals the change in equilibrium expenditure ____ (minus; divided by; multiplied by) the change in autonomous expenditure. The multiplier is ____ (less; greater) than 1. The greater the marginal propensity to consume, the ____ (larger; smaller) the multiplier. Imports and income taxes make the multiplier ____ (larger; smaller). A recession starts with ____ (an increase; a decrease) in autonomous expenditure.

True or false

1. The multiplier is greater than 1.

2. If the multiplier equals 4, then a $0.25 trillion increase in investment will increase real GDP by $1.0 trillion.

3. The smaller the marginal propensity to consume, the larger is the multiplier.

4. When the marginal propensity to consume is 0.8, the multiplier is 5.0.

5. A country that has a high marginal tax rate has a larger multiplier than a country with a low marginal tax rate, other things being the same.

Multiple choice

1. The multiplier is equal to the change in _____ divided by the change in _____.

a. autonomous expenditure; equilibrium expenditure

b. dependent expenditure; autonomous expenditure

c. real GDP; equilibrium expenditure

d. equilibrium expenditure; autonomous expenditure.

2. The multiplier is larger than one because

a. an increase in autonomous expenditure induces further increases in aggregate expenditure.

b. additional expenditure induces lower incomes.

c. an increase in autonomous expenditure brings about a reduction in the real interest rate.

d. an increase in autonomous expenditure induces further decreases in aggregate expenditure.

3. The multiplier equals 5 and there is a $3 million increase in investment. Equilibrium expenditure

a. decreases by $15 million.
b. increases by $3 million.
c. increases by $5 million.
d. increases by $15 million.

4. In an economy with no income taxes or imports, the marginal propensity to consume is 0.80. The multiplier is

a. 0.20.
b. 0.80.
c. 1.25.
d. 5.00.

5. An increase in the marginal tax rate

a. increases the multiplier.
b. decreases the multiplier.
c. has no effect on the multiplier.
d. can increase or decrease the multiplier.

6. Which of the following increases the magnitude of the multiplier?

a. a decrease in the marginal propensity to consume
b. an increase in autonomous spending
c. an increase in the marginal tax rate
d. a decrease in the marginal propensity to import

7. If the slope of the AE curve is 0.5, then the multiplier equals

a. 5.
b. 4.
c. 3.
d. 2.

8. At the beginning of a recession, the multiplier

a. offsets the initial cut in autonomous expenditure and slows the recession.
b. reinforces the initial cut in autonomous expenditure and adds force to the recession.
c. offsets the initial cut in autonomous expenditure and reverses the recession.
d. reinforces the initial cut in autonomous expenditure and reverses the recession.

Complete the graph

1. Figure 13.5 shows an AE curve. Now suppose that government expenditure increases by $1.2 trillion at every level of real GDP.

■ FIGURE 13.5

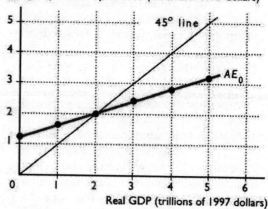

Aggregate planned expenditure (trillions of 1997 dollars)

a. Plot the new AE curve.
b. What is the new equilibrium expenditure? By how much does equilibrium expenditure change?
c. What is the slope of the AE curve?
d. What is the multiplier? Use the multiplier to find the change in equilibrium expenditure.

Short answer

1. The table gives various values for the marginal propensity to consume. Suppose there are no income taxes or imports. Complete the table. What is the relationship between the *MPC* and the multiplier?

Marginal propensity to consume, *MPC*	Multiplier
0.9	——
0.8	——
0.7	——
0.6	——
0.5	——
0.4	——

2. Why is the multiplier greater than 1?

CHECKPOINT 13.4

■ **Derive the *AD* curve from equilibrium expenditure.**

Practice Problem 13.4

1. An economy has the following aggregate expenditure schedules:

Real GDP (billions of 1997 dollars)	Aggregate planned expenditure in billions of 1997 dollars when the price level is		
	110	100	90
0	1.0	1.5	2.0
1	1.5	2.0	2.5
2	2.0	2.5	3.0
3	2.5	3.0	3.5
4	3.0	3.5	4.0
5	3.5	4.0	4.5
6	4.0	4.5	5.0

a. Make a graph to show three *AE* curves.

b. Find equilibrium expenditure at each price level.

c. Construct the aggregate demand schedule and plot the aggregate demand curve.

Solution to Practice Problem 13.4

This Practice Problem demonstrates how to derive the *AD* curve. The points on the aggregate demand curve are the points of equilibrium expenditure.

Quick Review

• *Equilibrium expenditure* The level of aggregate expenditure that occurs when aggregate planned expenditure equals real GDP.

a. **Make a graph to show three *AE* curves.**

The figure shows the three *AE* curves.

b. **Find equilibrium expenditure at each price level.**

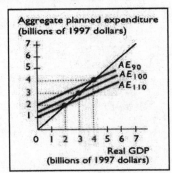

Equilibrium expenditure is determined where the *AE* curve intersects the 45° line. In the figure, when the price level is 90, equilibrium expenditure is $4 billion; when the price level is 100, equilibrium expenditure is $3 billion; and when the price level is 110, equilibrium expenditure is $2 billion.

c. **Construct the aggregate demand schedule and plot the aggregate demand curve.**

The table shows the aggregate demand schedule. The aggregate demand schedule is the combination of price level and equilibrium expenditure given in part b of the Practice Problem.

Price level	Quantity of real GDP demanded (billions of 1996 dollars)
90	4
100	3
110	2

The figure plots this aggregate demand schedule and shows the aggregate demand curve.

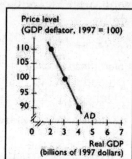

Additional Practice Problem 13.4a

1. Figure 13.6 shows the *AE* curve, AE_0 when the price level is 100.

■ FIGURE 13.6
Aggregate planned expenditure (trillions of 1997 dollars)

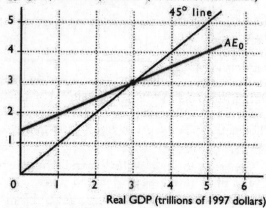

a. In Figure 13.6 show what occurs when the price level rises to 110 and aggregate planned expenditure decreases by $1 trillion at every level of real GDP. What is the new equilibrium expenditure?

b. In Figure 13.6, show what occurs when the price level falls to 90 and aggregate planned expenditure increases by $1 trillion at every level of real GDP. What is the new equilibrium expenditure?

c. Draw an aggregate demand curve in Figure 13.7 using the equilibrium expenditure from parts (a) and (b).

■ FIGURE 13.7
Price level (GDP deflator, 1997 = 100)

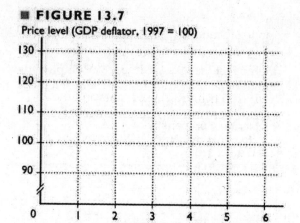

Solution to Additional Practice Problem 13.4a

a. Figure 13.8 shows the new aggregate expenditure curve, AE_1. The new equilibrium expenditure is $1 trillion, where the AE_1 curve intersects the 45° line.

b. Figure 13.8 shows the new aggregate expenditure curve, AE_2. The new equilibrium expenditure is $5 trillion, where the AE_2 curve intersects the 45° line.

■ FIGURE 13.8
Aggregate planned expenditure (trillions of 1997 dollars)

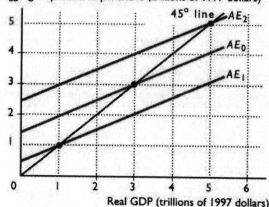

c. Each point of equilibrium expenditure corresponds to a point on the *AD* curve. When the price level is 110, real GDP is $1 trillion. When the price level is 100, real GDP is $3 trillion. And when the price level is 90, real GDP is $5 trillion. These points and the aggregate demand curve are shown in Figure 13.9.

■ **FIGURE 13.9**

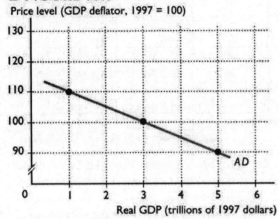

■ **Self Test 13.4**

Fill in the blanks

The ____ (*AE*; *AD*) curve is derived from the ____ (*AE*; *AD*) curve. The ____ (*AE*; *AD*) curve is the relationship between aggregate planned expenditure and real GDP. The ____ (*AE*; *AD*) curve is the relationship between the quantity of real GDP demanded and the price level. The ____ (*AE*; *AD*) curve is upward sloping and the ____ (*AE*; *AD*) curve is downward sloping. The ____ (*AE*; *AD*) curve shifts when the price level changes.

True or false

1. There is no relationship between equilibrium expenditure and the *AD* curve.

2. A change in the price level results in a movement along the *AD* curve.

3. A change in the price level results in a movement along the *AE* curve.

4. Each point of equilibrium expenditure on the *AE* curve corresponds to a point on the *AD* curve.

Multiple choice

1. A movement along the *AE* curve arises from a change in _____ and a movement along the *AD* curve arises from a change in _____.

a. real GDP; the price level
b. the price level; the price level
c. the price level; real GDP
d. equilibrium expenditure; autonomous expenditure

2. The level of equilibrium expenditure at each price level determines

a. the points on the *AD* curve.
b. aggregate planned production.
c. the price level.
d. full employment.

3. A change in the price level

a. shifts the *AE* curve and creates a movement along the *AD* curve.
b. creates a movement along the *AE* curve and shifts the *AD* curve.
c. shifts the *AE* curve and the *AD* curve in the same direction.
d. shifts the *AE* curve and the *AD* curve in opposite directions.

Short answer

1. What is the relationship between the *AE* curve and the *AD* curve?

2. What is the effect on the *AE* curve and the *AD* curve when the price level falls?

SELF TEST ANSWERS

■ CHECKPOINT 13.1

Fill in the blanks

Aggregate planned expenditure <u>does not always equal</u> GDP. The components of aggregate expenditure that change when real GDP changes are <u>induced</u> expenditure. The <u>consumption</u> function is the relationship between consumption expenditure and disposable income, other things remaining the same. The marginal propensity to consume equals the change in consumption expenditure <u>divided by</u> the change in disposable income that brought it about. The slope of the consumption function equals <u>the MPC</u>. A change in disposable income is shown by a <u>movement along</u> the consumption function and a change in the buying power of money is shown by a <u>shift of</u> the consumption function.

True or false

1. True;   page 320
2. True;   page 321
3. False;   page 321
4. False;   page 322
5. False;   page 322

Multiple choice

1. c;   page 318
2. d;   page 319
3. c;   page 319
4. d;   page 320
5. b;   page 320
6. c;   page 320
7. b   page 322
8. b;   page 323

Complete the graph

1. a. Figure 13.10 plots the consumption function, labelled CF_0; page 320.

■ FIGURE 13.10

Consumption expenditure (trillions of 1997 dollars)

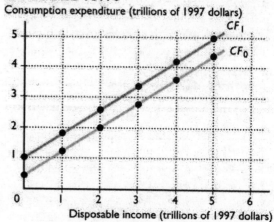

Disposable income (trillions of 1997 dollars)

b. Autonomous consumption is $0.4 trillion, the y-intercept of curve CF_0 in Figure 13.10; page 320.

c. If disposable income is $1.0 trillion, consumption expenditure is $1.2 trillion and saving is –$0.2 trillion. If disposable income is $4.0 trillion, consumption expenditure is $3.6 trillion and saving is $0.4 trillion; page 320.

d. When disposable income increases from $2.0 trillion to $3.0 trillion along curve CF_0, an increase of $1.0 trillion, consumption expenditure increases from $2.0 trillion to $2.8 trillion, an increase of $0.8 trillion. The marginal propensity to consume equals $0.8 trillion ÷ $1.0 trillion, which equals 0.8 ; page 322.

e. The new consumption function is labelled CF_1 in Figure 13.10. Autonomous consumption is $1 trillion; page 320, 323.

Short answer

1. Actual aggregate expenditure always equals real GDP. Aggregate planned expenditure does not necessarily equal real GDP. If aggregate planned expenditure exceeds real GDP, firms' inventories are smaller than

planned; and if aggregate planned expenditure is less than real GDP, firms' inventories are larger than planned. Real GDP equals aggregate planned expenditure plus the unplanned change in firms' inventories; page 319.

2. Autonomous expenditure is the components of aggregate expenditure that do not change when real GDP changes. Induced expenditure is the components of aggregate expenditure that change when real GDP changes; page 320.

3. The *MPC* equals the slope of the consumption function. Autonomous consumption equals the *y*-axis intercept; pages 320, 322.

4. The marginal propensity to consume is the change in consumption expenditure divided by the change in disposable income that brought it about; page 322.

Change in disposable income (trillions of 1997 dollars)	Change in consumption expenditure (trillions of 1997 dollars)	Marginal propensity to consume, *MPC*
2	1.8	0.90
1	0.9	0.90
4	3.0	0.75

■ **CHECKPOINT 13.2**

Fill in the blanks

As real GDP increases, aggregate planned expenditure <u>increases</u>. Equilibrium expenditure is the level of aggregate expenditure that occurs when aggregate planned expenditure equals <u>real</u> GDP. If aggregate planned expenditure exceeds real GDP, an unplanned <u>decrease</u> in inventories occurs and firms <u>increase</u> production.

True or false

1. True; page 328

2. False; page 329

3. True; page 329

4. False; page 329

5. True; page 329

Multiple choice

1. c; page 326

2. a; page 326

3. a; page 328

4. c; page 329

5. a; page 329

6. c; page 329

7. b; page 329

8. b; page 329

Complete the graph

1. a. Aggregate planned expenditure equals $C + I + G + X - M$. The completed table is below; page 326.

GDP	C	I	G	X	M	AE
0.0	0.6	0.4	0.2	0.2	0.2	<u>1.2</u>
1.0	1.2	0.4	0.2	0.2	0.4	<u>1.6</u>
2.0	1.8	0.4	0.2	0.2	0.6	<u>2.0</u>
3.0	2.4	0.4	0.2	0.2	0.8	<u>2.4</u>
4.0	3.0	0.4	0.2	0.2	1.0	<u>2.8</u>
5.0	3.6	0.4	0.2	0.2	1.2	<u>3.2</u>

b. Figure 13.11 shows the *AE* curve; page 326.

■ **FIGURE 13.11**

Aggregate planned expenditure (trillions of 1997 dollars)

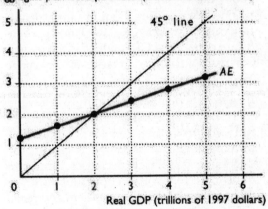

c. Equilibrium expenditure occurs in Figure 13.11 at the point where the 45° line intersects the *AE* curve. Equilibrium expenditure is $2 trillion; page 328.

d. An unplanned increase in inventories occurs when real GDP exceeds planned expenditure. In Figure 13.11, real GDP exceeds planned expenditure when real GDP is greater than $2 trillion.

An unplanned decrease in inventories occurs when real GDP is less than planned expenditure. In Figure 13.11, real GDP is less than planned expenditure when real GDP is less than $2 trillion; page 329.

e. When GDP is $3 trillion, planned investment is $0.4 trillion. When GDP is $3 trillion, aggregate planned expenditure is $2.4 trillion, so there is an unplanned increase in inventories of $0.6 trillion. Actual investment is $1 trillion, the sum of planned investment and the unplanned change in inventories; page 329.

Short answer

1. As real GDP increases, aggregate planned expenditure increases, so there is a positive relationship between real GDP and aggregate planned expenditure. Aggregate planned expenditure increases when real GDP increases because as real GDP increases, induced expenditure increases; page 326.

2. Along the 45° line real GDP equals aggregate planned expenditure. Equilibrium expenditure occurs when aggregate planned expenditure equals real GDP, which is the point where the *AE* curve intersects 45° line; page 328.

3. If aggregate planned expenditure is less than real GDP, people are spending less than firms are producing. There is an unplanned increase in inventories. Firms decrease production, and real GDP decreases. Firms continue to decrease production until the unplanned inventory change is zero and real GDP equals aggregate planned expenditure; page 329.

■ **CHECKPOINT 13.3**

Fill in the blanks

The multiplier equals the change in equilibrium expenditure <u>divided by</u> the change in autonomous expenditure. The multiplier is <u>greater</u> than 1. The greater the marginal propensity to consume, the <u>larger</u> the multiplier. Imports and income taxes make the multiplier <u>smaller</u>. A recession starts with <u>a decrease</u> in autonomous expenditure.

True or false

1. True; page 334
2. True; page 333
3. False; page 334
4. True; page 334
5. False; page 335

Multiple choice

1. d; page 333
2. a; page 334
3. d; page 333
4. d; page 334
5. b; page 335
6. d; page 335
7. d; page 335
8. b; page 336

Complete the graph

1. a. Figure 13.12 has the original *AE* curve labelled AE_0 and the new *AE* curve labelled AE_1; page 332.

■ FIGURE 13.12

Aggregate planned expenditure (trillions of 1997 dollars)

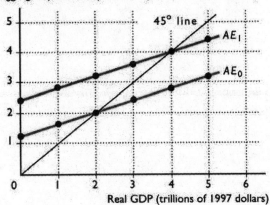

b. Equilibrium expenditure increases by $2 trillion to $4 trillion; page 332.

c. The slope of the *AE* curve equals ($0.4 trillion) ÷ ($1.0 trillion), which is 0.40; page 335.

d. The multiplier is

$$\frac{1}{(1-\text{slope of the } AE \text{ curve})}, \text{ which is}$$

$\frac{1}{(1-0.4)} = 1.67$. The change in equilibrium expenditure is equal to the multiplier multiplied by the change in autonomous expenditure, which is $(1.67) \times (\$1.2$ trillion). The change in equilibrium expenditure is $2.0 trillion; page 335.

Short answer

1. The multiplier equals $1/(1-MPC)$. The completed table is in the next column. As the *MPC* increases, the multiplier increases; page 334.

Marginal propensity to consume, *MPC*	Multiplier
0.9	10.0
0.8	5.0
0.7	3.3
0.6	2.5
0.5	2.0
0.4	1.7

2. The multiplier is greater than 1 because an increase in autonomous expenditure induces further increases in aggregate expenditure — induced expenditure increases; page 334.

■   CHECKPOINT 13.4

Fill in the blanks

The *AD* curve is derived from the *AE* curve. The *AE* curve is the relationship between aggregate planned expenditure and real GDP. The *AD* curve is the relationship between the quantity of real GDP demanded and the price level. The *AE* curve is upward sloping and the *AD* curve is downward sloping. The *AE* curve shifts when the price level changes.

True or false

1. False; page 338

2. True; page 338

3. False; page 338

4. True; page 338

Multiple choice

1. a; page 338

2. a; page 338

3. a; page 338

Short answer

1. The *AE* curve is used to derive the *AD* curve. Each point of equilibrium expenditure on the *AE* curve corresponds to a point on the *AD* curve; page 338.

2. When the price level falls, the *AE* curve shifts upward and there is a movement down along the *AD* curve; page 338.

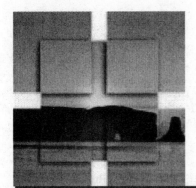

Fiscal and Monetary Policy

Chapter 14

Chapter 14 describes fiscal and monetary processes, policies, and limitations. The chapter uses the *AD-AS* model to study the effects of stabilization policies on real GDP and the price level. ...

■ **Describe the federal budget process and explain the effects of fiscal policy.**

The federal budget is an annual statement of the payments, receipts, and surplus or deficit of the government of Canada. If receipts exceed payments, the government has a budget surplus and if payments exceed receipts, the government has a budget deficit. Fiscal policy can be discretionary, which is a fiscal policy action that is initiated by an act of Parliament, or automatic, which is a fiscal policy action that is triggered by the state of the economy. The government expenditure multiplier is the magnification effect of a change in government expenditure on goods and services on aggregate demand. The tax multiplier is the magnification effect of a change in taxes on aggregate demand. A cut in taxes or an increase in government expenditure on productive services increases aggregate supply and aggregate demand. Automatic stabilizers are features of fiscal policy that stabilize real GDP without explicit action by the government.

■ **Describe the Bank of Canada's monetary policy process and explain the effects of monetary policy.**

The Bank of Canada makes monetary policy. In the long run, the real interest rate is determined in global financial markets. In the short run, the Bank of Canada can determine the nominal interest rate by undertaking open market operations. When the Bank of Canada raises the interest rate, investment and consumption expenditure decrease; the Canadian dollar rises, and net exports decrease; a multiplier process induces a further decrease in consumption expenditure and aggregate demand. To fight inflation, the Bank of Canada conducts an open market sale. The quantity of investment decreases. The multiplier decreases aggregate demand by a greater amount than the decrease in investment. The *AD* curve shifts leftward, real GDP decreases and the price level falls. To fight recession, the Bank of Canada conducts an open market purchase. Aggregate demand increases, real GDP increases and the price level rises.

■ **Describe the main debates about how fiscal and monetary policy should be used to improve**

   macroeconomic performance.

Monetarists favour a target growth rate for the quantity of money. Keynesians favour a target for the interest rate. When real GDP falls below potential GDP, Keynesians want to cut the interest rate and perhaps increase government expenditure. When the inflation rate rises, monetarists want swift action to slow it regardless of the state of real GDP. And if the inflation rate falls, monetarists want to take either no action or at most cautious action to stimulate the economy.

EXPANDED CHAPTER CHECKLIST

When you have completed this chapter, you will be able to

1 Describe the federal budget process and explain the effects of fiscal policy.

- Define budget surplus, budget deficit, and balanced budget.

- Define discretionary fiscal policy and automatic fiscal policy.

- Describe the government expenditure multiplier and the tax multiplier.

- Describe the balanced budget multiplier.

- Explain how fiscal policy can eliminate a deflationary gap and an inflationary gap.

- State why discretionary fiscal policy has supply-side effects.

- Discuss the limitations to discretionary fiscal policy.

- Explain the action of automatic stabilizers.

2 Describe the Bank of Canada's monetary policy process and explain the effects of monetary policy.

- Describe the Bank of Canada's monetary policy process.

- Explain the Bank of Canada's influence on the interest rate in the short run and long run.

- Describe how the Bank of Canada raises the interest rate and lowers the interest rate.

- Discuss the ripple effects of the Bank of Canada's actions.

- Describe how the Bank of Canada fights inflation and recession.

- Describe the limitations of monetary stabilization policy.

3 Describe the main debates about how fiscal and monetary policy should be used to improve macroeconomic performance.

- Explain why monetarists favour a target growth rate for the quantity of money and Keynesians favour a target for the interest rate.

- Discuss the weights placed on real GDP and the inflation rate by modern Keynesians and monetarists.

KEY TERMS

- Automatic fiscal policy (page 348)
- Automatic stabilizers (page 355)
- Balanced budget (page 346)
- Balanced budget multiplier (page 350)
- Budget deficit (page 346)
- Budget surplus (page 346)
- Discretionary fiscal policy (page 348)
- Federal budget (page 346)
- Fiscal policy (page 346)
- Government expenditure multiplier (page 349)
- Induced taxes (page 355)
- Induced transfer payments (page 356)
- Tax multiplier (349)

CHECKPOINT 14.1

■ Describe the federal budget process and explain the effects of fiscal policy.

Practice Problems 14.1

1. Classify each of the following as discretionary fiscal policy or automatic fiscal policy or neither

a. A decrease in tax receipts in a recession.

b. Additional expenditure to upgrade highways.

c. An increase in the public education budget.

d. A purchase of $10 million of medicines to treat AIDS sufferers in Africa.

e. A cut in funding for national defence during an expansion.

2. Explain the change in aggregate demand when

a. Government expenditure on goods and services increases by $100 billion.

b. Taxes are increased by $100 billion.

c. Both (a) and (b) occur simultaneously.

Solution to Practice Problems 14.1

An example of discretionary fiscal policy is an increase in defence spending because this spending requires an act of Parliament. An example of automatic fiscal policy, fiscal policy that is triggered by the state of the economy, is an increase in payments to the unemployed when unemployment increases in a recession.

Quick Review

- *Discretionary fiscal policy* A fiscal policy action that is initiated by an act of Parliament.

- *Automatic fiscal policy* A fiscal policy action that is triggered by the state of the economy, such as an increase in payments to the unemployed and a decrease in tax receipts triggered by recession.

- *Government expenditure multiplier* The magnification effect a change in government expenditure on goods and services on aggregate demand.

- *Tax multiplier* The magnification effect of a change in taxes on aggregate demand.

1. **Classify each of the following as discretionary fiscal policy or automatic fiscal policy or neither**

a. **A decrease in tax receipts in a recession.**

During a recession, tax receipts automatically fall as workers are laid off and their incomes decrease. So the decrease in tax receipts is an example of induced taxes and is an automatic fiscal policy.

b. **Additional expenditure to upgrade highways.**

To upgrade highways, the government initiates a change in spending. Additional expenditure to upgrade highways is a discretionary fiscal policy.

c. **An increase in the public education budget.**

An increase in the public education budget is initiated by government. So an increase in the public education budget is a discretionary fiscal policy.

d. **A purchase of $10 million of medicines to treat AIDS sufferers in Africa.**

The purchase of medicines for AIDS sufferers is initiated by an act of Parliament, so the policy is a discretionary fiscal policy.

e. **A cut in funding for national defence during an expansion.**

A cut in funding for national defence is initiated by an act of Parliament. The policy is a discretionary fiscal policy.

2. **Explain the change in aggregate demand when**

a. **Government expenditure on goods and services increases by $100 billion.**

The $100 billion increase in government expenditure increases aggregate demand by more than $100 billion because of the government expenditure multiplier. The initial government expenditure of $100 billion induces an increase in consumption expenditure, which brings a further increase in aggregate demand. A multiplier process ensues.

b. Taxes are increased by $100 billion.

The tax hike decreases aggregate demand by more than $100 billion because of the tax multiplier. The tax hike decreases disposable income, which decreases consumption expenditure. With decreased consumption expenditure, employment and incomes fall, and consumption expenditure falls further. A multiplier process ensues.

c. Both (a) and (b) occur simultaneously.

Aggregate demand increases. The increase in aggregate demand from the increase in government expenditure is larger than the decrease in aggregate demand from the tax hike. The balanced budget multiplier is positive—a simultaneous and equal increase in government expenditure and taxes brings an increase in aggregate demand.

Additional Practice Problem 14.1a

What is the balanced budget multiplier and why is it greater than zero?

Solution to Additional Practice Problem 14.1a

The balanced budget multiplier is the magnification effect on aggregate demand of *simultaneous* changes in government expenditure and taxes that leave the budget balance unchanged. The balanced budget multiplier is positive because the size of the government expenditure multiplier is larger than the size of the tax multiplier. That is, a $1 increase in government expenditure increases aggregate demand by more than a $1 increase in taxes decreases aggregate demand. So when both government expenditure and taxes increase by $1, aggregate demand still increases.

■ **Self Test 14.1**

Fill in the blanks

The national debt is ____ (total receipts minus payments; the total amount of debt outstanding that accumulates from past budget deficits). ____ (Automatic; Discretionary) fiscal policy is a fiscal policy action that is initiated by an act of Parliament. The government expenditure multi-plier is the magnification effect of a change in government expenditure on goods and services on aggregate ____ (demand; supply). A tax cut ____ (increases; decreases) aggregate supply and shifts the *AS* curve ____ (rightward; leftward). One limitation of discretionary fiscal policy is the ____ (stabilization; law-making time) lag.

True or false

1. Fiscal policy is the adjusting of the federal budget to eliminate unemployment.

2. A reduction in the federal personal income tax rates is an example of discretionary fiscal policy.

3. The government expenditure multiplier is the magnification effect of a change in aggregate demand on government expenditure on goods and services.

4. The magnitude of the tax multiplier is smaller than the government expenditure multiplier.

5. If government expenditure and taxes increase by the same amount, aggregate demand does not change.

6. To eliminate an inflationary gap, the government could decrease its expenditure on goods and services.

7. A tax cut increases aggregate supply but does not increase aggregate demand so it increases real GDP and lowers the price level.

8. Automatic stabilizers are features of fiscal policy that work to stabilize real GDP without explicit action by the government.

Multiple choice

1. The annual statement of the payments, tax receipts, and the surplus or deficit of the government of Canada is the federal

   a. surplus.
   b. deficit.
   c. budget.
   d. spending.

2. When payments are less than tax receipts, the government has a budget

a. that is balanced.
b. deficit.
c. surplus.
d. with a negative debt.

3. National debt decreases in a given year when a country has a

a. budget deficit.
b. balanced budget.
c. budget supplement.
d. budget surplus.

4. In _____ the federal government published a White Paper called *Employment and Incomes* that set the stage for the federal government to actively change its _____ to manage the level of aggregate demand.

a. 1945; expenditure and taxes
b. 1945; expenditure only
c. 1960; expenditure and taxes
d. 1960; taxes only

5. The central player in the process of determining fiscal policy in Canada is the

a. Prime Minister.
b. Minister of Finance.
c. Bank of Canada.
d. Department of Finance.

6. An example of automatic fiscal policy is

a. an interest rate cut, initiated by an act of Parliament.
b. an increase in the quantity of money.
c. a tax cut, initiated by an act of Parliament.
d. a decrease in tax receipts, triggered by the state of the economy.

7. The government expenditure multiplier is the magnification effect of a change in government expenditure on goods and services on

a. aggregate demand.
b. the budget deficit.
c. tax receipts.
d. the national debt.

8. The magnitude of the tax multiplier is ____ the magnitude of the government expenditure multiplier.

a. equal to
b. greater than
c. smaller than
d. the inverse of

9. Discretionary fiscal policy works to close a deflationary gap by shifting the

a. *AD* curve leftward.
b. *AS* curve leftward.
c. *AD* curve leftward and the *AS* curve leftward.
d. *AD* curve rightward.

10. According to the conventional view, a tax cut _____ real GDP and _____ the price level.

a. increases; raises
b. increases; lowers
c. decreases; raises
d. decreases; lowers

11. If the economy is at an above full-employment equilibrium _____ gap exists and discretionary fiscal policy that _____ aggregate demand will return real GDP to potential GDP.

a. an inflationary; increases
b. an inflationary; decreases
c. a deflationary; increases
d. a deflationary; decreases

12. Discretionary fiscal policy is hampered by

a. law-making time lags, induced taxes, and automatic stabilizers.

b. law-making time lags, estimating potential GDP, and economic forecasting.

c. economic forecasting, law-making time lags, and induced taxes.

d. automatic stabilizers, law-making time lags, and estimating potential GDP.

Complete the graph

1. Figure 14.1 illustrates an economy.

■ FIGURE 14.1

Price level (GDP deflator, 1997 = 100)

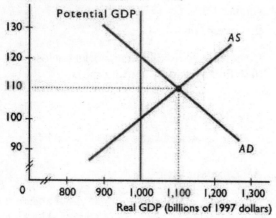

a. Is there an inflationary gap or a deflationary gap present?

b. Describe the fiscal policy that will restore the economy to full employment.

c. In Figure 14.1, illustrate the effect of the policy you suggested in your answer to part (b).

Short answer

1. What happens to the national debt if the government has a $100 million budget deficit?

2. How can the government use fiscal policy to eliminate a deflationary gap?

3. What are the demand side effects of a tax cut? What are the supply-side effects? Why does a tax cut have supply-side effects?

4. It is not easy to determine potential GDP. Why does this fact hamper the use of discretionary fiscal policy?

5. What are automatic stabilizers? Can they eliminate a recession?

CHECKPOINT 14.2

■ Describe the Bank of Canada's monetary policy process and explain the effects of monetary policy.

Practice Problems 14.2

1. If the Bank of Canada reduces the quantity of money, explain how each of the following items changes:

a. Businesses' purchases of new capital equipment.

b. Households' purchases of new cars and houses.

c. Foreigners' purchases of Canadian-made goods and services.

d. Canadians' purchases of imported goods and services.

2. What is the multiplier effect of monetary policy? How does it work? How does the size of the autonomous expenditure multiplier influence the size of the multiplier effect of monetary policy?

Solution to Practice Problems 14.2

The first Practice Problem studies the ripple effects of the Bank of Canada's actions. The second Practice Problem shows how the multiplier process magnifies the effect of a change in the interest rate.

Quick Review

• *Ripple effects from monetary policy* When the Bank of Canada raises the interest rate three main events follow: investment and consumption expenditure decrease; the Canadian dollar rises, and net exports decrease;

and a multiplier process induces a further decrease in consumption expenditure and aggregate demand.

1. **If the Bank of Canada reduces the quantity of money, explain how each of the following items changes:**

a. **Businesses' purchases of new capital equipment.**

A reduction in the quantity of money raises the interest rate. The interest rate is the opportunity cost of the funds used to finance investment. When the opportunity cost of investment increases, businesses delay their purchases of new capital equipment.

b. **Households' purchases of new cars and houses.**

A reduction in the quantity of money raises the interest rate. The interest rate is the opportunity cost of the funds used to finance the purchase of big-ticket consumer items. When the opportunity cost of purchasing big-ticket items increases, households delay their purchases of new cars and houses.

c. **Foreigners' purchases of Canadian-made goods and services.**

When the interest rate in Canada rises relative to the interest rate in other countries, people buy Canadian dollars and sell other currencies. With more Canadian dollars demanded, the price of the Canadian dollar rises on the foreign exchange market. The higher price of the Canadian dollar means that foreigners must now pay more for Canadian-made goods and services. Canadian exports decrease.

d. **Canadians' purchases of imported goods and services.**

When the interest rate in Canada rises relative to the interest rate in other countries, people buy Canadian dollars and sell other currencies. With more Canadian dollars demanded, the price of the Canadian dollar rises on the foreign exchange market. The higher price of the Canadian dollar means that Canadians now pay less for imported

goods and services. Canadians' purchases of imported goods and services increase.

2. **What is the multiplier effect of monetary policy? How does it work? How does the size of the autonomous expenditure multiplier influence the size of the multiplier effect of monetary policy?**

When the Bank of Canada increases the quantity of money, the interest rate falls. Consumption expenditure and investment increase. The foreign exchange value of the dollar falls. Canadian exports increase and Canadian imports decrease. Aggregate expenditure increases. The multiplier effect of monetary policy is the increase in aggregate expenditure divided by the increase in the quantity of money.

When the interest rate falls, part of autonomous expenditure increases and the autonomous expenditure multiplier determines the increase in aggregate demand. The larger the autonomous expenditure multiplier, the larger the increase in aggregate demand and the larger is the multiplier effect of monetary policy.

Additional Practice Problem 14.2a

What is an advantage that monetary policy has over fiscal policy?

Solution to Additional Practice Problem 14.2a

Monetary policy has an advantage over fiscal policy because it cuts out the law-making time lags. The actual actions that change the quantity of money are taken daily by the Bank of Canada. So monetary policy is a continuous policy process and is not subject to the long decision lag associated with discretionary fiscal policy.

■ **Self Test 14.2**

Fill in the blanks

In the _____ (long; short) run, the Bank of Canada has no control over the real interest rate. To raise the interest rate, the Bank of Canada _____ (purchases; sells) government securities in the open market. When the interest rate rises, investment and consumption expenditure ____ (increase; decrease) and net exports ____ (increase; decrease). When the Bank of Canada eases to fight recession, the aggregate ____ (demand; supply) curve shifts ____ (leftward; rightward). Monetary policy ____(is; is not) subject to the same law-making time lag as fiscal policy.

True or false

1. The Bank of Canada's Board of Directors meets once a year in January to approve interest rate decisions.

2. In the short run, when the Bank of Canada changes the nominal interest rate, the real interest rate also changes.

3. If the Bank of Canada fears a recession, it will conduct an open market purchase that lowers the interest rate.

4. A change in the interest rate changes net exports.

5. The Bank of Canada's monetary policy works by changing aggregate supply.

6. If the Bank of Canada conducts an open market operation that raises the interest rate, aggregate demand decreases.

7. To combat a recession, the Bank of Canada lowers taxes, which increases aggregate demand and shifts the aggregate demand curve rightward.

8. Monetary policy is a perfect stabilization tool because it does not have law-making time lags.

Multiple choice

1. The Bank of Canada's Board of Directors consists of the Governor and

a. Senior Deputy Governor, and the Deputy Minister of Finance.

b. the Minister of Finance, and twelve bureaucrats from the Bank of Canada.

c. Senior Deputy Governor, the Deputy Minister of Finance, and twelve prominent Canadians with varied backgrounds.

d. the Minister of Finance, and twelve bureaucrats from the Department of Finance.

2. The Bank of Canada changes aggregate demand through monetary policy by changing

a. the quantity of money and influencing the interest rate.

b. tax rates and influencing disposable income.

c. government expenditure.

d. the budget balance.

3. If the Bank of Canada sells government securities, the interest rate

a. rises.

b. is not affected.

c. falls.

d. might either rise or fall.

4. When the Bank of Canada raises the nominal interest rate, the real interest rate

a. temporarily rises.

b. permanently rises.

c. temporarily falls.

d. permanently falls.

5. If the Bank of Canada lowers the interest rate

a. investment increases.

b. consumption expenditure decreases.

c. exports do not change.

d. net exports decrease.

6. If the Bank of Canada raises the interest rate,

a. the price of the Canadian dollar on the foreign exchange market increases.

b. investment increases.

c. aggregate demand increases.

d. net exports increase.

7. The Bank of Canada will raise the interest rate when it

a. fears recession.

b. wants to increase the quantity of money.

c. fears inflation.

d. wants to encourage bank lending.

8. Decreasing the quantity of money shifts the aggregate demand curve ____ so that real GDP ____ and the price level ____.

a. rightward; increases; rises

b. leftward; decreases; rises

c. rightward; increases; falls

d. leftward; decreases; falls

9. To fight recession, the Bank of Canada can _____ the interest rate by _____ government securities.

a. lower; buying

b. lower; selling

c. raise; buying

d. raise; selling

10. In a recession, the Bank of Canada can ____ the interest rate, which ____ aggregate demand and ____ real GDP.

a. lower; increases; decreases

b. raise; decreases; increases

c. lower; increases; increases

d. raise; increases; decreases

11. An advantage monetary policy has over fiscal policy is that monetary policy

a. can be quickly changed and implemented.

b. is coordinated with fiscal policy.

c. is approved by the Minister of Finance.

d. changes consumption expenditure and investment but does not change net exports.

Complete the graph

1. Figure 14.2 illustrates an economy.

■ FIGURE 14.2

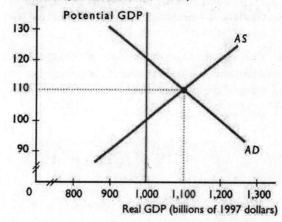
Price level (GDP deflator, 1997 = 100)

a. Describe the monetary policy that will restore the economy to full employment.

b. In Figure 14.2 illustrate the effect of the policy you suggested in your answer to part (a).

c. Compared to fiscal policy, what is an advantage of using monetary policy to restore the economy to potential GDP? What is an additional limitation faced by monetary policy?

Short answer

1. How does the Bank of Canada keep the public informed about the state of the economy and its monetary policy decisions?

2. How does the Bank of Canada influence the real interest rate in the short run and in the long run?

3. Suppose the Bank of Canada increases the quantity of money. What is the effect on the

interest rate? On investment? On aggregate demand?

4. How does monetary policy affect the price of the Canadian dollar on the foreign exchange market?

5. Suppose the Bank of Canada is concerned that the economy is entering a recession. What policy can the Bank of Canada pursue and what is the effect of the policy on real GDP and the price level?

CHECKPOINT 14.3

■ Describe the main debates about how fiscal and monetary policy should be used to improve macroeconomic performance.

Practice Problem 14.3

1. Suppose that the inflation rate is 4 percent a year and real GDP exceeds potential GDP.
a. What would a Keynesian prescribe?
b. What would a monetarist prescribe?
c. What would the government of Canada most likely do?
d. What would the Bank of Canada most likely do?

Solution to Practice Problem 14.3

This Practice Problem studies the debate between Keynesians and monetarists and the use of fiscal policy and monetary policy to influence real GDP and the price level.

Quick Review

- *Keynesians* When real GDP rises above potential GDP, Keynesians want cautious action to slow the growth of aggregate demand and eliminate the inflationary gap.

- *Monetarists* When the inflation rate rises, monetarists want swift action to slow it regardless of the state of real GDP.

1. Suppose that the inflation rate is 4 percent a year and real GDP exceeds potential GDP.

a. **What would a Keynesian prescribe?**

A Keynesian would prescribe a cautious rise in the interest rate, which would slow the growth of aggregate demand.

b. **What would a monetarist prescribe?**

A monetarist would want swift action to slow the inflation rate. So a monetarist would prescribe an aggressive slowing of money growth.

c. **What would the government of Canada most likely do?**

The government of Canada would most likely do nothing.

d. **What would the Bank of Canada most likely do?**

The Bank of Canada is monetarist in its views and actions on the inflation rate. The Bank of Canada would want to lower the inflation rate, so it would most likely raise the overnight rate.

Additional Practice Problem 14.3a

In what aspect is the Bank of Canada Keynesian?

Solution to Additional Practice Problem 14.3a

Keynesians favour a target for the interest rate. They believe that aggregate demand can be controlled more accurately by preventing the interest rate from fluctuating too wildly, which it might do with strict targeting of the quantity of money and its growth rate. The Bank of Canada is Keynesian in the respect that it sets a target for the overnight rate and hits this target exactly by its setting of bank rate.

■ **Self Test 14.3**

Fill in the blanks

Historically, Keynesians favoured _____ (fiscal; monetary) policy and monetarists favoured _____ (fiscal; monetary) policy as the tool for stabilizing aggregate demand. Monetarists favour a target _____ (for the interest rate;

growth rate for the quantity of money). The Bank of Canada _____ (does not set; sets) a specific target for the growth rate of the quantity of money. When real GDP falls below potential GDP _____ (Keynesians; monetarists) want to take swift action to stimulate the economy. The Bank of Canada is _____ (Keynesian; monetarist) in its views and actions on a rising inflation rate.

True or false

1. Keynesians favour a target for the interest rate.

2. The Bank of Canada is monetarist in the respect that its sets a target for the overnight rate.

3. The Bank of Canada sets a target for the overnight rate and a target for the growth rate of the quantity of money.

4. Monetarists favour an inflation target at a low inflation rate.

5. Keynesians are concerned about any fluctuations in the inflation rate.

Multiple choice

1. Monetary policy influences

a. the allocation of resources between consumption and investment.
b. the exchange rate.
c. exports and imports.
d. all of the above.

2. Monetarists favour a target _____ and Keynesians favour a target _____.

a. growth rate for the quantity of money; for the interest rate.
b. growth rate for the quantity of money demanded; for the interest rate
c. for the interest rate; growth rate for the quantity of money
d. for the interest rate; growth rate for the quantity of money demanded

3. The greatest divide that defines modern Keynesians and monetarists arises from views about the appropriate weights to place on

a. monetary policy and fiscal policy.
b. real GDP and unemployment.
c. real GDP and the inflation rate.
d. the price level and the inflation rate.

4. When real GDP falls below potential GDP _____ want to take swift action to stimulate the economy.

a. monetarists
b. Keynesians
c. monetarists and Keynesians
d. the Bank of Canada

5. The Bank of Canada is _____ in its view of setting a target for the overnight rate and _____ in its view and actions in keeping the inflation rate in check.

a. Keynesian; monetarist
b. monetarist; Keynesian
c. Keynesian; Keynesian
d. monetarist; monetarist

Short answer

1. Why do monetarists favour a target growth rate for the quantity of money?

2. Why do Keynesians favour a target for the interest rate?

3. How do monetarists react to changes in the inflation rate?

SELF TEST ANSWERS

■ CHECKPOINT 14.1

Fill in the blanks

The national debt is <u>the total amount of debt outstanding that accumulates from past budget deficits</u>. <u>Discretionary</u> fiscal policy is a fiscal policy action that is initiated by an act of Parliament. The government expenditure multiplier is the magnification effect of a change in government expenditure on goods and services on aggregate <u>demand</u>. A tax cut <u>increases</u> aggregate supply and shifts the *AS* curve <u>rightward</u>. One limitation of discretionary fiscal policy is the <u>law-making time</u> lag.

True or false

1. False; page 346
2. True; page 348
3. False; page 349
4. True; page 349
5. False; page 350
6. True; page 352
7. False; pages 349, 353
8. True; page 355

Multiple choice

1. c; page 346
2. c; page 346
3. d; page 346
4. a; page 348
5. b; page 348
6. d; page 348
7. a; page 349
8. c; page 349
9. d; page 351
10. a; page 354
11. b; page 352

12. b; page 355

Complete the graph

1. a. There is an inflationary gap because real GDP exceeds potential GDP; page 352.

   b. The economy will return to full employment with a tax hike or a decrease in government expenditure; page 352.

   c. Figure 14.3 shows the results of the policy in part (b). Aggregate demand decreases and the *AD* curve shifts leftward from AD_0 to AD_1. Real GDP decreases from $1,100 billion to $1,000 billion and the price level falls from 110 to 100; page 352.

■ FIGURE 14.3

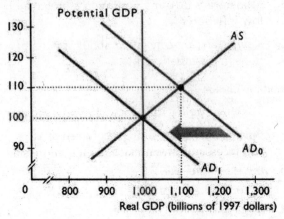

Price level (GDP deflator, 1997 = 100)

Short answer

1. If the government has a $100 million budget deficit, the national debt increases by $100 million; page 346.

2. A deflationary gap exists when real GDP is less than potential GDP. The government can eliminate the deflationary gap by increasing aggregate demand. The government increases aggregate demand by increasing its expenditure on goods and services or by cutting taxes; page 351.

3. A tax cut increases disposable income, which increases consumption expenditure and aggregate demand. A tax cut creates an incentive to work and save. So a tax cut increases the supply of labour and the supply of saving. An increase in the supply of labour decreases the equilibrium real wage rate and increases the equilibrium quantity of labour employed. An increase in the supply of saving decreases the equilibrium real interest rate and increases the equilibrium quantity of investment and capital employed. With larger quantities of labour and capital, potential GDP increases and so does aggregate supply. So a decrease in taxes increases aggregate supply; pages 349, 352.

4. It is not easy to tell whether real GDP is below, above, or at potential GDP. So a discretionary fiscal action can move real GDP *away* from potential GDP instead of towards it; page 355.

5. Automatic stabilizers are features of fiscal policy that stabilize real GDP without explicit action by the government. Automatic stabilizers include induced taxes and induced transfer payments. Induced taxes and induced transfer payments decrease the multiplier effect of a change in autonomous expenditure. So they moderate both expansions and recessions and make real GDP more stable. But they cannot eliminate a recession; page 355.

■ **CHECKPOINT 14.2**

Fill in the blanks

In the <u>long</u> run, the Bank of Canada has no control over the real interest rate. To raise the interest rate, the Bank of Canada <u>sells</u> government securities in the open market. When the interest rate rises, investment and consumption expenditure <u>decrease</u> and net exports <u>decrease</u>. When the Bank of Canada eases to fight recession, the aggregate <u>demand</u> curve shifts <u>rightward</u>. Monetary policy <u>is not</u> subject to the same lawmaking time lag as fiscal policy.

True or false

1. False; page 358
2. True; page 359
3. True; page 360
4. True; page 361
5. False; page 363
6. True; page 363
7. False; page 364
8. False; page 365

Multiple choice

1. c; page 358
2. a; page 359
3. a; page 359
4. a; page 359
5. a; page 360
6. a; page 361
7. c; page 363
8. d; page 363
9. a; page 364
10. c; page 364
11. a; page 365

Complete the graph

1. a. The economy will return to full employment with a decrease in the quantity of money; page 363.

   b. Figure 14.4 shows the results of the decrease in the quantity of money. Aggregate demand decreases and the *AD* curve shifts leftward from AD_0 to AD_1. Real GDP decreases from $1,100 billion to potential GDP of $1,000 billion and the price level falls from 110 to 100; page 363.

■ **FIGURE 14.4**

Price level (GDP deflator, 1997 = 100)

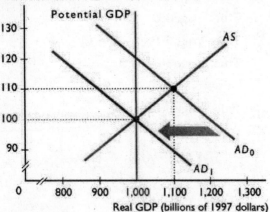

Real GDP (billions of 1997 dollars)

c. The advantage of using monetary policy is that there is no law-making lag. The actions that change the quantity of money are taken daily by the Bank of Canada. The effects of monetary policy, unlike fiscal policy, are indirect and depend on how private decisions respond to a change in the interest rate. These responses are hard to forecast and vary from one situation to another in unpredictable ways; page 365.

Short answer

1. The Bank of Canada provides a running commentary on the state of the economy in the form of the data that it publishes on its Web site and less formally in the speeches made by the Governor and other senior officials.

    Twice a year, in May and November, the Bank of Canada prepares a *Monetary Policy Report*. And at other times of the year, the Bank publishes a *Monetary Policy Report Update*. These reports provide a detailed summary of the Bank's policies and of the Bank's strategic thinking. They also provide a detailed description of the current state of the economy and the outlook for future inflation; page 358.

2. In the short run, the Bank of Canada can determine the nominal interest rate by undertaking open market operations that change the quantity of money. In the short run, the expected inflation rate is determined by recent monetary policy and inflation experience. So when the Bank of Canada changes the nominal interest rate, the real interest rate also changes, temporarily.

    In the long run, the real interest rate is determined in global financial markets. So in the long run, the Bank of Canada influences the nominal interest rate by the effects of its policies on the inflation rate. But it does not directly control the nominal interest rate, and it has no control over the real interest rate; page 359.

3. If the Bank of Canada increases the quantity of money, the interest rate falls, investment increases, and aggregate demand increases; page 360.

4. Suppose the interest rate rises relative to the interest rates in other countries. Some people will want to move funds into Canada from other countries to take advantage of the higher interest rate they can now earn on their Canadian bank deposits and bonds. When money is moved into Canada, people buy Canadian dollars and sell other currencies. With more Canadian dollars demanded, the price of the Canadian dollar rises on the foreign exchange market; page 361.

5. When the Bank of Canada is concerned that the economy is entering a recession, it makes an open market purchase. The interest rate falls. Investment and expenditure on consumer durables increases. The dollar falls on the foreign exchange market and net exports increase. Aggregate expenditure increases and the multiplier increases aggregate demand. Real GDP increases and the price level rises; page 364.

■ **CHECKPOINT 14.3**

Fill in the blanks

Historically, Keynesians favoured <u>fiscal</u> policy and monetarists favoured <u>monetary</u> policy as the tool for stabilizing aggregate demand. Monetarists favour a target <u>growth rate for the quantity of money</u>. The Bank of Canada <u>does not set</u> a specific target for the growth rate of the quantity of money. When real GDP falls below potential GDP <u>Keynesians</u> want to take swift action to stimulate the economy. The Bank of Canada is <u>monetarist</u> in its views and actions on a rising inflation rate.

True or false

1. True; page 367
2. False; page 367
3. False; page 367
4. True; page 368
5. False; page 368

Multiple choice

1. d; page 367
2. a; page 367
3. c; page 368
4. b; page 368
5. a; page 367

Short answer

1. Monetarists favour a target growth rate for the quantity of money because of the fact that the quantity theory of money provides a good explanation for the decade by decade changes in the inflation rate. And they say that not keeping money growth on target risks outburst of inflation; page 367.

2. Keynesians favour a target for the interest rate because they say that aggregate demand can be controlled more accurately by preventing the interest rate from fluctuating too wildly. And the interest rate may fluctuate wildly with strict targeting of the quantity of money and its growth rate; page 367.

3. When the inflation rate rises, monetarists want swift action to slow it regardless of the state of real GDP. And if the inflation rate falls, monetarists want to take either no action or at most cautious action to stimulate the economy; page 368.

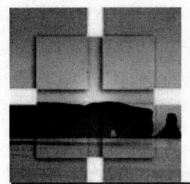

International Trade

Chapter
15

Chapter 15 shows that all countries can benefit from international trade. The chapter also demonstrates the effects of trade barriers, and explains the arguments countries use to justify these trade barriers.

■ **Describe the patterns and trends in international trade.**

The goods and services that we buy from people in other countries are called imports. The goods and services that we sell to people in other countries are called exports. Total trade in goods accounts for 88 percent of Canadian exports and 85 percent of Canadian imports. The rest of Canada's international trade is in services. From 1960 to 2003 exports have grown from about 17 percent of Canada's GDP to 38 percent and imports have grown from 18 percent of GDP to 31 percent of GDP. The United States is Canada's biggest trading partner. In 2003, Canada has a trade surplus.

■ **Explain why nations engage in international trade and why trade benefits all nations.**

A country has a comparative advantage in producing a good if it can produce that good at a lower opportunity cost than another country. To achieve the gains from trade, a country specializes in the production of the goods and services in which it has a comparative advantage and then trades with other countries. By specializing and trading, a country can consume at a point beyond its production possibilities frontier.

■ **Explain how trade barriers reduce international trade.**

A tariff is a tax on a good that is imposed by the importing country when an imported good crosses its international boundary. A tariff on a good reduces imports of that good, increases domestic production of the good, and reduces the gains from trade. A quota is a specified maximum amount of a good that may be imported in a given period of time.

■ **Explain the arguments used to justify trade barriers and show why they are incorrect but also why some barriers are hard to remove.**

The three main arguments for protection and restricting international trade are the employment argument, the infant-industry argument, and the dumping argument. Other arguments for restricting international trade are that protection: maintains national security; allows us to compete with cheap foreign labour; brings diversity and stability; penalizes lax environmental standards; protects national culture; and prevents rich countries from exploiting developing countries. Each of these arguments is flawed. Tariffs are imposed in some nations to gain revenue for the government. The major reason why international trade is restricted is because of rent seeking.

EXPANDED CHAPTER CHECKLIST

When you have completed this chapter, you will be able to

1 **Describe the patterns and trends in international trade.**

- Discuss Canada's international trade in goods and services and describe the trends in the volume of trade between 1960 and 2003.

- Discuss Canada's trading partners and the trading blocs in which Canada is a member.

- Define balance of trade.

2 **Explain why nations engage in international trade and why trade benefits all nations.**

- Discuss the relationship between comparative advantage and opportunity cost.

- Explain how to determine the goods in which Canada has a comparative advantage by comparing the Canadian supply curve and the world price line.

- Demonstrate how the production possibilities frontier can be used to determine the opportunity cost of producing a good.

- Use the production possibilities frontier to demonstrate the gains from trade.

3 **Explain how trade barriers reduce international trade.**

- Define tariff, nontariff barrier, and quota.

- Explain the effects on domestic consumers, domestic producers, and the domestic government of a tariff and a quota.

4 **Explain the arguments used to justify trade barriers and show why they are incorrect but also why some barriers are hard to remove.**

- Discuss the three main arguments for protection and explain why each is invalid.

- Discuss six other arguments for protection.

- Explain why governments and rent seekers are in favour of protection.

KEY TERMS

- Balance of trade (page 377)
- Dumping (page 392)
- Dynamic comparative advantage (page 384)
- Infant-industry argument (page 391)
- Learning-by-doing (page 384)
- Nontariff barrier (page 386)
- Quota (page 388)
- Rent seeking (page 396)
- Tariff (page 386)

CHECKPOINT 15.1

■ **Describe the patterns and trends in international trade.**

Practice Problem 15.1

Use the link on your Foundations Web site to answer the following questions.

a. In 1999, what percentage of Canadian production was exported to the United States and what percentage of total goods and services bought by Canadians was imported from the United States?

b. In 2002, what percentage of Canadian production was exported to the United States and what percentage of total goods and services bought by Canadians was imported from the United States?

Solution to Practice Problem 15.1

Canada participates more heavily in international trade than most nations. This Practice

Problem emphasizes the role of the United States as Canada's biggest trading partner.

Quick Review

- *Imports* The goods and services that we buy from people in other countries are called imports.

- *Exports* The goods and services that we sell to people in other countries are called exports.

a. In 1999, what percentage of Canadian production was exported to the United States and what percentage of total goods and services bought by Canadians was imported from the United States?

In 1999, Canadian exports to the United States were 31.5 percent of total Canadian production and imports from the United States were 25.4 percent of the total goods and services bought by Canadians.

b. In 2002, what percentage of Canadian production was exported to the United States and what percentage of total goods and services bought by Canadians was imported from the United States?

In 2002, Canadian exports to the United States were 30 percent of total Canadian production and imports from the United States were 22 percent of the total goods and services bought by Canadians.

Additional Practice Problem 15.1a

The Bank of Montreal provides financial services to firms in the Bahamas. How do Canada and the Bahamas categorize these financial services?

Solution to Additional Practice Problem 15.1a

Canada considers the services rendered by the Bank of Montreal as exports from Canada to the Bahamas. The Bahamas considers the services as imports from Canada.

■ Self Test 15.1

Fill in the blanks

Manufactured goods account for more than ____ (one-half; two-thirds) of Canadian imports. ____ (Japan; Mexico; The United States) is Canada's biggest trading partner. Canada ____ (is; is not) a member of the Asia-Pacific Economic Cooperation. In Canada between 1960 and 2003, trade ____ (decreased; increased) as a fraction of GDP.

True or false

1. Canada exports more services than goods.

2. In 1960, Canadian exports were about 1 percent of Canada's GDP.

3. Canada is a member of NAFTA and APEC.

4. In 2003, Canada had a trade surplus.

Multiple choice

1. Goods and services that we buy from people in other countries are called

a. imports.

b. exports.

c. inputs.

d. raw materials.

2. The largest fraction of Canadian imports is ____ and the largest fraction of Canadian exports is ____.

a. resource products; agricultural products

b. resource products; manufactured goods

c. manufactured goods; agricultural products

d. manufactured goods; manufactured goods

3. Goods account for about ____ percent of Canadian exports and services account for about ____ percent of Canadian exports.

a. 50; 50

b. 88; 12

c. 12; 88

d. 100; 0

4. If a Canadian student vacations in Germany, the money spent in Germany are services

a. exported to Canada.

b. imported to Germany.

c. exported to Germany.

d. exported from Canada.

5. Canada's largest trading partner is

a. the United States.

b. Mexico.

c. Japan.

d. the European Union.

6. The balance of trade equals the value of

a. imports minus the value of exports.

b. exports minus the value of imports.

c. imports.

d. exports.

Short answer

1. French cheese is flown to Canada aboard an Air Canada plane. Classify these transactions as exports or imports.

2. How has the amount of international trade changed in Canada between 1960 and 2003?

3. What is NAFTA and what is its goal?

CHECKPOINT 15.2

■ **Explain why nations engage in international trade and why trade benefits all nations.**

Practice Problems 15.2

During most of the Cold War, North America and Russia did not trade with each other. North America produced manufactured goods and farm produce. Russia produced manufactured goods and farm produce. Suppose that in the last year of the Cold War, North America could produce 100 million units of manufactured goods or 50 million units of farm produce and Russia

could produce 30 million units of manufactured goods or 10 million units of farm produce.

a. What was the opportunity cost of 1 unit of farm produce in North America?

b. What was the opportunity cost of 1 unit of farm produce in Russia?

c. Which country had a comparative advantage in producing farm produce?

d. With the end of the Cold War and the opening up of trade between Russia and North America, which good did North America import from Russia?

e. Did North America gain from this trade? Explain why or why not.

f. Did Russia gain from this trade? Explain why or why not.

Solution to Practice Problem 15.2

This Practice Problem shows that when opportunity costs between countries diverge, comparative advantage enables countries to gain from international trade.

Quick Review

• *Comparative advantage* A country has a comparative advantage in a good when its opportunity cost of producing the good is lower than another country's opportunity cost of producing the good.

a. What was the opportunity cost of 1 unit of farm produce in North America?

In North America when 50 million units of farm produce are produced, 100 million units of manufactured goods are forgone. The opportunity cost of 1 unit of farm produce is (100 million units of manufactured goods) ÷ (50 million units of farm produce), which is 2 units of manufactured goods.

b. What was the opportunity cost of 1 unit of farm produce in Russia?

In Russia, when 10 million units of farm produce are produced, 30 million units of manufactured goods are forgone. The opportunity cost of 1 unit of farm produce is (30 million units of manufactured goods) ÷ (10 million units of farm produce), which is 3 units of manufactured goods.

c. Which country had a comparative advantage in producing farm produce?

The opportunity cost of producing farm produce was less in North America than in Russia, so North America had the comparative advantage in farm produce.

d. With the end of the Cold War and the opening up of trade between Russia and North America, which good did North America import from Russia?

Russia had the comparative advantage in producing manufactured goods. The opportunity cost of producing 1 unit of manufactured goods in Russia was 1/3 of a unit of farm produce. The opportunity cost of producing 1 unit of manufactured goods in North America was 1/2 of a unit of farm produce. So North America imported manufactured goods from Russia.

e. Did North America gain from this trade? Explain why or why not.

North America gained from this trade because it ended up with more of both goods. When countries specialize in the good in which they have a comparative advantage and then trade, both countries gain.

f. Did Russia gain from this trade? Explain why or why not.

Russia gained from this trade because it ended up with more of both goods. When countries specialize in the good in which they have a comparative advantage and then trade, both countries gain.

Additional Practice Problem 15.2a

In Practice Problem 15.2, suppose that new technology becomes available so that the production of manufactured goods doubles in North America and in Russia. Now which good does North America import from Russia?

Solution to Additional Practice Problem 15.2a

In North America when 200 million units of manufactured goods are produced, 50 million units of farm produce are forgone. The opportunity cost of 1 unit of manufactured goods is (50 million units of farm produce) ÷ (200 million units of manufactured goods), which is 1/4 of a unit of manufactured goods.

In Russia when 60 million units of manufactured goods are produced, 10 million units of farm produce are forgone. The opportunity cost of 1 unit of manufactured goods is (10 million units of farm produce) ÷ (60 million units of manufactured goods), which is 1/6 of a unit of manufactured goods.

Russia still has the lower opportunity cost and the comparative advantage in manufactured goods. So North America continues to import manufactured goods from Russia.

■ Self Test 15.2

Fill in the blanks

A country has a comparative advantage in producing a good if it can produce the good at a _____ (higher; lower) opportunity cost than another country. If the world price of clothing is less than the price in Canada with no international trade and Canada imports clothing from Asia, Canadian buyers of clothing _____ (gain; lose) and Asian producers of clothing _____ (gain; lose). Trade _____ (allows; does not allow) a country to produce at a point beyond its production possibilities frontier. Trade _____ (allows; does not allow) a country to consume at a point beyond its production possibilities frontier.

True or false

1. Only the exporting country gains from free international trade because it has a comparative advantage.

2. Canada has a comparative advantage in the production of a good if the opportunity cost of producing that good is higher in Canada than in most other countries.

3. A country cannot reap any gains from international trade if it has an absolute advantage in producing all goods and services.

4. Hong Kong, South Korean, and Taiwan have become low opportunity cost producers in electronics and biotechnology industries through learning-by-doing.

Multiple choice

1. The fundamental force that drives trade between nations is

a. the government.

b. NAFTA.

c. absolute advantage

d. comparative advantage.

2. A country will import a good if its

a. no-trade, domestic price is equal to the world price.

b. no-trade, domestic price is less than the world price

c. no-trade, domestic price is greater than the world price.

d. All of the above answers are correct.

3. When Italy buys GM locomotives produced in Canada, the price Italy pays is ____ than if they produced their own locomotives and the price GM receives is ____ than it could receive from an additional Canadian buyer.

a. lower; lower

b. higher; higher

c. lower; higher

d. higher; lower

4. When a good is imported, domestic production ____ and domestic consumption ____.

a. increases; increases

b. increases; decreases

c. decreases; increases

d. decreases; decreases

5. You can tell that specialization and trade make a country better off because then the country can consume at a point

a. outside its production possibilities frontier.

b. inside its production possibilities frontier.

c. on its production possibilities frontier.

d. on the trading partner's production possibilities frontier.

6. People can become more productive just by repeatedly producing a particular good or service. This is called

a. learning-by-doing.

b. learning-by-boredom.

c. absolute advantage.

d. dynamic absolute advantage.

Complete the graph

1. Figure 15.1 shows the Canadian demand and supply curves for apples.

■ **FIGURE 15.1**

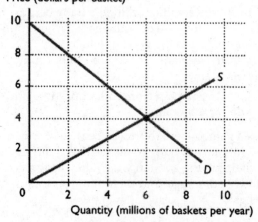

a. In the absence of international trade, what is the equilibrium price of a basket of apples in Canada?

b. If the world price of a basket of apples is $6 a basket, will Canada import or export apples? Above what world price for apples will Canada export apples? Below what world price for apples will Canada import apples?

2. Figure 15.2 shows the *PPF*s for Canada and France.

■ FIGURE 15.2

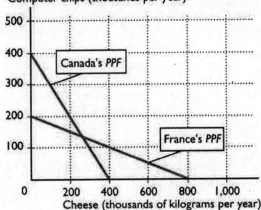

Computer chips (thousands per year)

Canada's *PPF*

France's *PPF*

Cheese (thousands of kilograms per year)

a. What is the opportunity cost of a computer chip in Canada? In France? Who has the comparative advantage in producing computer chips?

b. What is the opportunity cost of a kilogram of cheese in Canada? In France? Who has the comparative advantage in producing cheese?

c. When Canada and France trade, who exports computer chips and who exports cheese?

d. Canada produced 200,000 computer chips and 200,000 kilograms of cheese before trade. France produced 100,000 computer chips and 400,000 kilograms of cheese. Label as point *A* the point that shows the total computer chip and cheese production before trade.

e. Canada and France both specialize according to comparative advantage and trade. Label as point *B* the point that shows the total computer chip and cheese production after trade. How does point *B* compare to point *A*?

Short answer

1. The table shows the Canadian demand and supply schedules for potatoes.

Price (dollars per tonne)	Quantity supplied (tonnes per year)	Quantity demanded (tonnes per year)
400	38	58
500	42	52
600	46	46
700	50	40
800	54	34
900	58	28

a. If there is no international trade, what is the equilibrium price and quantity?

b. If the world price of potatoes is $800 a tonne, what is the quantity supplied and the quantity demanded in Canada? Does Canada import or export potatoes? What quantity?

c. If the world price of potatoes rises to $900 a tonne, what is the quantity supplied and the quantity demanded in Canada? Does Canada import or export potatoes? What quantity?

d. Would Canada ever import potatoes?

2. Suppose Canada and France produce only ice cream and cheese. Canada can produce 50 tonnes of ice cream or 100 tonnes of cheese and France can produce 20 tonnes of ice cream or 120 tonnes of cheese.

a. What is the opportunity cost of a tonne of ice cream in France? In Canada? Which country has the comparative advantage in producing ice cream?

b. What is the opportunity cost of a tonne of cheese in France? In Canada? Which country has the comparative advantage in producing cheese?

c. If France and Canada trade, what does Canada import? What does it export?

d. Before trade Canada produced 25 tonnes of ice cream and 50 tonnes of cheese and France produced 10 tonnes of ice cream and 60 tonnes of cheese. What is the total production of ice cream? Of cheese?

e. After trade, France and Canada specialize according to comparative advantage. What is the total amount of ice cream produced? Of cheese?

f. Compare your answers to (d) and (e).

3. What are the gains from trade? How do countries obtain the gains from trade?

4. What is dynamic comparative advantage?

CHECKPOINT 15.3

■ **Explain how trade barriers reduce international trade.**

Practice Problems 15.3

1. Before 1995, Canada imposed tariffs on goods imported from Mexico. In 1995, Mexico joined NAFTA. Canadian tariffs on imports from Mexico and Mexican tariffs on imports from Canada are gradually being removed. Explain how the removal of tariffs will change

a. The price that Canadian consumers pay for goods imported from Mexico.

b. The quantity of imports from Mexico into Canada.

c. The quantity of Canadian exports to Mexico.

d. The Canadian government's tariff revenue from trade with Mexico.

2. Almost all U.S. imports of potatoes come from Canada. In 1999-2000, the U.S. government banned potato imports from Prince Edward Island. Explain how this ban would have influenced

a. The price that U.S. consumers paid for potatoes.

b. The quantity of potatoes consumed in the United States.

c. The price received by Canadian potato growers.

d. The U.S. and Canadian gains from trade.

Solution to Practice Problems 15.3

To solve these Practice Problems, think in terms of supply and demand. Imposing a tariff raises the domestic price, which changes the domestic quantity demanded and the domestic quantity supplied.

Quick Review

*   *Tariff* A tariff is a tax on a good that is imposed by the importing country when an imported good crosses its international boundary.

*   *Quota* A quota is a specified maximum amount of a good that may be imported in a given period of time.

1. **Before 1995, Canada imposed tariffs on goods imported from Mexico. In 1995, Mexico joined NAFTA. Canadian tariffs on imports from Mexico and Mexican tariffs on imports from Canada are gradually being removed. Explain how the removal of tariffs will change**

a. **The price that Canadian consumers pay for goods imported from Mexico.**

When the tariff is removed Canadian consumers pay less for goods imported from Mexico.

b. **The quantity of imports from Mexico into Canada.**

As the price falls, the quantity of Mexican goods demanded by Canadian consumers increases. So the quantity of imports from Mexico into Canada increases.

c. **The quantity of Canadian exports to Mexico.**

As Mexican tariffs on imports from Canada are removed, the price of Canadian exports to Mexico falls and the quantity of Canadian goods demanded by Mexican consumers increases. So the quantity of Canadian exports to Mexico increases.

d. **The Canadian government's tariff revenue from trade with Mexico.**

As the tariff falls, tariff revenue falls. When the tariff reaches zero, so that trade is totally free of tariffs, the Canadian government's tariff revenue is zero.

2. **Almost all U.S. imports of potatoes come from Canada. In 1999–2000, the U.S. government banned potato imports from Prince Edward Island. Explain how this ban would have influenced**

a. **The price that U.S. consumers paid for potatoes.**

The ban decreases the supply of imported potatoes and raises the price paid by U.S. consumers.

b. **The quantity of potatoes consumed in the United States.**

As the price of potatoes rises, the quantity of potatoes consumed in the United States falls.

c. **The price received by Canadian potato growers.**

Because Canadian producers cannot export their potatoes to the United States, the supply of potatoes in Canada increases and the price of potatoes falls.

d. **The U.S. and Canadian gains from trade.**

The U.S. and Canadian gains from trade are decreased. Anything that limits international trade decreases the gains from trade.

Additional Practice Problem 15.3a

If Canada has a quota on eggs entering Canada from the United States, what happens to the price of eggs for Canadian consumers? What is the difference between a quota on eggs and a tariff?

Solution to Additional Practice Problem 15.3a

A quota restricts imports. When a quota is implemented, the domestic price of eggs rises. In the case of a tariff, the Canadian government collects tariff revenue. In the case of a quota, there is no tariff revenue and the difference between the world price and the Canadian price goes to the

person who has the right to import the eggs under the import quota regulations.

■ Self Test 15.3

Fill in the blanks

A tax on a good that is imposed by the importing country when an imported good crosses its international boundary is a ____ (quota; tariff). A tariff ____ (raises; lowers) the price paid by domestic consumers and ____ (increases; decreases) the quantity produced by domestic producers. A quota ____ (raises; lowers) the price paid by domestic consumers and ____ (increases; decreases) the quantity produced by domestic producers.

True or false

1. If Canada imposes a tariff on a good, the price paid by Canadian consumers for that good does not change.

2. If a country imposes a tariff on pasta imports, domestic production of pasta will increase and domestic consumption of pasta will decrease.

3. A tariff on imports decreases the gains from trade for the importing country but not for the exporting country.

4. A quota on imports of a particular good specifies the minimum quantity of that good that can be imported in a given period.

Multiple choice

1. A tax that is imposed by the importing country when an imported good crosses its international boundary is known as a

a. quota.
b. nontariff barrier.
c. tariff.
d. sanction.

2. A nontariff barrier

a. is used by the government to restrict international trade.

b. is imposed by the exporting country.

c. lowers the price of the imported good.

d. is always a quantitative restriction.

3. Suppose the world price of a shirt is $10. If Canada imposes a tariff of $5 a shirt, then the price of a shirt in

a. Canada falls to $5.

b. Canada rises to $15 if $15 a shirt is less than the price in Canada without international trade.

c. the world falls to $5.

d. the world rises to $5.

4. When a tariff is imposed on a good, the _____ increases.

a. domestic quantity purchased

b. domestic quantity produced

c. quantity imported

d. quantity exported

5. When a tariff is imposed on a good, Canadian consumers _____ because they pay _____ then the opportunity cost of the good.

a. win; less

b. lose; more

c. win; more

d. lose; less

6. Which of the following parties benefits from a quota but not from a tariff?

a. the government

b. domestic producers

c. domestic consumers

d. the person with the right to import the good

Complete the graph

1. Figure 15.3 shows the supply of and demand for sugar in Canada.

■ **FIGURE 15.3**

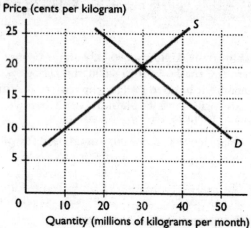

a. If the world price of sugar is 10¢ a kilogram, draw the world price line in the figure. What is the quantity consumed in Canada, the quantity produced in Canada, and the quantity imported?

b. Suppose the government imposes a 5¢ a kilogram tariff on sugar. Show the effect of the tariff in Figure 15.3 After the tariff, what is the quantity consumed in Canada, the quantity produced in Canada, and the quantity imported?

Short answer

1. Suppose the Canadian government imposes a tariff on steel. How does the tariff affect the price of steel, Canadian consumers, and Canadian steel producers?

2. Suppose the Canadian government imposes a quota on steel. How does the quota affect the price of steel, Canadian consumers, and Canadian steel producers?

3. Why do consumers lose from a tariff?

CHECKPOINT 15.4

■ **Explain the arguments used to justify trade barriers and show why they are incorrect but also why some barriers are hard to remove.**

Practice Problems 15.4

1. Japan sets quotas on imports of rice. California rice growers would like to export more rice to Japan. What are Japan's arguments for restricting imports of Californian rice? Are these arguments correct? Who loses from this restriction in trade?

2. In March 2003, steel producers in Canada asked the federal government to put a tariff on steel imports from all offshore countries (countries other than the United States). What was the argument for a tariff? Who will gain and who will lose?

3. The United States maintains a quota on imports of textiles. What is the argument for this quota? Is this argument flawed? If so, explain why.

Solution to Practice Problems 15.4

Free trade promotes prosperity for all countries. Protection reduces the potential gains from trade. These Practice Problems discuss the arguments for protection.

Quick Review

*   *Rent seeking* Lobbying and other political activity that seeks to capture the gains from trade.

1. **Japan sets quotas on imports of rice. California rice growers would like to export more rice to Japan. What are Japan's arguments for restricting imports of Californian rice? Are these arguments correct? Who loses from this restriction in trade?**

Japan has used number of arguments, but they are all incorrect. Japan has argued that Japanese rice is of a higher quality than U.S. rice, but if

Japanese consumers detect a quality difference, they can purchase Japanese rice rather than U.S. rice. Japan has argued that rice is part of Japanese national heritage, but if Japanese consumers want to protect this part of their heritage, they can buy exclusively Japanese rice rather than U.S. rice. The major losers from the Japanese quota are Japanese consumers who must pay a higher price for rice.

2. **In March 2003, steel producers in Canada asked the federal government to put a tariff on steel imports from all offshore countries (countries other than the United States). What was the argument for a tariff? Who will gain and who will lose?**

The argument for a tariff on steel imports is that foreign producers are dumping steel in Canada. By imposing a tariff on steel, Canadian steel producers face less competition from foreign firms. Canadian jobs are saved. The winners from the tariffs are the steel producers and steel workers. The losers are all Canadian steel consumers.

3. **The United States maintains a quota on imports of textiles. What is the argument for this quota? Is this argument flawed? If so, explain why.**

The argument for a quota on U.S. imports of textiles is the existence of cheap foreign labour in the textile industry in third world countries. This employment argument is flawed. The United States does not have a comparative advantage in textile production. Because of the quota the U.S. textile industry continues to produce. Without a quota, the U.S. textile industry would be smaller.

Additional Practice Problem 15.4a

In each of the three Practice Problems, identify who is rent seeking.

Solution to Additional Practice Problem 15.4a

In Practice Problem 1, the Japanese rice farmers are rent seeking. In Practice Problem 2, the Canadian steel producers and Canadian steel workers are rent seeking. And in Practice Problem 3, U.S. textile producers and U.S. textile workers are rent seeking.

■ Self Test 15.4

Fill in the blanks

The argument that it is necessary to protect a new industry to enable it to growth into a mature industry that can compete in world markets is the ____ (infant-industry; maturing-industry) argument. Protection ____ (is; is not) necessary to bring diversity and stability to our economy. Protection ____ (is; is not) necessary to prevent rich countries from exploiting developing countries. The major reason why international trade is restricted is because ____ (foreign countries protect their industries; of rent seeking).

True or false

1. The employment argument is the only valid argument for protection.

2. Dumping by a foreign producer is easy to detect.

3. Protection allows us to compete with cheap foreign labour.

4. International trade is an attractive base for tax collection in developing countries.

Multiple choice

1. The three main arguments for protection include all of the following except the

a. employment argument.
b. infant-industry argument.
c. rent-seeking argument.
d. dumping argument.

2. What is the major reason international trade is restricted?

a. rent seeking
b. to bring diversity and stability
c. to save jobs
d. to prevent dumping

3. The argument that it is necessary to protect a new industry to enable it to grow into a mature industry that can compete in world markets is the

a. national security argument.
b. diversity argument.
c. infant-industry argument.
d. environmental protection argument.

4. _____ occurs when a foreign firm sells its exports at a lower price than the price in the foreign firm's domestic market.

a. Dumping
b. The trickle-down effect
c. Rent seeking
d. Tariff avoidance

5. Canada

a. needs tariffs to allow us to compete with cheap foreign labour.
b. does not need tariffs to allow us to compete with cheap foreign labour.
d. should not trade with developing countries.
d. does not benefit from trade with developing countries .

6. Why do governments in developing countries impose tariffs on imported goods and services?

a. International transactions are well recorded and audited.
b. Tariffs protect jobs.
c. The country's total income is increased.
d. National security of the country is improved.

Short answer

1. What is the dumping argument for protection? What is its flaw?

2. Does Canada need to limit auto imports from Japan to save Canadian jobs?

3. Explain why trade with developing countries does not exploit workers in these countries.

SELF TEST ANSWERS

■ CHECKPOINT 11.1

Fill in the blanks

Manufactured goods account for more than <u>one-half</u> of Canadian imports. <u>The United States</u> is Canada's biggest trading partner. Canada <u>is</u> a member of the Asia-Pacific Economic Cooperation. In Canada between 1960 and 2003, trade <u>increased</u> as a fraction of GDP.

True or false

1. False; page 374
2. False; page 374
3. True; page 375
4. True; page 377

Multiple choice

1. a; page 374
2. d; page 374
3. b; page 374
4. a; page 374
5. a; page 375
6. b; page 377

Short answer

1. From the Canadian vantage, the cheese is an imported good and the air transportation is an exported service. From the French vantage, the cheese is an exported good and the air transportation is an imported service; page 374.

2. Between 1960 and 2003, international trade in Canada expanded. In 1960, Canadian exports were about 17 percent of Canada's GDP and imports were 18 percent of GDP. In 2000, the numbers peaked at 40 percent of GDP exported and 34 percent imported. In 2003, 38 percent of GDP was exported and 31 percent was imported; page 374.

3. NAFTA is the North American Free Trade Agreement. It is an agreement between Canada, the United States, and Mexico to make trade among the three nations easier and freer; page 376.

■ CHECKPOINT 15.2

Fill in the blanks

A country has a comparative advantage in producing a good if it can produce the good at a <u>lower</u> opportunity cost than another country. If the world price of clothing is less than the price in Canada with no international trade and Canada imports clothing from Asia, Canadian buyers of clothing <u>gain</u> and Asian producers of clothing <u>gain</u>. Trade <u>does not allow</u> a country to produce at a point beyond its production possibilities frontier. Trade <u>allows</u> a country to consume at a point beyond its production possibilities frontier.

True or false

1. False; page 383
2. False; page 379
3. False; page 383
4. True; page 384

Multiple choice

1. d; page 378
2. c; page 381
3. c; page 378
4. c; page 381
5. a; page 383
6. a; page 384

Complete the graph

1. a. In the absence of international trade, the equilibrium price of a basket of apples in Canada is $4; page 378.

b. If the world price of a basket of apples is $6 a basket, Canada will export apples because the world price exceeds the no-trade price. If the price of a basket of apples exceeds $4, Canada will export apples. If the price of a basket of apples is less than $4, Canada will import apples; pages 378-381.

2. a. The opportunity cost of a computer chip in Canada is 1 kilogram of cheese. In France, the opportunity cost of a computer chip is 4 kilograms of cheese. Canada has the comparative advantage in producing computer chips; pages 381, 383.

b. The opportunity cost of a kilogram of cheese in Canada is 1 computer chip. In France, the opportunity cost of a kilogram of cheese is 1/4 of a computer chip. France has the comparative advantage in producing cheese; pages 381, 383.

c. Canada has the comparative advantage in producing computer chips, so it will specialize in producing computer chips and export computer chips to France. France will specialize in cheese and export cheese to Canada; page 383.

d. The point is point A in Figure 15.4; page 383.

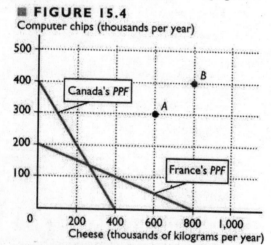

■ FIGURE 15.4

e. Canada produces 400,000 computer chips and no cheese and France produces 800,000 kilograms of cheese and no computer chips. Total production is 400,000

computer chips and 800,000 kilograms of cheese, labelled B in Figure 15.4. More computer chips *and* more cheese are produced at point B after trade than are produced at point A before trade; page 383.

Short answer

1. a. In the absence of international trade, the equilibrium price is $600 a tonne and the equilibrium quantity is 46 tonnes; page 378.

b. In Canada, the quantity supplied is 54 tonnes and the quantity demanded is 34 tonnes. Canada exports 20 tonnes of potatoes; page 378.

c. In Canada, the quantity supplied is 58 tonnes and the quantity demanded is 28 tonnes. Canada exports 30 tonnes of potatoes; page 378.

d. Canada imports potatoes if the world price is less than $600 a tonne; page 381.

2. a. In France, the opportunity cost of a tonne of ice cream is 6 tonnes of cheese; in Canada, the opportunity cost of a tonne of ice cream is 2 tonnes of cheese. Canada has the comparative advantage in producing ice cream; page 383.

b. In France, the opportunity cost of a tonne of cheese is 1/6 of a tonne of ice cream; in Canada, the opportunity cost of a tonne of cheese is 1/2 of a tonne of ice cream. France has the comparative advantage in producing cheese; page 383.

c. Canada imports cheese and exports ice cream; page 383.

d. 35 tonnes of ice cream are produced and 110 tonnes of cheese are produced; page 383.

e. 50 tonnes of ice cream are produced in Canada and 120 tonnes of cheese are produced in France; page 383.

f. The world production of ice cream *and* cheese increased, which demonstrates the gains from trade; page 383.

3. The gains from trade occur because after specialization and trade, a country can increase its consumption so that it can consume at a point beyond its production possibilities frontier. To obtain the gains from trade a country must specialize and trade; page 383.

4. Dynamic comparative advantage is a comparative advantage that a person (or country) obtains by specializing in an activity, resulting from learning-by-doing; page 384.

■ CHECKPOINT 15.3

Fill in the blanks

A tax on a good that is imposed by the importing country when an imported good crosses its international boundary is called a <u>tariff</u>. A tariff <u>raises</u> the price paid by domestic consumers and <u>increases</u> the quantity produced by domestic producers. A quota <u>raises</u> the price paid by domestic consumers and <u>increases</u> the quantity produced by domestic producers.

True or false

1. False; pages 386-388

2. True; pages 386-388

3. False; pages 386-388

4. False; page 388

Multiple choice

1. c; page 386

2. a; page 386

3. b; page 388

4. b; pages 386-388

5. b; pages 386-388

6. d; pages 388-389

Complete the graph

1. The world price line is shown in Figure 15.5.

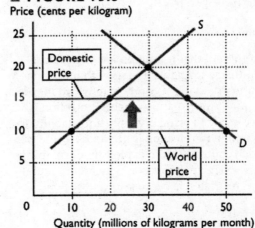

■ FIGURE 15.5

Price (cents per kilogram)

Quantity (millions of kilograms per month)

a. 50 million kilograms of sugar are consumed in Canada, 10 million kilograms are produced in Canada, and 40 million kilograms are imported into Canada; pages 386-388.

b. The tariff increases the domestic price to 15¢ a kilogram in Figure 15.5. The quantity consumed in Canada decreases to 40 million kilograms, the quantity produced in Canada increases to 20 million kilograms, and the amount imported decreases to 20 million kilograms; pages 386-388.

Short answer

1. The tariff raises the price of steel. Canadian steel consumers decrease the quantity they purchase and Canadian steel producers increase the quantity they produce; pages 386-388.

2. The quota has the same effects as the tariff in the previous question. The quota increases the price of steel. Canadian steel consumers decrease the quantity purchased and Canadian steel producers increase the quantity produced; pages 388-389.

3. Consumers lose from a tariff because the tariff raises the price they must pay and the quantity bought decreases. The tariff makes people pay more than the opportunity cost of the good; page 388.

■ **CHECKPOINT 15.4**

Fill in the blanks

The argument that it is necessary to protect a new industry to enable it to growth into a mature industry that can compete in world markets is the <u>infant-industry</u> argument. Protection <u>is not</u> necessary to bring diversity and stability to our economy. Protection <u>is not</u> necessary to prevent rich countries from exploiting developing countries. The major reason why international trade is restricted is because <u>of rent seeking</u>.

True or false

1. False; page 391
2. False; page 392
3. False; page 393
4. True; page 395

Multiple choice

1. c; page 391
2. a; page 396
3. c; page 391
4. a; page 392
5. b; page 393
6. a; page 395

Short answer

1. Dumping occurs when a foreign firm sells its exports at a lower price than the price in the foreign firm's domestic market. The dumping argument is flawed for the following reasons. First, it is virtually impossible to detect dumping. Second, it is hard to think of a good that is produced by a natural global monopoly. Third, if a good or service were a truly global natural monopoly, the best way to deal with it would be by regulation; page 392.

2. Saving jobs is one of the oldest arguments in favour of protection. It is also incorrect. Protecting a particular industry likely will save jobs in that industry but will cost many other jobs in other industries. The cost to consumers of saving a job is many times the wage rate of the job saved; page 391.

3. Trade with developing countries does not exploit workers in these countries. Wage rates in some developing countries are very low. But by trading with developing countries, we increase the demand for the goods that these countries produce, and we increase the demand for their labour. When the demand for labour in developing countries increases, the wage rate also increases. So instead of exploiting people in developing countries, trade improves their opportunities and increases their income; page 395.

International Finance

CHAPTER IN PERSPECTIVE

Chapter 16 studies international accounts, what determines the balance of payments accounts, and how the value of the Canadian dollar is determined in the foreign exchange market.

■ **Describe a country's balance of payments accounts and explain what determines the amount of international borrowing and lending.**

The three balance of payments accounts are the current account, the capital account, and the official settlements account. The current account records international receipts and payments in a given period—current account balance equals exports minus imports, plus net interest and transfers received from abroad. The capital account records foreign investment into Canada minus Canadian investment abroad in a given period. The official settlements account records the change in Canadian official reserves. The sum of the balances on the three accounts always equals zero. The rest of the world pays for its imports of Canadian goods and services in excess of Canada's imports from the rest of the world by borrowing from Canada. A net borrower is a country that is borrowing more from the rest of the world than it is lending to the rest of the world and a net lender is a country that is lending more to the rest of the world than it is borrowing from the rest of the world. A debtor nation is a country that during its entire history has borrowed more from the rest of the world than it has lent to it and a creditor nation is a country that during its entire history has invested more in the rest of the world than other countries have invested in it. Net exports equals the sum of the private sector balance and the government sector balance.

■ **Explain how the exchange rate is determined and why it fluctuates.**

Foreign currency is needed to buy foreign goods and to invest in another country. The foreign exchange rate is the price at which one currency exchanges for another. The quantity of dollars demanded increases when the exchange rate falls. The demand for dollars changes and the demand curve for dollars shifts if the Canadian interest rate differential or the expected future exchange rate changes. The quantity of dollars supplied increases when the exchange rate rises. The supply of dollars changes and the supply curve of dollars shifts if the Canadian interest rate differential or the expected future exchange rate changes. At the equilibrium exchange rate, the quantity of dollars demanded equals the quantity of dollars supplied. The exchange rate is volatile because factors that change demand also change supply. Exchange rate expectations are influenced by purchasing power parity, a situation in which money buys the same amount of goods and services in different currencies, and interest rate parity, a situation in which the interest rate in one currency equals the interest rate in another currency when exchange rate changes are taken into account. The Bank of Canada can intervene directly in the foreign exchange market.

EXPANDED CHAPTER CHECKLIST

When you have completed this chapter, you will be able to

1 Describe a country's balance of payments accounts and explain what determines the amount of international borrowing and lending.

- Define the balance of payment accounts, the current account, the capital account, and the official settlements account.
- Define net borrower, net lender, creditor nation, and debtor nation.
- State the relationship between net exports, the private sector balance, and the government sector balance.

2 Explain how the exchange rate is determined and why it fluctuates.

- Explain the role of the foreign exchange market.
- Define currency appreciation and currency depreciation.
- Discuss the relationship between the exchange rate and the quantity of dollars demanded.
- Discuss the relationship between the exchange rate and the quantity of dollars supplied.
- Explain how a change in the Canadian interest rate differential or in the expected future exchange rate changes the demand for dollars and the supply of dollars.
- Illustrate equilibrium in the foreign exchange market and show how a change in the demand for dollars or supply of dollars changes the exchange rate.
- Explain how the Bank of Canada intervenes in the foreign exchange market.

KEY TERMS

- Balance of payments accounts (page 404)
- Canadian interest rate differential (page 414)
- Canadian official reserves (page 404)
- Capital account (page 404)
- Creditor nation (page 406)
- Currency appreciation (page 411)
- Currency depreciation (page 412)
- Current account (page 404)
- Debtor nation (page 406)
- Foreign exchange market (page 411)
- Foreign exchange rate (page 411)
- Government sector balance (page 408)
- Interest rate parity (page 422)
- Net borrower (page 406)
- Net lender (page 406)
- Official settlements account (page 404)
- Private sector balance (page 408)
- Purchasing power parity (page 420)

CHECKPOINT 16.1

1 Describe a country's balance of payments accounts and explain what determines the amount of international borrowing and lending.

Practice Problem 16.1

It is 2006 and the Canadian economy records the following transactions:

Imports of goods and services, $200 billion; interest paid to the rest of the world, $50 billion; interest received from the rest of the world, $40 billion; decrease in Canadian official reserves, $1 billion; government sector balance, $20 billion;

saving, $180 billion; investment, $200 billion; net transfers, zero.

a. Calculate the current account balance, the capital account balance, the official settlements account balance, and exports of goods and services.

b. Is Canada a debtor or a creditor nation in 2006?

c. If government expenditure increases by $10 billion, what happens to the current account balance?

Solution to Practice Problem 16.1

Problems such as this Practice Problem are straightforward to solve. Remember that the three balance of payments accounts are the current account, the capital account, and the official settlements account, and that the sum of the balances on these three accounts always equals zero.

Quick Review

*   *Current account* The current account records receipts from the sale of goods and services to other countries (exports), minus payments for goods and services bought from other countries (imports), plus the net amount of interest and transfers (such as foreign aid payments) received from and paid to other countries.

    It is 2006 and the Canadian economy records the following transactions:

    Imports of goods and services, $200 billion; interest paid to the rest of the world, $50 billion; interest received from the rest of the world, $40 billion; decrease in Canadian official reserves, $1 billion; government sector balance, $20 billion; saving, $180 billion; investment, $200 billion; net transfers, zero.

a. **Calculate the current account balance, the capital account balance, the official settlements account balance, and exports of goods and services.**

The current account balance equals net exports plus net interest, which is –$10 billion, plus net

transfers, which is zero. Net exports equals the sum of the private sector balance and the government sector balance. The private sector balance equals saving minus investment, which is $180 billion minus $200 billion = –$20 billion. The government sector balance is $20 billion. The sum of the private sector balance and the government sector balance is zero. So net exports are zero and the current account balance is –$10 billion.

When net exports are zero, exports equal imports, which is $200 billion.

The official settlements account is a surplus of $1 billion.

The sum of the current account balance, the capital account balance, and the official settlements account balance is zero. The current account balance is –$10 billion and the official settlements account balance is $1 billion, so the capital account balance is $9 billion.

b. **Is Canada a debtor or a creditor nation in 2006?**

Interest payments reflect the value of outstanding debts. Canada is a debtor nation because the value of interest payments received from the rest of the world is less than the value of interest payments made to the rest of the world.

c. **If government expenditure increases by $10 billion, what happens to the current account balance?**

Net exports equals the sum of the private sector balance and the government sector balance. The current account balance equals net exports plus net interest and transfers received from abroad. When government expenditure increases by $10 billion, the government sector balance decreases by $10 billion, which reduces net exports by $10 billion. The current account balance decreases by $10 billion and so the current account deficit increases by $10 billion.

Additional Practice Problem 16.1a

Suppose the official settlements account balance equals zero. In this case, what is the relationship between the current account and the capital account? Why does this relationship exist?

Solution to Additional Practice Problem 16.1a

If the official settlements account balance equals zero, then a deficit in the current account equals the surplus in the capital account or the surplus in the current account equals the deficit in the capital account. This relationship exists because the sum of the balances on the current account, the capital account, and the official settlements account equals zero. If the official settlements account equals zero, the current account balance equals the negative of the capital account balance.

■ Self Test 16.1

Fill in the blanks

The ____ (current; capital) account records payments for the imports of goods and services. The ____ (current; capital; official settlements) account records foreign investment into Canada minus Canadian investment abroad. The sum of the balances of the current account, capital account, and the official settlements account always equals ____ (1; real GDP; zero).

True or false

1. If foreign investment into Canada increases, and Canadian investment in the rest of the world decreases, the current account shows an increase in exports and a decrease in imports.

2. The official settlements account balance is positive if Canada's official reserves decrease.

3. In the year 2002, Canada had a current account surplus.

4. If Canada has a surplus in its capital account and a deficit in its current account, the balance in its official settlements account is zero.

5. In the years following World War II, Canada has mostly been a net lender.

6. If a country starts to run a current account surplus, which continues indefinitely, it would become a net lender and eventually a creditor nation.

7. Net exports equals the private sector balance minus the government sector balance.

8. The private sector balance equals saving minus investment.

Multiple choice

1. A country's balance of payments accounts records its _____ in a given period.
   a. tax receipts and government expenditure
   b. tariffs and nontariff revenue and government expenditure
   c. international trading, borrowing, and lending
   d. exports and imports, and its holdings of international currency and gold

2. All the following are balance of payments accounts EXCEPT the
   a. capital account.
   b. labour account.
   c. official settlements account.
   d. current account.

3. Which balance of payments account records payments for imports and receipts for exports?
   a. current account
   b. capital account
   c. official settlements account
   d. reserves account

4. The current account balance is equal to

a. imports – exports + net interest + net transfers.

b. imports – exports + net interest – net transfers.

c. exports – imports – net interest + net transfers.

d. exports – imports + net interest + net transfers.

5. If an investment of $100 million from the United Kingdom is made into Canada, the $100 million is listed as a ____ entry in Canada's ____ account.

a. positive; current

b. negative; capital

c. positive; capital

d. negative; current

6. If Canada receives $20 billion of foreign investment and at the same time invests $16 billion abroad, then Canada's

a. capital account balance increases by $4 billion.

b. current account must be in surplus.

c. balance of payments must be negative.

d. capital account balance decreases by $4 billion.

7. In the balance of payments accounts, changes in Canadian official reserves are recorded in the

a. current account.

b. capital account.

c. official settlements account.

d. international currency account.

8. If a country has a current account balance of $100 billion and the official settlements account balance equals zero, then the country's capital account balance must be

a. equal to $100 billion.

b. positive but not necessarily equal to $100 billion.

c. equal to –$100 billion.

d. zero.

9. A country that is borrowing more from the rest of the world than it is lending to the rest of the world is called a

a. net lender.

b. net borrower.

c. net debtor.

d. net creditor.

10. A debtor nation is a country that

a. borrows more from the rest of the world than it lends to it.

b. lends more to the rest of the world than it borrows from it.

c. during its entire history has invested more in the rest of the world than other countries have invested in it.

d. during its entire history has borrowed more from the rest of the world than it has lent to it.

11. Borrowing and lending are _____, and debts are _____.

a. flows; flows

b. flows; stocks

c. stocks; flows

d. stocks; stocks

12. Net exports increase when

a. the private sector balance increases by more than the government sector balance decreases.

b. the government sector balance increases by more than the private sector balance decreases.

c. the government sector balance increases and the private sector balance does not change.

d. All of the above

Short answer

1. What is recorded in Canada's current account? In its capital account? In its official settlements account?

2. If the official settlements account balance equals zero, what will a country's capital account balance equal if it has a $350 billion current account deficit?

3. The table has balance of payment data for Canada in 2000.

Item	(billions of dollars)
Canadian investment abroad	129
Exports of goods and services	478
Net transfers	1
Official settlements account balance	−5
Statistical discrepancy in capital account	−7
Net interest	−27
Foreign investment into Canada	114

a. What is the capital account balance?

b. What is the current account balance?

c. What is the value of imports of goods and services?

4. What is a net borrower? A debtor nation? Is it possible for a nation to be net borrower and yet not be a debtor nation?

5. The table has data for the Canada in 2000.

Item	(billions of dollars)
Saving	207
Investment	191
Government expenditure	218
Net taxes	255

a. What is the private sector balance?

b. What is the government sector balance?

c. What is net exports?

CHECKPOINT 16.2

■ **Explain how the exchange rate is determined and why it fluctuates.**

Practice Problem 16.2

Suppose that yesterday, the Canadian dollar was trading on the foreign exchange market at 75 U.S. cents per dollar. Today, the Canadian dollar is trading at 80 U.S. cents per dollar.

a. Which of the two currencies (the Canadian dollar or the U.S. dollar) has appreciated and which has depreciated today?

b. List the events that could have caused today's change in the value of the Canadian dollar on the foreign exchange market.

c. Did the events that you have listed in part (b) change the demand for Canadian dollars, the supply of Canadian dollars, or both the demand for and supply of Canadian dollars?

d. If the Bank of Canada had tried to stabilize the value of the Canadian dollar at 75 U.S. cents per dollar, what action would it have taken?

e. In part (d), what effect would the Bank of Canada's actions have had on Canadian official reserves?

Solution to Practice Problem 16.2

To solve this Practice Problem, remember that the demand for and supply of Canadian dollars changes when the Canadian interest rate differential changes and when the expected future exchange rate changes.

Quick Review

• *Canadian interest rate differential* On the foreign exchange market, an increase in the Canadian interest rate differential, which is the Canadian interest rate minus the foreign interest rate increases the demand for Canadian dollars and decreases the supply of Canadian dollars.

- *Expected future exchange rate* On the foreign exchange market, a rise in the expected future exchange rate increases the demand for Canadian dollars and decreases the supply of Canadian dollars.

  Suppose that yesterday, the Canadian dollar was trading on the foreign exchange market at 75 U.S. cents per dollar. Today, the Canadian dollar is trading at 80 U.S. cents per dollar.

a. **Which of the two currencies (the Canadian dollar or the U.S. dollar) has appreciated and which has depreciated today?**

The Canadian dollar has risen from 75 U.S. cents per dollar yesterday to 80 U.S. cents per dollar today. There has been a rise in the value of the Canadian dollar in terms of the U.S. dollar. The Canadian dollar has appreciated. The U.S. dollar has depreciated because it buys fewer Canadian dollars.

b. **List the events that could have caused today's change in the value of the Canadian dollar on the foreign exchange market.**

The factors that change the demand for and supply of Canadian dollars are the Canadian interest rate differential and the expected future exchange rate. Because the Canadian dollar rose in value, an increase in the Canadian interest rate differential, which could be the result of either a rise in the Canadian interest rate or a fall in the U.S. interest rate, or a rise in the expected future Canadian dollar exchange rate could be the events that changed the value of the dollar.

c. **Did the events that you have listed in part (b) change the demand for Canadian dollars, the supply of Canadian dollars, or both the demand for and supply of Canadian dollars?**

The events change *both* the demand for Canadian dollars and the supply of Canadian dollars. Both

events increase the demand for Canadian dollars and decrease the supply of Canadian dollars.

d. **If the Bank of Canada had tried to stabilize the value of the Canadian dollar at 75 U.S. cents per dollar, what action would it have taken?**

The Canadian dollar increased in value. To prevent the Canadian dollar from rising in value, the Bank of Canada would have sold dollars to increase the supply of dollars and keep the value at 75 U.S. cents per dollar.

e. **In part (d), what effect would the Bank of Canada's actions have had on Canadian official reserves?**

In part (d), when the Bank of Canada sells Canadian dollars it buys foreign currency. Canadian official reserves would have increased.

Additional Practice Problem 16.2a

How and why does an increase in the expected future exchange rate change the demand for Canadian dollars and the demand curve for dollars? How and why does an increase in the expected future exchange rate change the supply of Canadian dollars and the supply curve of dollars? What is the effect on the equilibrium exchange rate?

Solution to Additional Practice Problem 16.2a

An increase in the expected future exchange rate increases the demand for Canadian dollars and shifts the demand curve for dollars rightward. The demand for dollars increases because at the current exchange rate people want to buy Canadian dollars now and sell them in the future at the higher expected exchange rate. An increase in the expected future exchange rate decreases the supply of Canadian dollars and shifts the supply curve of dollars leftward. The supply of dollars decreases because people prefer to keep Canadian dollars until they can sell them in the future at the higher expected exchange rate. Because the demand for dollars increases and the supply of dollars decreases, the equilibrium exchange rises.

■ Self Test 16.2

Fill in the blanks

The price at which one currency exchanges for another is called a foreign ____ (exchange; interest) rate. If the dollar falls in value against the Mexican peso, the dollar has ____ (appreciated; depreciated). An increase in the demand for dollars shifts the demand curve for dollars ____ (leftward; rightward) and an increase in the supply of dollars shifts the supply curve of dollars ____ (leftward; rightward). The exchange rate is volatile because supply and demand in the foreign exchange market ____ (are; are not) independent of each other. An increase in the expected future exchange rate ____ (raises; lowers) the equilibrium exchange rate. Purchasing power parity is equal value of ____ (interest rates; money). If the Bank of Canada buys dollars on the foreign exchange market, the exchange rate ____ (rises; falls).

True or false

1. The foreign exchange market is located in London, England.

2. If the exchange rate increases from 78 yen per Canadian dollar to 84 yen per Canadian dollar, the dollar has appreciated.

3. The larger the value of Canadian exports, the larger is the quantity of Canadian dollars demanded.

4. An increase in the Canadian exchange rate increases the supply of Canadian dollars and shifts the supply curve of dollars rightward.

5. A rise in the expected future exchange rate increases the demand for dollars and the supply of dollars and might raise or lower the exchange rate.

6. The equilibrium Canadian exchange rate is the exchange rate that sets the quantity of Canadian dollars demanded equal to the quantity of Canadian dollars supplied.

7. An increase in the Canadian interest rate differential raises the Canadian exchange rate.

8. To prevent the price of the euro from falling, the European Central Bank might sell euros on the foreign exchange market.

Multiple choice

1. The foreign exchange market is the market in which

a. all international transactions occur.

b. currencies are exchanged solely by governments.

c. goods are exchanged between governments.

d. the currency of one country is exchanged for the currency of another.

2. When E.D. Smith, a Canadian company, purchases Mexican strawberries, E.D. Smith pays for the strawberries with

a. Canadian dollars.

b. Mexican pesos.

c. gold.

d. Mexican goods and services.

3. If today the exchange rate is 73 U.S. cents per Canadian dollar and tomorrow the exchange rate is 72 U.S. cents per Canadian dollar, then the Canadian dollar ____ and the U.S. dollar ____.

a. appreciated; appreciated

b. appreciated; depreciated

c. depreciated; appreciated

d. depreciated; depreciated

4. In the foreign exchange market, as the Canadian exchange rate rises, other things remaining the same, the

a. quantity of Canadian dollars demanded increases.

b. demand curve for Canadian dollars shifts rightward.

c. demand curve for Canadian dollars shifts leftward.

d. quantity of Canadian dollars demanded decreases.

5. In the foreign exchange market, the demand curve for Canadian dollars shifts rightward if the

a. Canadian interest rate differential increases.
b. expected future exchange rate falls.
c. foreign interest rate rises.
d. Canadian interest rate falls.

6. As the exchange rate _____ the quantity supplied of Canadian dollars _____.

a. rises; increases
b. falls; increases
c. falls; remains the same
d. rises; decreases

7. In the foreign exchange market, the supply curve of dollars is

a. upward sloping.
b. downward sloping.
c. vertical.
d. horizontal.

8. If the _____, everything else remaining the same, the supply of Canadian dollars increases in the foreign exchange market.

a. U.S. interest rate rises
b. expected future exchange rate rises
c. Canadian interest rate rises
d. Canadian interest rate differential increases

9. When there is a shortage of Canadian dollars in the foreign exchange market, the

a. demand curve for Canadian dollars shifts leftward to restore the equilibrium.
b. Canadian exchange rate will appreciate.
c. Canadian exchange rate will depreciate.
d. supply curve of Canadian dollars shifts leftward to restore the equilibrium.

10. In the foreign exchange market, when the Canadian interest rate rises, the supply of Canadian dollars _____ and the foreign exchange rate _____.

a. increases; rises
b. increases; falls
c. decreases; rises
d. decreases; falls

11. A situation in which money buys the same amount of goods and services in different currencies is called

a. exchange rate equilibrium.
b. purchasing power parity.
c. exchange rate surplus.
d. exchange rate balance.

12. Interest rate parity occurs when

a. the interest rate in one currency equals the interest rate in another currency when exchange rate changes are taken into account.
b. interest rate differentials are always maintained across nations.
c. interest rates are equal across nations.
d. prices are equal across nations when exchange rates are taken into account.

Complete the graph

1. Figure 16.1 shows the foreign exchange market for Canadian dollars.

■ FIGURE 16.1

Exchange rate (U.S. cents per Canadian dollar)

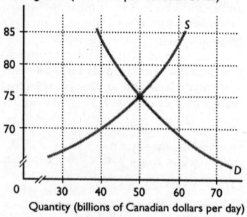

Quantity (billions of Canadian dollars per day)

a. What is the equilibrium exchange rate?
b. The Canadian interest differential rises. In Figure 16.1, illustrate the effects of this change. What happens to the exchange rate?

2. Figure 16.2 shows the foreign exchange market for Canadian dollars.

■ FIGURE 16.2

Exchange rate (U.S. cents per Canadian dollar)

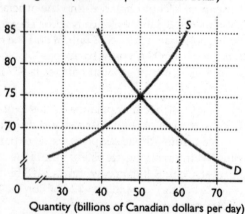

Quantity (billions of Canadian dollars per day)

Suppose people expect that the future exchange rate will be lower. In Figure 16.2, illustrate the effects of this change. What happens to the exchange rate? Has the exchange rate appreciated or depreciated?

Short answer

1. If the exchange rate rises from 73 U.S. cents per Canadian dollar to 75 U.S. cents per Canadian dollar, has the Canadian dollar appreciated or depreciated? Has the U.S. dollar appreciated or depreciated?

2. What is the relationship between the value of Canadian exports and the quantity of Canadian dollars demanded? Why does this relationship exist?

3. What is the relationship between the value of Canadian imports and the quantity of Canadian dollars supplied? Why does this relationship exist?

4. How will a rise in the U.S. interest rate, everything else remaining the same, affect the demand for Canadian dollars, the supply of Canadian dollars, and the Canadian exchange rate?

5. If the Bank of Canada believes the exchange rate is too low and wants to raise it, what action does the Bank undertake in the foreign exchange market? What limits the extent to which the Bank can undertake this action?

SELF TEST ANSWERS

■ CHECKPOINT 16.1

Fill in the blanks

The <u>current</u> account records payments for the imports of goods and services. The <u>capital</u> account records foreign investment into Canada minus Canadian investment abroad in a given period. The sum of the balances of the current account, capital account, and the official settlements account always equals <u>zero</u>.

True or false

1. False; page 404
2. True; page 404
3. True; page 404
4. False; page 404
5. False; page 406
6. True; page 406
7. False; page 407
8. True; page 408

Multiple choice

1. c; page 404
2. b; page 404
3. a; page 404
4. d; page 404
5. c; page 404
6. a; page 404
7. c; page 404
8. c; page 404
9. b; page 406
10. d; page 407
11. b; page 407
12. d; page 407

Short answer

1. The current account records receipts from the sale of goods and services to other countries (exports), minus payments for goods and services bought from other countries (imports), plus the net amount of interest and transfers (such as foreign aid payments) received from and paid to other countries. The capital account records foreign investment into Canada minus Canadian investment abroad in a given period. The official settlements account records the change in Canada's official reserves; page 404.

2. The current account balance plus capital account balance plus the official settlements account balance sum to zero. So if the official settlements account balance equals zero, a $350 billion current account deficit means there is a $350 billion capital account surplus; page 404.

3. a. The capital account balance equals foreign investment into Canada, $114 billion, minus Canadian investment abroad, $129 billion, plus the statistical discrepancy, –$7 billion, which is –$22 billion; page 404.

   b. The sum of the current account balance, the capital account balance, and the official settlements account balance is zero. The capital account balance is –$22 billion and the official settlements account balance is–$5 billion, so the current account balance is $27 billion; page 404.

   c. The current account balance equals exports minus imports plus net interest and transfers received from abroad. Imports equal exports plus net interest plus transfers minus the current account balance, which is $478 billion + (–$27 billion) +$1 billion –$27 billion = $425 billion; page 404.

4. A net borrower is a country that is borrowing more from the rest of the world than it is lending to the rest of the world. A debtor nation is a country that during its entire history

has borrowed more from the rest of the world than it has lent to it. It is possible for a nation to be a net borrower but not be a debtor nation. A country can be a creditor nation and a net borrower. This situation occurs if a creditor nation is, during a particular year, borrowing more from the rest of the world than it is lending to the rest of the world; page 406.

5. a. The private sector balance equals saving minus investment, so the private sector balance is $207 billion – $191 billion = $16 billion; page 407.

   b. The government sector balance equals net taxes minus government expenditure, so the government sector balance is $255 billion – $218 billion = $37 billion; page 407.

   c. The sum of the private sector balance and the government sector balance equals net exports, so net exports equals $16 billion + $37 billion = $53 billion; page 407.

■ **CHECKPOINT 16.2**

Fill in the blanks

The price at which one currency exchanges for another is called a foreign exchange rate. If the dollar falls in value against the Mexican peso, the dollar has depreciated. An increase in the demand for dollars shifts the demand curve for dollars rightward and an increase in the supply of dollars shifts the supply curve of dollars rightward. The exchange rate is volatile because supply and demand in the foreign exchange market are not independent of each other. An increase in the expected future exchange rate raises the equilibrium exchange rate. Purchasing power parity is equal value of money. If the Bank of Canada buys dollars on the foreign exchange market, the exchange rate rises.

True or false

1. False; page 411
2. True; page 411
3. True; page 412

4. False; page 415
5. False; pages 414, 417
6. True; page 418
7. True; page 419
8. False; page 422

Multiple choice

1. d; page 411
2. b; page 411
3. c; page 411
4. d; page 412
5. a; page 414
6. a; page 415
7. a; page 415
8. a; page 417
9. b; page 418
10. c; page 419
11. b; page 420
12. a; page 422

Complete the graph

1. a. In Figure 16.3 the equilibrium exchange rate is 75 U.S. cents per Canadian dollar at the intersection of the D_0 and S_0 curves; page 418.

   b. The increase in the Canadian interest rate differential increases the demand for Canadian dollars and decreases the supply of Canadian dollars. In Figure 16.3, the demand curve shifts rightward from D_0 to D_1 and the supply curve shifts leftward from S_0 to S_1. The exchange rate rises. In the figure, the exchange rate rises to 80 U.S. cents per Canadian dollar; page 419.

■ FIGURE 16.3

Exchange rate (U.S. cents per Canadian dollar)

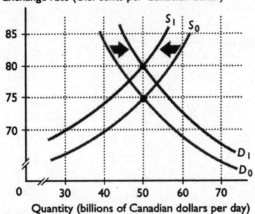

Quantity (billions of Canadian dollars per day)

2. The fall in the expected future exchange rate decreases the demand for Canadian dollars and increases the supply of Canadian dollars. In Figure 16.4, the demand curve shifts leftward from D_0 to D_1 and the supply curve shifts rightward from S_0 to S_1. The exchange rate falls in the figure from 75 U.S. cents per dollar to 70 U.S. cents per dollar. The exchange rate depreciates; page 419.

■ FIGURE 16.4

Exchange rate (U.S. cents per Canadian dollar)

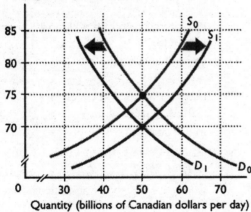

Quantity (billions of Canadian dollars per day)

Short answer

1. When the exchange rate rises from 73 U.S. cents per dollar to 75 U.S. cents per dollar,

the Canadian dollar appreciates because one Canadian dollar buys more U.S. dollars. The U.S. dollar depreciates because it now takes 75 U.S. cents to buy a Canadian dollar instead of 73 U.S. cents; pages 411-412.

2. The larger the value of Canadian exports, the larger is the quantity of Canadian dollars demanded. This relationship exists because Canadian firms want to be paid for their goods and services in Canadian dollars; page 412.

3. The larger the value of Canadian imports, the larger the quantity of Canadian dollars supplied. This relationship exists because Canadian consumers must pay for their imports in foreign currency. To obtain foreign currency, Canadian consumers supply Canadian dollars; page 415.

4. An increase in the U.S. interest rate decreases the Canadian interest rate differential. The smaller the Canadian interest rate differential, the smaller is the demand for Canadian assets and the smaller the demand for Canadian dollars.

   The smaller the Canadian interest rate differential, the greater is the demand for foreign assets and the greater is the supply of Canadian dollars.

   So when the U.S. interest rate rises, the demand for Canadian dollars decreases, the supply of Canadian dollars increases, and the equilibrium exchange rate falls; page 419.

5. If the Bank of Canada wants to raise the exchange rate, it will buy Canadian dollars to decrease supply. The Bank sells Canadian official reserves to buy Canadian dollars. The Bank is limited by its quantity of official reserves. If the Bank persists in this action, eventually it will run out of foreign currency; page 422.